Praise for

The
MAP THIEF

A New England Independent Booksellers Association Bestseller
An NPR Best Book of 2014

"The book offers a brisk, engaging introduction to the slippery world of rare maps and map stewardship. . . . Library crimes aren't cinematic, but . . . *The Map Thief* more than makes up for [that] with the details of the strange world of tweed-collar crime." —*The Boston Globe*

"Truth is much stranger than fiction. . . . In the normally dry world of cartography, Smiley's story makes for a riveting read." —*Town & Country*

"The best glimpse yet of the social-climbing sneak thief who stole millions of dollars in rare maps from Yale University and other institutions a decade ago." —*New Haven Register*

"[An] incredible and sometimes-tawdry tale" —Cleveland.com, *The Plain Dealer*

"[Blanding's] book is as much a riveting true-crime tale as it is a fascinating peek inside the little-seen world of mapmaking and collecting." —*Booklist*

"Brain kale. . . . Bizarre, fascinating, and 100 percent true." —*Mental_Floss*

"An enthralling look at a famous case." —*Boston Common*

"Old maps tug powerfully at the imagination, and not always in healthy ways. Nothing makes that clearer than the strange, unsettling case of Forbes Smiley, whose story Michael Blanding has pieced together in captivating detail. This is an unforgettable and cautionary tale, told by an expert investigative reporter who writes with the narrative flair of a novelist. A great read!" —Toby Lester, author of *The Fourth Part of the World: An Astonishing Epic of Global Discovery, Imperial Ambition, and the Birth of America*

© KEVIN DAY PHOTOGRAPHY

Michael Blanding is an award-winning magazine writer with nearly twenty years of experience writing long-form narrative and investigative journalism. A senior fellow at the Schuster Institute for Investigative Journalism at Brandeis University, he is the author of *The Coke Machine: The Dirty Truth Behind the World's Favorite Soft Drink* (Avery/Penguin 2010) as well as numerous articles for publications including *The Nation, The New Republic, Consumers Digest, Boston,* and *The Boston Globe Magazine.* Blanding is also an avid map lover, with a collection of international subway maps covering the walls of his home.

www.michaelblanding.com
www.twitter.com/michaelblanding

The
MAP
THIEF

THE GRIPPING STORY OF AN ESTEEMED RARE-MAP DEALER

WHO MADE MILLIONS STEALING PRICELESS MAPS

Michael Blanding

AVERY
an imprint of Penguin Random House
New York

an imprint of Penguin Random House LLC
375 Hudson Street
New York, New York 10014

Previously published in hardcover by Gotham Books
First trade paperback edition, June 2015
Copyright © 2014 by Blanding Enterprises, LLC

Most Avery books are available at special quantity discounts for bulk purchase for sales promotions, premiums, fund-raising, and educational needs. Special books or book excerpts also can be created to fit specific needs. For details, write SpecialMarkets@penguinrandomhouse.com.

Frontispiece and figures 2, 8, and 12 original illustrations by Jelmer Noordeman and Koen Harmsma, Bier en Brood. Figures 1, 18, A, and C courtesy of Beinecke Rare Book & Manuscript Library. Figure 3 courtesy of Bedford Historical Society. Figures 4 and 5 courtesy of Library of Congress, g3200 ct000725C. Figures 6, 10, E, G, and L map reproduction courtesy of the Norman B. Leventhal Map Center at the Boston Public Library. Figure 7 courtesy of Library of Congress, g3710 070900. Figure 9 from *Recollections of Sebec, Maine: Stories Across Two Generations* by Shirley Nason Wright, courtesy of Shirley Nason Wright. Figure 11 courtesy of Library of Congress, g3710 ct003573a. Figure 13 courtesy of the Library of Virginia. Figure 14 courtesy of Library of Congress, g3700 ct000675. Figure 15 courtesy of Library of Congress, France in America collection. Figure 16 courtesy of the author. Figures 17, B, H, and N courtesy of Barry Lawrence Ruderman Antique Maps Inc., www.raremaps.com. Figure D from Wikimedia Commons. Figure F courtesy of Library of Congress, g3200 ct000270. Figure I courtesy of Sterling Memorial Library Map Collection, Yale University Library. Figure J courtesy of Library of Congress, g3300 ct000232. Figure K courtesy of Library of Congress, g3700 ct000666. Figure M courtesy of Kris Butler and Shipyard Brewery. Figure O courtesy of Connecticut State's Attorney, New Haven Judicial District. Figure P AP Photo/Fred Beckham.

The Library of Congress has catalogued the hardcover edition as follows:

Blanding, Michael.
The map thief : the gripping story of an esteemed rare-map dealer who made millions stealing priceless maps / Michael Blanding.
   p.   cm.
Includes bibliographical references and index.
ISBN 978-1-59240-817-7 (hardback)
1. Smiley, E. Forbes.   2. Map dealers—United States.   3. Map industry and trade—United States.   4. Map thefts—United States.   5. Book thefts—United States.   I. Title.
Z286.M3B53   2014   2014005305
364.16'289120973—dc23

ISBN 978-1-59240-940-2 (paperback)

Printed in the United States of America
3 5 7 9 10 8 6 4

Book design by Patrice Sheridan

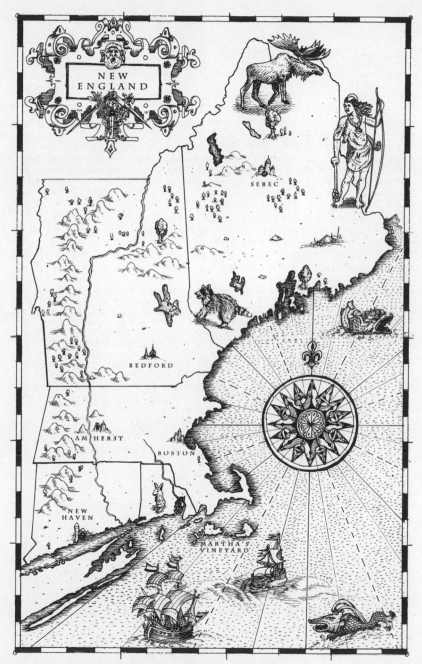

SMILEY'S NEW ENGLAND.

To Zachary and Cleo

May you always find your way.

Contents

List of Characters

ALL TITLES AS OF JUNE 2005, unless otherwise noted.

The Dealers

MARTHA'S VINEYARD
Edward Forbes Smiley III

NEW YORK

B. Altman and Co. (closed 1985)

Rosejeanne Slifer (d. 1989)

Arader Galleries

Graham Arader

The Old Print Shop

Harry Newman
Robert Newman

Richard B. Arkway, Inc.

Dick Arkway
Paul Cohen
Henry Taliaferro

NEW HAVEN

Bill Reese

LONDON

Philip Burden
Ashley Baynton-Williams
Jonathan Potter
R.V. "Mick" Tooley (d. 1986)

CHICAGO

Ken Nebenzahl

SAN DIEGO

Barry Ruderman

The Libraries

YALE UNIVERSITY
Alice Prochaska, head of libraries

Beinecke Rare Book and Manuscript Library

Frank Turner, director
E.C. Schroeder, head of technical services
Ellen Cordes, head of public services
Naomi Saito, library services assistant
Ralph Mannarino, supervisor of building operations and security

Sterling Memorial Library Map Collection

Fred Musto, curator
Margit Kaye, library services assistant
Abe Parrish, GIS specialist

Yale Police Department

Martin Buonfiglio, detective
Bill Holohan, lieutenant

NEW YORK PUBLIC LIBRARY

Paul LeClerc, president
David Ferriero, director of the research libraries
Bill Walker, former director of the research libraries

Map Division

Alice Hudson, chief
Matt Knudsen, assistant chief
Nancy Kandoian, map cataloger

Rare Book Division

Michael Inman, curator

BOSTON PUBLIC LIBRARY

Bernard Margolis, president

Norman B. Leventhal Map Center

Ron Grim, curator

Rare Books Department

Earle Havens, curator of manuscripts
Roberta Zonghi, keeper of rare books

HARVARD UNIVERSITY

Nancy Cline, head of libraries

Houghton Library

Bill Stoneman, librarian

Map Collection

David Cobb, curator

BRITISH LIBRARY

Clive Field, director of scholarship and collections

Map Library

Peter Barber, director
Tony Campbell, former director (retired)

NEWBERRY LIBRARY

Charles Cullen, president

Maps Section

Bob Karrow, curator

Collectors

Norman Leventhal (Boston)
Lawrence Slaughter (Larchmont, New York)
Harold Osher (Portland, Maine)
Barry McLean (Chicago)
Bob Gordon (New York)
Jim Curtis (Boston)

Smiley's Family and Friends

FAMILY
Edward Forbes Smiley II, father
Adele Smiley, mother
Edward "Ned" Forbes Smiley IV, son
Marion Smiley, sister
Marilyn (Smiley) Phillips, sister
Susan (Smiley) Burns, twin sister
Lisa Smiley, wife

DERRYFIELD SCHOOL

Paul Statt
Hilary Chaplain

HAMPSHIRE COLLEGE

Scott Slater
Bennett Fischer
Scott Haas
Fred Melamed
Dick Cantwell

OTHER

Bob von Elgg, Slater's brother-in-law

In Sebec

Glen Fariel, next-door neighbor, former selectman
David Mallett, president, Sebec Historical Society
Jayne Lello, manager, Sebec post office
Bill and Charlene Moriarty, owners, Sebec Village Marina
Buzz Small, selectman
Susan Dow, selectman
Walt Emmons, member, planning department
Louisa Finnemore, president, Sebec Reading Room Association (now Sebec Village Associates)

The Law

Stephen Kelleher, special agent, New Haven field office, FBI
Christopher "Kit" Schmeisser, assistant US attorney
Janet Bond Arterton, judge, US Court, District of Southern Connecticut
Michael Dearington, state's attorney, state of Connecticut
Richard Damiani, judge, Connecticut District Court
Bob Goldman, former special trial attorney, US Justice Department, now managing partner, Goldman Law Offices

SELECTED MAPMAKERS, 1470–1860

Name	Nationality	Dates*
Martin Waldseemüller	German	1470–1520
Hernán Cortés	Spanish	1485–1547
Oronce Fine	French	1494–1555
Peter Apian	German	1495–1552
Gerard de Jode	Flemish	1509–1591
Gerard Mercator	Flemish	1509–1591
Abraham Ortelius	Flemish	1527–1598
Theodor de Bry	Flemish	1528–1598
Robert Dudley	English	1531–1588
Jacques Le Moyne	French	1533–1588
John White	English	1540–1593
John Speed	English	1542–1629
Richard Hakluyt	English	1552–1616
George Best	English	1555–1584
Edward Wright	English	1561–1615
Henry Briggs	English	1561–1630
Jodocus Hondius	Flemish	1563–1612
William Alexander	English	1567–1640
Cornelius de Jode	Dutch	1568–1600
Willem Blaeu	Dutch	1571–1638
Samuel de Champlain	French	1574–1635
John Smith	English	1580–1631
William Wood	English	1580–1639
Luke Foxe	English	1586–1635
Hendrik Hondius	Dutch	1587–1651
Jan Jansson	Dutch	1588–1664
Jodocus Hondius II	Dutch	1593–1629
Joan Blaeu	Dutch	1596–1673
Nicolas Sanson	French	1600–1667
John Ogilby	English	1600–1676
Cornelius Blaeu	Dutch	1616–1648
Claude Dablon	French	1618–1697

Name	Nationality	Dates*
Claude Allouez	French	1622–1689
Thomas Holme	English	1624–1695
Hendrick Doncker	Dutch	1626–1699
John Seller	English	1630–1697
William Berry	English	1639–1718
John Thornton	English	1641–1708
John Bonner	English	1643–1726
John Foster	English	1648–1681
Herman Moll	English	1654–1732
Robert Morden	English	1668–1703
Guillaume De L'Isle	French	1675–1726
Joshua Fry	English	1699–1754
Lewis Evans	English	1700–1756
Peter Jefferson	American	1708–1757
Thomas Jefferys	English	1710–1771
Joseph F.W. Des Barres	English	1721–1824
William Scull	American	1739–1784
Thomas Jefferson	American	1743–1826
Reading Howell	English	1743–1827
Henry Pelham	American	1748–1806
John Norman	American	1748–1817
James Madison	American	1749–1812
William Faden	English	1750–1836
Andrew Ellicott	American	1754–1820
John Collet	English	1756–1789
William Norman	American	1770–1807
John Melish	Scottish	1771–1822
William Darby	American	1775–1854

* Some dates are approximate.

The
MAP THIEF

[A]s Geography without History seemeth a carkasse without motion; so History without Geography, wandreth as a Vagrant without a certaine habitation.

—CAPTAIN JOHN SMITH, 1624

INTRODUCTION

THE FIRST TIME I HEARD Forbes Smiley's voice was at six o'clock on a summer Friday as I was drinking a martini at a Boston bar. It was a warm night after a long week, and I was almost down to the olive when I got the call. "This is Forbes Smiley, from the Vineyard," he intoned, speaking in that rich, nasally voice I had heard so many people imitate in the months I'd spent researching a magazine article about his case. Though he'd been caught stealing millions in rare maps nearly ten years earlier, at the height of his career as a rare-map dealer, he'd never spoken to a journalist until now. With some persistence—and help from an old friend of his named Scott Slater—I'd finally gotten him to contact me.

"I understand that Scott met with you and you had a conversation and that he thought it would be a good idea that I speak with you," he continued. Maybe it was just the buzz from the martini, but I found myself having difficulty following his circuitous language. "Frankly I wish these kinds of things would go away and one might move forward. What I understand is that people are interested in the human story. When someone crashes and burns as I did, you learn certain things, and that may be interesting to some people."

After a bit more back and forth, he agreed to an interview, and we settled on some ground rules, chief among them that I would not report on his wife and son any more than necessary in order to tell his own story. A week later I was on a ferry to the island of Martha's Vineyard, off the south coast of Massachusetts, to meet him. We talked for four hours at an outdoor picnic table, where I found him to be candid, thoughtful, and even funny. By the end of the interview, I was convinced that an article wasn't enough space to tell his story. After a second interview a few months later, I broached the subject of a book.

He initially threw cold water on the idea. "I'll be straight up right now; I think it would be difficult to write without me saying a lot more than I am willing to say," he said, adding tantalizingly, "I could tell you stories that would make your hair curl." After a few months, however, he agreed through Slater to participate. I secured a book contract and began talking to friends, map dealers, librarians, and law enforcement officers. Only after I was well into the reporting did the stalling begin. We made another date to meet on the Vineyard, which he canceled. We set a time to meet in Boston, which he canceled.

Finally, the night before another scheduled meeting in a Boston suburb, I received an e-mail from him. After speaking to his "closest confidant & adviser," he said, he decided not to participate any further. "After talking it through, he is of the strong opinion that I am unable to [distance] myself from the emotional pain of these events to [ensure] that I remain within appropriate bounds. He considers the harm I might do to others, to my wife and family, friends, dealers & old clients—in something as involved as a book—too great a risk." I wrote back immediately, expressing my disappointment but also telling him it was too late now to scuttle the project. Though I would like to have his participation, I'd be writing the book regardless. Despite several more attempts to contact him, I never heard from Smiley again.

Over the next year, I persisted in filling in the gaps of the narrative that had been left open after our conversations. After talking with a wider circle of people, investigating a paper trail of court documents, and spending hours sifting through library archives and volumes of old maps, I began to piece together an answer to my biggest question: Why did a respected map dealer at the height of his profession betray those closest to him—and deface the artifacts he spent his life preserving? The more I researched his story, however, the more questions I uncovered—to the point where I began to suspect that his reasons for cutting off our correspondence had less to do with the advice of his advisor or the impact on his family, and more to do with his own fears of exposing secrets he had never revealed.

IN HIS ONE-PARAGRAPH short story, "On Exactitude in Science," surrealist writer Jorge Luis Borges imagined an empire so advanced in the science of mapmaking that it was able to produce a map on a one-to-one scale—that is, as large as the empire itself. Such a feat, of course, is as impossible as it is undesirable. The very point of a map is to re-create an area in miniature, allowing us to envision, navigate, and control our world.

The paradox of mapmaking, however, is that as soon as you begin shrinking a geography down to usable size, you necessarily are forced to misrepresent it. By making choices about what to include and what to leave out, you change the map from a document faithfully documenting an area to one furthering a particular point of view. Writing contains the same paradox. As soon as we start picking and choosing relevant details to "propel the story forward" (literally or figuratively), we change the story to fit the narrative.

When I was growing up, I always found that the best books were those with maps in them. Like many children, I pored over the "There and Back Again" map in J.R.R. Tolkien's *The Hobbit*, which both allows the reader to follow along with the journey and also plays an essential role in the plot. Personally, though, I was always more captivated by the sprawling map of Middle-earth in Tolkien's *The Lord of the Rings*, thrilling to the long leagues of jagged mountains and dark-shaded forests bleeding off the margins of the page. That open-ended geography consciously raised the specter of other stories in adjacent territories occurring at the same time as the events described in the trilogy. That appeal to imagination made the world of the novels both less knowable and more real.

I can still see the two-tone version of the map that folded out of a red leather–bound edition of *The Lord of the Rings* that sat on my father's highest shelf. In those days, I suppose, reading fantasy novels was for me a way to grow closer to my father, who like many men of his generation seemed to me a distant territory. He had piles and piles of them stacked by his bed, stuffed into overflowing bookcases in the den, and filling shelf after shelf in the basement. Most of them contained maps, and I can still see the borders of their imagined earths in my mind—Cimmeria and Amber, Shannara and Xanth, Prydain and Pern. And I can still smell their musty pages as I opened them to the maps—always first to the maps—and began navigating their geographies before reading their stories.

The other love my father and I shared was for traveling. He worked as a sales rep for a computer company and continued to make sales calls across New England as president of his own company. We hit the road for family vacations as well, and I can clearly see him in his cockpit, with everything he needed close by—the radio, a bag of salted peanuts, and that sheaf of folding state maps simultaneously offering freedom and control. I loved sitting next to him in the passenger seat, folding and unfolding the maps as the trip itself unfolded. It gave me a feeling of control over the landscape—and maybe some control over our relationship as well, navigating a simpler topography than our familial bond.

As I got older, I continued to love maps. In junior high school, I spent hours creating my own fantasy worlds on hexagonal graph paper, piling continents full of cities, mountains, forests, of my own invention. In high school, I plotted my own road trips with friends, and after college, I traveled farther afield, backpacking across France and India, always with map in hand. In those days before Google Earth and GPS, I felt like I could find my way anywhere as long as I had a map, offering me ownership of places where I didn't even speak the language.

Eventually, I began collecting maps as well, focusing on subway maps of places I've lived or traveled over the years—Washington, Paris, London, Barcelona, Moscow. They line the walls of my apartment as I write this, each a skeleton of a city reduced to its essential form. I like reading the names of the stops on their colored lines: L'Enfant Plaza, Charing Cross, Passeig de Gràcia, conjuring up worlds in my imagination as efficiently as the fantasy maps of my youth.

I know I'm not alone in feeling that cartographic allure—since I started working on this book, countless people have shared with me their own enthusiasm for maps. Some love them for the beauty they express, others for the sense of order they represent. Some thrill to their promise of adventure, armchair or otherwise, and others cherish their familiar depiction of a territory close to home. For everyone I've spoken with, however, there is something intensely personal about this cartographic connection. Despite the way they express a shared geography, maps are tools of the imagination first, mediating a relationship between an individual and a place.

GIVEN THE LOVE I've always had for maps, it was natural that I'd become intrigued by the story of E. Forbes Smiley III—that deliciously old-money name opening the door to the rarified world of map collecting and map collectors. I read about him in *The New Yorker* in October 2005 with fascination—first, for the maps themselves, these historical documents that were at once beautiful and flawed, and second, for this strange character at the center of the crime, so mysterious in his decision to despoil the world he loved.

The *New Yorker* article, however, was written before the case went to court, and without Smiley's voice to offer his explanation. When I heard Boston Public Library was opening a new map center in which Smiley had played a bit of a role, it seemed opportune to revisit the story. Initially, the timing seemed good, since Smiley had decided he finally wanted to tell his story. His son, E. Forbes Smiley IV, was getting old enough to use Google, and he wanted at least one chance to offer his version of what had occurred.

As I spoke with Smiley, I found a mass of contradictions—someone who was at once so capable and at the same time so deeply flawed. The irony of the story, as I came to understand it, is that this man who was stealing maps had so clearly lost his own way. Perhaps what made maps so appealing to him was the same thing that made them appealing to me—that sense of control they give over our surroundings, no matter how much control we have over our own lives. Researching his story, I became just as intrigued with the stories of those who made the maps he stole, each with their own passions and rivalries. As I spoke with Smiley and those around him, I found myself writing the map of a man, a profession, and an obsession. And like any good map, his story ultimately bleeds off into the margins between the known and the unknowable.

Chapter 1

THE EXPLORER AND THE THIEF

FIGURE 1 JOHN SMITH. "NEW ENGLAND," FROM
ADVERTISEMENTS FOR THE UNEXPERIENCED PLANTERS OF
NEW ENGLAND. LONDON, 1631.

June 8, 2005

E. FORBES SMILEY III couldn't stop coughing. No matter how much he tried to suppress it, the tickle in the back of his throat kept breaking out into a hacking cough, drawing glances from the patrons sitting around him. The glass fishbowl of a reading room at the Beinecke Rare Book and Manuscript Library at Yale University was quiet except for the low hum of the air-conditioning and the clicking of fingers on keyboards, making Smiley painfully aware of the noise he was making. At one point, he pulled a handkerchief out of his pocket to muffle the sound. As he did, an X-Acto knife blade wrapped inside fell softly onto the carpeted floor. He folded the cloth and put it back in his pocket, oblivious to what had just happened.

Smiley was in the Beinecke this morning to study some rare atlases in preparation for the London Map Fair, an annual gathering of hundreds of map collectors who came to the British capital to buy, sell, and trade antiquarian maps. As one of the top dealers in the field, Smiley hoped to use the event to climb out of the financial hole into which he'd recently sunk. Over the years, he'd become expert at recognizing different versions of the same map from subtle typographical variations, an ability that could translate into thousands of dollars when deployed at the right moment. By refamiliarizing himself with some select maps, he hoped to be ready for any opportunity in London.

So far, the trip hadn't gone well. The previous night, he'd woken up miserable in a cheap hotel. It wasn't the kind of place he'd usually stay. He favored luxury hotels, where he could see the look of surprise and interest flit across the faces of people when he let it be known he was a map dealer. He looked the part, too, with graying hair swept back over his ears and a long, oval face ending in a narrow, patrician chin. A pair of silver wire-framed glasses perched on his nose, and he invariably wore tweed or navy blue blazers. That, along with his Yankee-sounding name, usually caused people to assume he was from "old money," an impression Smiley did nothing to correct.

When people thought of Forbes Smiley—as he was universally known by friends, dealers, librarians, and clients—a few words inevitably sprang to mind: gregarious; jolly; larger-than-life. He spoke with the resonance of an Italian tenor mangled by a nasally Waspish affectation. His voice, like Daisy Buchanan's, was "full of money." When he made phone calls, he made sure to announce that he was calling "from the Vineyard." His upper-crust affectations, however, were tempered by a charming self-deprecation. He'd ingratiated himself with many a librarian by inquiring after her spouse or children, and reciprocated with entertaining stories of travels around the world or the progress of the new home he was building on the Vineyard.

Most of all, people thought of his laugh. For years, friends had reveled in Smiley's laugh, which rolled up out of his belly and wracked his body in a cackle that only increased in volume the longer it went on. It was the kind of laugh that in college had earned him free tickets from theater producers, who sat him in the front row to egg on the audience. And it generally caused people to excuse the pretension that crept into his voice when he was expounding on any of his obsessions—architecture, New England history, the blues, and, of course, maps. Whether they liked him or not, his colleagues and rivals in the map business had all been seduced by his knowledge, which in certain areas exceeded that of anyone else in the world.

On the morning of June 8, 2005, however, none of the librarians at the Beinecke's public services desk recognized him. Had they known him, they would have been shocked at the transformation he'd undergone. In addition to the cough that had developed overnight, he was suffering from a splitting headache left over from a night of drinking. Smiley had been drinking a lot these days—it was the only thing that took his thoughts away from the problems that multiplied in his mind whenever he was sober. As gifted as he was at remembering details about maps, he was abysmal at managing the details of the business through which he earned his livelihood. No matter how entertaining his stories, the truth was that he was overextended and hemorrhaging money.

The stress had taken a physical toll, leading to a constant pain in his back for the past two years. This morning, it was particularly awful. Each time a cough wracked his body, fresh bullets of pain rocketed up his spine. Smiley made two phone calls that morning: one to his wife and one to a client; neither ended well. His spirits were already sinking as he headed across town to Yale's campus. If anyone had stopped to wonder, they might have thought he looked strange in a tweedy olive blazer on this warm summer day. Then again, Yale was full of eccentric professors who might be found doing just that. Probably no one gave him a second glance as he crossed the Beinecke's broad plaza to enter the building.

THE BEINECKE LIBRARY'S modern architecture is an anomaly among Yale's predominantly Gothic-style buildings. A heavy granite lattice creates a series of squares on its façade, each framing a thin, octagonal sheet of translucent white marble. On a sunny day, the sun bathes the interior mezzanine in a soft, church-like light. Inside, the library resembles nothing so much as a giant literary aquarium, with a rectangular tank of steel and glass stacked with five stories of weathered bindings—a literal tower of knowledge. Completed in the 1960s, the Beinecke remains one of the largest libraries in the world devoted exclusively to rare books. Nearly two hundred thousand volumes fill its tower, with space for a half million more in its subterranean stacks.

Smiley entered at the mezzanine and headed downstairs, where a much smaller aquarium tank houses the library's reading room. On his way, he passed by one of the jewels of the Beinecke's collection: a six-foot-long framed world map by Henricus Martellus dating from 1489. As Smiley—and few other visitors—knew, the one-of-a-kind map is the closest representation we have to Europeans' worldview on the eve of Christopher Columbus's first voyage. Smiley stopped at the public services desk to request the books and atlases he'd come to see, then headed into the reading room, where he sat at a window table looking out on a sunken courtyard of white marble sculptures. For a while he worked, leaning over books hundreds of years old, carefully taking notes in pencil.

As studious as he looked, he was feeling a fresh sense of desperation by the time he left to get lunch around eleven. Sitting in a coffee shop around the corner, he turned his options over in his mind. He could take the train to New York today and fly to London a day early in hopes of putting together a deal before the map fair began. Or he could abandon the whole plan and head back to the Vineyard, saving the expense and hoping to find another way out of his financial mess.

While he sat pondering his predicament without reaching a conclusion, the situation in the reading room had changed radically in his absence. Smiley may have missed the X-Acto knife blade that fell from his pocket, but a librarian named Naomi Saito had not. The Beinecke's librarians make regular sweeps of the room to ensure that materials are handled properly—and to subtly alert patrons they are being watched. As Saito had entered to make her check, she immediately spied the blade on the floor. Few objects could be more disturbing to someone who works in a building full of rare books than a tool that can separate the pages of a book from its binding. Saito picked up the blade in a tissue and walked back out of the room.

When her supervisor, Ellen Cordes, arrived shortly after noon, Saito showed her what she'd found. Cordes knew that custodians had cleaned the room in the morning—so whoever had dropped the blade was probably still there. She scanned through several dozen reader cards and immediately focused on Smiley, who had by now returned to examine more books. Looking up his website and seeing he was a dealer of rare maps made her even more nervous. Cordes called over to Sterling Memorial Library, which houses Yale's main map collection, and wasn't reassured. The head of the department told her that Smiley had recently looked at some folders later found to be missing several maps, but the matter had been dropped for lack of proof. Finally, Cordes contacted the Beinecke's head of security, Ralph Mannarino, who kept watch over Smiley at the front desk while Cordes went into the back room to look at the materials Smiley had examined.

Smiley continued his research, oblivious to the attention he'd attracted. He requested more items, among them a dark brown leather case with raised ridges along the spine. He slid it open in the middle, a musty odor wafting from an olive-green cloth case inside. Smiley folded out the sides into an irregularly shaped cross, uncovering a sheaf of rough-cut manuscript pages inside.

On its title page were the words:

ADVERTISEMENTS

For the unexperienced Planters of

New England, or any where.

OR,

The Path-way to experience to erect a

PLANTATION.

Below them was written an even more unwieldy subtitle:

With the yearely proceedings of this Country in Fifhing

and Planting, fince the yeare 1614. to the yeare 1630.

and their prefent eftate.

Alfo how to prevent the greateft inconveniences, by their

proceedings in Virginia, and other Plantations,

by approved examples.

With the Countries Armes,
a defcription of the Coaft,

Harbours, Habitations, Land-markes, Latitude and

Longitude :

and, to Smiley's purpose:

with the Map, allowed by our Royall

King C H A R L E S.

Below that, finally, was the name of the author:

By Captaine I o h n S m i t h, fometimes Governour
of

V i r g i n i a, and Admirall of N e vv-E n g l a n d.

CAPTAIN JOHN SMITH was a soldier, explorer, writer, and part founder
of Jamestown, the first permanent English settlement in North America.
He's probably best known, however, for his association with the story of
Pocahontas, the Powhatan Indian maiden who supposedly saved him
from death. The truth of that story has been hotly debated over the
years—especially since the only source for it is Smith himself, who first
told it seventeen years after the supposed event. One fact seems clear,
however: The two never had a romantic affair, despite numerous depictions to the contrary. Smith was twenty-eight and Pocahontas only
eleven, and nothing in the historical record suggests they were ever anything more than chaste friends.

The real-life story of John Smith, in fact, is more colorful and complicated than a Disney-fied tale of interracial love. The son of a yeoman
farmer, he pined for overseas adventure from a young age. After a brief
sojourn as a teenage mercenary for the Dutch, he designed his own
crash-course curriculum in the military arts, covering everything from
Roman military strategy to demolitions. From there (again, according to
Smith) he fought in European battles against the Turks, earning the rank

of captain before being captured and held as a slave in Istanbul. After killing his master, he escaped into Transylvania and briefly sojourned through Russia and North Africa, returning to England in late 1604.

Smith never explained what made him sign up with the Virginia Company's expedition to America in December 1606. It doesn't take much, however, to imagine how irresistibly the lure of that adventure must have tugged at him. If even half his later accounts can be believed, he had seen firsthand how knowledge, bravery, and hard work paid off in his promotion from a common soldier to an officer. Here, now, was a chance to distinguish himself in the New World, where the old social strata wouldn't apply. Some historians have, in fact, seen Smith as one of the very first adherents of the American Dream, championing a new meritocracy to replace the aristocracy of Europe.

The idea didn't go over so well. Clashing from the beginning with the higher-ranking "gentlemen" aboard ship, Smith was clapped in irons barely a month out of England and accused of instigating a mutiny. By the time the expedition arrived in the Caribbean, one of his chief accusers had erected a gallows, and Smith only narrowly avoided being hung. After that inauspicious start, the expedition's leaders must have gotten a shock when they touched land at the mouth of Chesapeake Bay and opened the sealed orders to reveal the names of the seven men chosen by the Virginia Company to govern the colony. There, among the names of the rich and highborn gentlemen, was one exception: John Smith.

Smith gained his release and cleared his name to take his place among the governors of the colony—but wasted no time in stirring up a coup against the colony's president, whom he accused of hogging the colony's meager stores. By all accounts, the first year in Jamestown was a disaster. The gentlemen farmers who ran the colony placed their hopes on a resupply from England, rather than planting and harvesting their own fields. When that relief didn't come, starvation and disease set in. Within twelve months, half the original 105 colonists were dead. At the same time, the settlers had to deal with Native American tribes, who carried out repeated raids on the colonists occupying their land.

That the colonists survived at all was probably thanks to Smith, who was put in charge of relations with the tribes. No matter how much Smith caused trouble or puffed himself up, there was no denying his singular gifts as a colonist. Through a combined strategy of trading with friendly tribes and preemptively attacking hostile villages, he kept the colonists protected and ensured enough food to make it through the first years of settlement.

It was at this time the Pocahontas legend was born. Just before New Year's in 1608, Smith was captured by the Native American chief Powhatan, regional overlord of the area's many tribes, who laid him out on a pair of rocks for execution. At that moment, the chief's daughter Pocahontas interceded, begging her father to spare his life. Later biographers have surmised that the whole affair may have been a ritual involving a mock execution that Smith mistook for the real thing. But whatever the truth, Powhatan became a sometime friend to the English and Smith walked free of captivity once again. Over the next two years, Pocahontas served as an invaluable aide to Smith in negotiating with the natives and supposedly saved his life a second time by warning him of an ambush set by her temperamental father.

The colonists eventually elected Smith president, and he simultaneously made Virginia both a meritocracy and a dictatorship with his famous edict: "He that will not work shall not eat." His leadership, however, was all too brief. Never one to disguise his contempt for his social betters, he made a long list of enemies, who were by now actively lobbying in England for his removal. The Virginia Company had already sent a new governor to replace him when Smith suffered a tragic accident. On an expedition upriver, his powder bag accidentally caught fire, badly burning him. He left the New World injured and disgraced, just two and a half years after he had arrived.

BACK IN LONDON, Smith nursed his wounds and his resentments against the Virginia Company. The following winter, he saw his convictions sadly vindicated when the new leaders' ineptness led to a famine known as the Starving Time. The population, which now numbered five hundred, plummeted to sixty as colonists resorted to boiling boot leather, and in some cases each other, to survive.

For the next few years, Smith busied himself writing books about Virginia, criticizing his enemies and building up his own role in the enterprise. In one of them, published in 1612, he included a map of Virginia produced from his surveys and conversations with natives. Not only was it the most accurate map of the region to date, but also it remained in use for more than three hundred years. In time, he learned to play the political game well enough to secure another expedition, funded by a group of investors out of Plymouth. They gave him orders to explore the coast of "North Virginia" for whale oil, fish, and furs. But Smith saw another opportunity: to correct the Virginia colony's mistakes and claim a new settlement for England—and for himself.

He set sail with two ships in 1614, reaching the coast of what is now Maine and sailing a small boat in and out of harbors, making careful notes of fishing banks, anchorages, and native settlements. As he did, he grasped for a new name to solidify England's claim on the area—and separate it from Virginia. With a bold stroke, Smith coined a new title for the entire region from Maine to Cape Cod: New England.

The name stuck. The Plymouth Company officially confirmed it upon Smith's return and gratefully appointed him "admiral" of the new territory. They even outfitted him with a small fleet for his return journey, consisting of two ships and sixteen colonists. Unfortunately, they never made it. French pirates captured his ship off the Azores and took Smith captive again for several months. True to form, he escaped by taking advantage of a storm to commandeer one of the ship's boats, taking with him a manuscript he'd started about his latest expeditions. Published in 1616 as *A Description of New England*, the book was part adventure yarn, with him as the swashbuckling main character, and part advertisement for the virtues of the region, which he breathlessly extolled as an unspoiled paradise of codfish and pine.

"Could I have but the means to transport a colony, I would rather live here than anywhere," he gushed, baldly spelling out his heretical notion of a country based on merit. "Here every man may be master and owner of his own labour and land," he wrote. "If he have nothing but his hands, he may set up this trade; he may by industry quickly grow rich." To further promote the area, he worked with a Dutch engraver named Simon van de Passe to produce a detailed map of the coastline (Figure 1). Though an American Indian guide had helped him affix native names to the villages they had seen, he decided a bit of sycophancy couldn't hurt his cause. So he sent out a copy of the map to the fifteen-year-old crown prince, Charles, to humbly request he add his own names.

The prince obliged, naming the Charles River after himself, Cape Anna after his mother, and Cape James (previously known as Cape Cod) after his father. Further asserting English dominance, he renamed various native set-tlements after English cities— changing Sagoquas to Oxford, Aggawom to Southampton, Anmoughcawgen to Cambridge, and so on—and added Lon-don to a blank spot along the coast. The resulting map is an unprecedented act of virtual colonization, claiming a huge swath of territory with a fictitious geography that served both Smith's and England's purposes.

In the end, however, Smith never saw his dream realized. After bad winds scuttled another expedition in 1617, Smith was never again able to navigate the political waters to fund a new voyage. He spent the remain-der of his life in England, dining out on his adventures and writing books to establish his legacy. His map of New England, however, did soon make it back to the New World. When the self-styled Pilgrims set out from Plymouth in 1620, they used it to steer the *Mayflower* around Cape Cod toward a site Smith had described as "an excellent good har-bor, good land; and no want of any thing but industrious people." Whether through coincidence or design, the harbor they chose had the same name on Smith's map as the city in England from which they'd set out. They took it up for their new colony: Plimouth.

More settlers followed in later years to found Massachusetts Bay Colony. Despite his contributions, however, Smith found his reputation slipping away in future years as both colonies prospered without him. The last book he wrote before his death in 1631, *Advertisements for the Un-experienced Planters of New-England, or Any Where,* was an anxious work, full of unsolicited advice drawn from Smith's experiences of more than a dozen years before. In it, he built up the Massachusetts colonists at the expense of the Virginians, even as he lost no opportunity to tout his own accom-plishments in establishing Virginia for what it was. And, so his contribu-tions to New England wouldn't be forgotten, he also included an updated version of the map he'd created of that territory fifteen years before.

SITTING IN THE READING ROOM of the Beinecke Library nearly four centuries later, Smiley carefully turned the water-stained frontispiece of the book to reveal a map folded into a rectangle about six by eight inches wide. He spread it out on the table, examining the copper-engraved image he prac-tically knew by heart. Unusual for maps of this time period—or any time period—a portrait of the mapmaker fills the entire upper left-hand corner of the page. It is the only known portrait of Smith, drawn by van de Passe when the captain was thirty-six. He looks proud and wary, with shoulders thrown back and piercing eyes staring over a bushy beard and waxed mustache. In the portrait Smith eschews the ruffled collar of a gentleman in favor of a patterned leather jerkin, his hand resting lightly on the pommel of his sword—solidifying his reputation as a soldier and adventurer.

Carved around the portrait are the pits and points of the New England coastline. Despite a few notable errors, the map is regarded as the first accurate depiction of the Massachusetts and Maine coastlines, and the foundation for generations of maps that would come after it—all the more remarkable considering the short period of time Smith spent surveying. On this new map, Smith updates some names, writing the word "New" above Plimouth, and adding the recent settlement of Salem. But he left the other names given by Charles, now King Charles I, in place, perhaps hoping settlers might one day adopt them. (In the end, the only ones that have survived are Plymouth, Cape Ann, and the Charles River.)

For generations of collectors, the map is also notoriously difficult to pin down. Smith produced no less than nine different versions, or states, of the map, with subtle updates and corrections between 1616 and 1631. Copies of the same book have different maps depending on who printed it and when. And copies of the map continued to be reproduced long after Smith's death. In some cases, booksellers peddling a copy of one of Smith's books inserted a state from another book or a facsimile copy, which an inexperienced eye might mistake for an original. To a serious collector, all these slight differences matter a great deal. The state of the map and its rarity could mean a difference of tens of thousands of dollars in a sale.

Smiley knew this well. In fact, he was one of the few people in the world who knew just how rare this map was. Smith's map of New England had become scarce on the market, with copies now coming up at auction once or twice in a generation and fetching anywhere from $50,000 to $100,000. With that thought in mind, Smiley refolded the map down into its original rectangle, about the size of a letter envelope. The map was already free in the book, its four-hundred-year-old glue long since having given way and separated from the binding. Smiley waited until he thought no one was looking and then quickly slipped the folded page into the pocket of his blazer.

At the circulation desk a dozen yards away, the Beinecke's head of security, Ralph Mannarino, was still watching Smiley for signs of suspicious behavior. Now as he watched Smiley get up to check something on the computer, he noticed that he seemed to be fidgeting with something inside his blazer pocket. That Smiley was even wearing a jacket on such a warm day seemed strange to him. As Smiley went to sit back down, Mannarino decided to call Yale Police for backup.

The call went to Detective Martin Buonfiglio, a tall officer with a gray mustache, who was dressed in a plainclothes uniform of a sports coat, tie, and khaki pants. He was just sitting down to lunch at a nearby pizza house. "Someone found a razor blade at the Beinecke," his sergeant told him.

Buonfiglio shrugged. "So?" he said. "Call someone on patrol."

"They are really upset down there," the caller insisted. "I need you to check it out."

With a glance at his uneaten pizza, Buonfiglio left the restaurant and walked the several blocks to the library, arriving by two o'clock. Once there, he went into the back office with Cordes, who explained the situation. "So what did he steal?" the detective asked.

"We don't know," answered Cordes. So far, she said, they hadn't seen him steal anything— they'd just seen the razor blade and the suspicious behavior.

Buonfiglio sighed. If he was going to arrest Smiley, he'd need more evidence than that, he said. "Do you have a camera?"

Cordes told him that the library did have security cameras but, due to patron complaints, didn't turn them on without permission from the president's office.

"Turn it on," Buonfiglio insisted, as he put in a call to his superior officer, Lieutenant Bill Holohan, for further instructions. The call went to voice mail, and so Buonfiglio waited along with the librarians. Around three o'clock he watched Smiley get up from his table and head back upstairs to the Beinecke's storage lockers, looking like he was ready to leave. Buonfiglio considered calling a patrol officer to intercept him, but he worried an officer might be too aggressive. Finally, he decided to follow himself, trailing a few paces behind as Smiley walked out the front door.

CICADAS WERE WHIRRING in the trees as Smiley left the library. He figured he had just enough time to visit the research library in the Yale

Center for British Art, which had one more atlas he wanted to examine before the fair in London. The day was now pushing eighty-five degrees, and Smiley started sweating almost immediately under his blazer. The long hours hunched over in the reading room had also taken their toll on his back, which throbbed with pain as he walked.

Detective Buonfiglio waited behind the corner of the building, watching through the glass as Smiley stopped and put his briefcase down on the low concrete wall edging the Beinecke's courtyard. Smiley opened the briefcase and looked around to either side before closing it and continuing. Buonfiglio followed twenty feet behind as Smiley crossed to a pedestrian walkway heading south toward the art museum, keeping a screen of pedestrians between Smiley and himself as they walked (Figure 2).

After a few dozen yards, the walkway opened up into a large courtyard in front of the Sterling Memorial Library. Buonfiglio was glad Smiley didn't enter the building, where it would be difficult to follow him

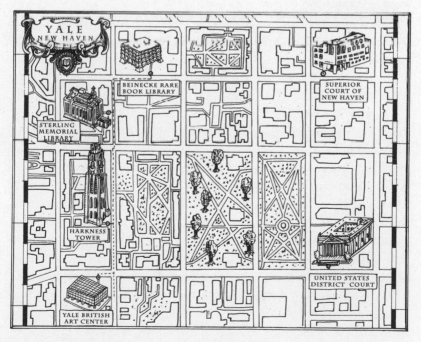

FIGURE 2 SMILEY'S NEW HAVEN (SHOWING SMILEY'S ROUTE, JUNE 8, 2005).

without being noticed. Even so, he faced a dilemma. If Smiley was heading to his car, then Buonfiglio had only a few moments in which to make an arrest. But without probable cause, he had no right to stop and search him. If it came to it, he could do an illegal search—at least he'd get back whatever Smiley stole, even if he failed to get the pinch.

As he followed behind Smiley, he kept trying to reach Lieutenant Holohan for orders, but again the calls went to voice mail. He had to make up his mind on his own. For a moment, he thought he lost Smiley as he reached the end of the pedestrian walkway at Elm Street, a busy avenue with three lanes of fast-moving traffic. Buonfiglio looked around wildly before just spying the back of Smiley's head continuing down High Street. The detective quickly crossed behind him. The street narrowed, with heavy stone buildings on both sides casting cool shadows over the sidewalk. Smiley stopped just before the Harkness Tower, Yale's landmark two-hundred-foot clock tower, where he once again put down his briefcase on another stone wall. Again he opened it, looked both ways, and closed it.

Smiley was oblivious to the detective on his tail, still preoccupied with the weight of his indecision about whether or not to go to London. He crossed the street and continued walking for a half block before realizing he'd passed his destination, the Yale Center for British Art. Walking down the other side of the street, Buonfiglio closed the distance, thinking Smiley was heading for a parking lot behind the museum. When Smiley turned around, Buonfiglio ducked into a barbershop, watching him as he entered the door to the museum on his left. Almost immediately, Smiley realized that he had entered the museum's gift shop, rather than the main entrance, and left as soon as he went in.

Warily, Buonfiglio crossed back to the other side of High Street and followed Smiley as he turned the corner and once again passed the museum. He froze as Smiley suddenly turned back, walking right past him, then finally turning right under a stone arcade that covered the entrance. Inside, the lobby of the museum was mercifully cool. Smiley crossed the lobby, passing by two sculptures—a bronze of an armored man striding confidently forward with laurels on his head, and a modern stone sculpture of a woman looking back over her shoulder, one eye a gaping hole.

He handed over his briefcase at the coat check and began walking toward the elevator. That was when he heard a voice behind him asking him to stop. He turned around to see a tall mustached man wearing a jacket and tie approaching him.

"Hi, I work for Yale. Were you just over at the Beinecke?" asked Buonfiglio.

"Yes," Smiley said quickly. "I'm a researcher. I go there a lot."

"Is this yours, by any chance?" Buonfiglio asked, unwrapping the X-Acto knife blade from the tissue paper and showing it to Smiley.

"Yes, it is. I must have dropped it," Smiley replied, adding a bit nonsensically, "I have a cold."

Buonfiglio tried his best to appear nonchalant, knowing Smiley had no obligation to cooperate. "Well, folks over there think you might have taken something by mistake," he said. "Do you mind if I take a look at your briefcase?"

"Of course," Smiley said. "No problem." He walked back to the desk, retrieved the briefcase, and opened it up to the policeman, revealing a jumble of papers that included several maps. "I'm a collector," Smiley said. "These are my maps."

Buonfiglio could see that Smiley had gone pale and that thick white saliva had begun to form in the corners of his mouth, sure signs of nervousness. "Look, I don't know what's what and who belongs to who," Buonfiglio said after a glance at the maps. "Would you mind coming back with me to the library?"

"Of course," Smiley said again.

As they were leaving, Buonfiglio finally received a call back from his superior, Lieutenant Holohan, who arranged to pick them up outside the museum. As they drove toward the Beinecke, Smiley mentioned that he might miss his train. "Don't worry," said Buonfiglio. "If I have to, I'll drive you to New York myself."

WHEN THEY ARRIVED at the Beinecke, the officers asked Smiley to stand in the back of the mezzanine near the lockers, while they spread out the maps from his briefcase atop a glass display case. While he'd been gone, staff members had been frantically looking through the books he'd examined to see if any maps were missing. That wasn't as straightforward as it might seem. Rare books might have any number of maps inside them—and different editions might have different maps, or have been missing maps before they even arrived at the library. Most of the cataloguing, meanwhile, was maddeningly incomplete, sometimes referring simply to the number of maps in a book, or including just the generic word "maps" without additional information.

One exception was the Smith book, which the catalog record clearly listed as containing his map of New England. Looking through the documents the police officers had recovered, however, library supervisor Ellen Cordes didn't see the Smith map among them. She asked Smiley if he had the map, and he demurred, only saying he knew of the map and it was rare. But he continued to insist he had brought with him all of the maps he had. By this time, Smiley felt strangely calm, his mind almost blank, as if the whole experience was happening to someone else. He'd get out of this, he told himself, and when he did, he would make some big changes in his life. The only strong sensation he felt was the pain in his back, which throbbed more acutely the longer he stood.

Holohan stayed upstairs with Smiley as Buonfiglio went back and forth to the office downstairs to consult with Cordes. "You've got to tell tell me what he stole," he said impatiently. "Otherwise I got to release this guy."

"Did you search him?" asked security head Ralph Mannarino, telling Buonfiglio how he had seen Smiley fidgeting with his coat.

"I'm lucky I even got him back here," said Buonfiglio. But when he got back upstairs, he mentioned Smiley's fidgeting to Holohan.

"Would you mind just showing us if you have anything in your pocket?" Holohan asked. Smiley pulled a credit card from the inside pocket of his blazer. As he did, however, Holohan noticed there was still a bulge there. "What else do you have in there?" he asked.

Smiley pulled out a folded piece of paper, saying, "Oh, I forgot about that."

Back in her office, Cordes unfolded the paper to see the portrait of John Smith staring out of the upper left-hand corner, along with the familiar outlines of the New England coast. In the bottom margin was writing in pencil she recognized as belonging to Henry C. Taylor, a benefactor of the Beinecke who had donated many maps and had a distinctive way of writing his *s*'s.

"That's our map!" she cried.

"Are you sure?" asked Buonfiglio.

"There is no doubt in my mind."

Buonfiglio brought the map back upstairs and asked Smiley where he'd gotten it.

"I bought it from Philip Burden, a map dealer in London," he answered.

Buonfiglio pressed him: "So if I call this guy, he's going to know you, and he's going to know you bought this map from him?"

Smiley put his hands to his head, pressing his fingers into his temples for a few moments. "I'm not sure," he said. "Maybe I didn't get it from him."

Buonfiglio had heard enough. "You are under arrest for larceny in the first degree," he said, turning him around as another officer handcuffed him. Buonfiglio led Smiley outside, reading him his Miranda rights as a cruiser from the New Haven Police Department pulled up to take him to headquarters to spend the night there in jail.

AS SMILEY WAS GRAPPLING with his sudden reversal of fortune, the librarians at the Beinecke were doing the same thing. They put the maps in a safe while continuing to go through the books Smiley had looked at that day. And they finally looked at the security tape from the reading room and saw what they'd missed before: Smiley furtively ripping another map out of an atlas.

Called *Speculum Orbis Terrarum* (Latin for "mirror of the world") and published by Flemish cartographer Gerard de Jode in Antwerp in 1578, the book contained dozens of exquisitely etched maps hand-painted in blues, greens, and pinks. Right after the cover page, de Jode had included a two-page world map copied from his fellow cartographer Abraham Ortelius before the two had become rivals (Figure A). After the first edition, he swapped it out for another world map, making copies of it extremely rare. On the open market, it could fetch as much as $150,000—if it could be sold. The trouble was, all the copies of de Jode's atlas had been well catalogued, making an unknown copy near impossible. Out of recklessness or desperation, Smiley had taken it anyway, ripping it from the binding of the 427-year-old book. As he did, some of the fragile paint flaked, opening a small tear in the middle of Persia.

The other maps from Smiley's briefcase that the Beinecke was able to claim after examination weren't quite as valuable, but they were still significant. One rare map came from a small book with a blue leather binding by English explorer Luke Foxe recounting his 1631 expedition to find the Northwest Passage across America. Due to its scarcity, the map was worth about $50,000. The last map the Beinecke identified came from a brown leather book redolent of tobacco smoke called *The Principall Navigations, Voiages and Discoveries of the English Nation.* Written by geographer Richard Hakluyt in 1589, it contained a rare world map copied from Ortelius that was worth more than $75,000.

As the librarians looked through Smiley's briefcase, however, they quickly realized it contained more maps than they could identify as their own. Of the eight maps inside, only four came from books Smiley had viewed that day. The fact begged the obvious questions: Where had the others come from? Had they been stolen too? Buonfiglio contacted the FBI, which sent out an alert to rare-book libraries around the country. One by one, they began to call with panicked reports of maps missing from books in their collections as well. As they did, more questions began to reverberate through the insular world of map libraries, collectors, and dealers: Why had a respected and successful antiquarian dealer turned against those who trusted him and stolen the things he loved most? And how long had he been getting away with it?

Chapter 2

SMALL HOPE

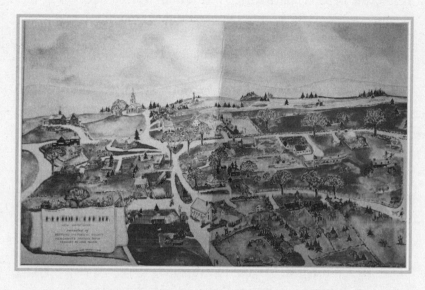

FIGURE 3 JEAN TALLMAN. "BEDFORD CENTER."
NEW HAMPSHIRE. 1979.

1956–1985

IT WAS IN AN effort to answer those questions that I found myself on a ferry from Cape Cod to the island of Martha's Vineyard on a shimmering August day in 2011. More than six years had passed since that day of his arrest at the Beinecke, and Smiley had never told his story to a reporter. I wanted to find out what had led him down the path to his crimes, turning him from map dealer to map thief. The boat glided past the breakwater into the harbor, where gray cottages and white church steeples climbed the hill. Finally it bumped up against the dock, where I joined a line of passengers clutching duffel bags and beach satchels on their way down the gangway.

I easily picked out Smiley's glasses and pushed-back gray hair on the other side of a line of waiting taxicabs. "Beautiful day, isn't it?" he said, greeting me with a wide grin. "Did you have a good trip in?" He seemed fit and tan, not at all the shrunken, defeated figure I'd seen in newspaper reports about his crimes. After some small talk, we drove ten minutes to a nearby café, where we took our coffees to an outside picnic table. Removing his wooden coffee stirrer, he began to worry it apart as he told me the story of his life—not stopping for nearly four hours.

He got into the map trade "by accident," he told me. After graduating from college in the spring of 1978, he followed a girlfriend to London, where she worked at Sotheby's auction house. The relationship didn't last, but Smiley's interest in the world of rare books and manuscripts had been piqued. "It was like buying and selling parts of puzzles," he said. "I began to understand how it worked, and how dynamic the relationship was between buyers and sellers, and I wanted to be a part of that world."

When he returned stateside in 1979 at age twenty-three, he looked for an entrée, finding it in the rare-books department of B. Altman and Co., a department store at Thirty-Fourth Street and Fifth Avenue in New York City. Founded just after the Civil War, Altman's was quieter and more elegant than its rivals in the Manhattan department store world, the bustling Macy's and Bloomingdale's. With plush, carpeted floors and Waterford chandeliers hanging from the ceiling, it was better known for furnishings than fashions—selling rugs, crystal, and china to the "carriage trade" of Upper East Side doyennes. Every winter, its windows filled with elaborate holiday displays featuring life-size figures of elves, animals, and people in traditional Christmas scenes.

The rare-books department was an afterthought, located on the eighth floor next to the Charleston Garden restaurant, a favorite rendezvous for the theater matinee crowd. On their way to or from lunch, some of its patrons would stop to flip through the books, autographs, and celebrity memorabilia lining the shelves. An even smaller division, where Smiley was placed, sold rare maps, atlases, and globes. Despite knowing little about the topic, he bent himself to the task. "Most maps are bad," his supervisor, Rosejeanne Slifer, told him. "But they are bad for a reason." French and English maps of the Ohio Valley drew different boundary lines in a cartographical land-grab before the French and Indian

War. English mapmakers kept the fantasy of the Northwest Passage alive for centuries to please the merchant companies that funded their expeditions. John Smith asked Prince Charles to put a fictitious London and Oxford in the middle of the wilderness of New England to spur his countrymen to colonization. Understand hidden motives like those, and not only could you identify the stories behind the maps; you could also determine which were worth buying and selling.

He learned more technical lessons as well—such as how to tell the difference between the chunky lines of woodblock prints and the finely drawn curves of copper-plate engravings, and how to spot "original color," paint applied by hand at the time the map was made, over "modern color" applied decades or centuries after the fact. He learned to identify the "rhumb lines" that crisscrossed antique maps to provide bearings to navigators and the elaborately drawn "cartouches," containing the name of the map and its creators. Depending on the map, up to five people could take credit for making it—including the surveyor, cartographer, engraver, publisher, and map seller. Different maps were attributed differently according to the fame and influence of their contributors, making it difficult for novice map collectors to keep track of which map was whose.

Smiley became fascinated by the combination of history and craftsmanship that lay behind this specialized art. Since childhood, he had been drawn both to beautiful, well-made objects and to esoteric knowledge, and maps were the perfect manifestation of both. Here was a world where knowledge mattered, and not just for bragging rights, but for real money.

DESPITE HIS ELITIST-SOUNDING NAME, E. Forbes Smiley III grew up solidly middle class in suburban New Hampshire, the son of a physicist who worked for a local defense contractor. The original Edward Forbes Smiley—Smiley's grandfather—was born in Connecticut, descended from a line of Congregationalist ministers. After graduating from Harvard in 1917 he became one himself, spending most of his career as a small-town preacher. Smiley's father, Edward Forbes Smiley II, took a different tack, earning his degree in engineering from the University of Connecticut in 1946, followed by a master's from Brown in 1949 and a PhD from Catholic University in Washington, DC, in 1953.

The elder Smiley married young, fathering a daughter, Marilyn, who was born in May 1945 before his first wife died. A few years later, he met Adele Moreau, a Chicago girl who had married a military colonel and traveled with him as far afield as Panama before he, too, died suddenly in 1950. After a brief courtship, the two married and had three more children: Marion in July 1953, and Forbes and his twin sister, Susan, on April 13, 1956. By that time, Smiley had decided to leave the city and look for a small town close to his New England family roots.

He found it in Bedford, New Hampshire, where he began work as a physicist for nearby defense contractor Sanders Associates. Today, Bedford is a tony bedroom community next door to the City of Manchester, with winding back roads filled with big brick houses and a commercial district along the highway teeming with upscale shops. Islanded in their midst, the historic district where Smiley grew up consists of a square mile of older houses and municipal buildings ranged around the iconic white bell tower of the town's Presbyterian church (Figure 3).

The town was founded in 1750 by Scotch-Irish immigrants who planted hard-rock farms before expanding into gristmills and granite quarries. It hit its stride in the 1850s with the widespread planting of hops for making beer—briefly becoming the hops capital of New England. Another boom came a century later, in the 1950s, as a host of transplants came after World War II to work in jobs in Manchester's burgeoning manufacturing and technology center, and the population tripled from two thousand to six thousand in a matter of decades.

One of the newcomers was Smiley's father, who bought a white-and-pink farmhouse a half mile from the church in December 1958. The house was a classic New England farmhouse, combining two Greek Revival homes with an ell that has since been converted into a double garage. Behind it sprawled nearly two acres of rolling backyard with a swimming pool, some thickety woods, and a culvert on one side—a young boy's perfect playground.

SMILEY ALWAYS DESCRIBED his childhood as "idyllic." Even as Bedford rapidly expanded, it remained in many ways the classic New England village. The town had virtually no industry and only a few stores. One of them, French's, stood a mile from Smiley's home at the town's main intersection and housed the town post office and general store, where residents stopped by every weekend to pick up gossip along with their mail and groceries. Major issues were settled in town meetings, in which each citizen got one vote. Social life centered around the Presbyterian church, the venue for Boy and Girl Scout meetings, weddings, parties, club meetings, and a nonsectarian kindergarten.

Smiley's family life also centered around the church. His grandfather, who had moved with the family and occupied an attic apartment, served as an elder; his mother assisted with Sunday school; and Smiley himself was an altar boy. Smiley's father, meanwhile, tended to be shy and reserved—the kind of person who retreated into his office for hours to read after work. But he was also patient and kind with his children, teaching his son about history and instructing him how to carve and whittle. Smiley's father was an avid gardener and collected antique gardening books from England, which he eventually began buying and selling out of the back of a bookseller's trade magazine, *AB Bookman's Weekly.*

Prone to be overweight, Smiley, too, was bookish as a child, spending long afternoons in the library and scouring flea markets for old things to repair. But Smiley was hardly a loner. Unlike his father, his mother was outgoing and gregarious, teaching Sunday School and serving as a Cub Scout den mother, and Smiley picked up on her example as well. After school and on weekends, he and his sisters attracted a group of neighborhood kids who came to the farmhouse to play in the rambling backyard and swim in the pool while his mother made sandwiches in the kitchen.

Even as Smiley was growing up, however, Bedford was changing. The town established a full-time police department in 1964, around the same time the main thoroughfare, Route 101, was relocated outside the town center. A strip of commercial development sprouted, including a Jordan Marsh department store in 1968 and the heralded opening of the Bedford Mall a year later, complete with a supermarket, department store, and cinema. Smiley listened as his father lamented the changes, nostalgic for the small town of his own youth.

Smiley's father had always emphasized the importance of education while Smiley was growing up. He insisted on intelligent conversation at the dinner table and showed slides in the living room of countries he visited for work. In the early 1960s, Smiley's parents joined with several dozen like-minded families to found the Derryfield School, a private school in nearby Manchester, in order to provide their children with a better education than the one they thought the public education system could provide. Smiley's sister Marilyn started in the inaugural class in 1964, and Marion, Susan, and Forbes all followed in later years.

Situated on a curve of the Merrimack, it now looks like the quintessential New England prep school, with a sprawling campus of academic buildings, tennis courts, and sports fields. When first founded, though, it proudly called itself an "experimental" school, with a distinctly counterculture vibe. One of Smiley's friends, Paul Statt, clearly remembered starting at the school when he and his family moved into the area in 1971. There were two types of students, he recalled: children of the children of the sixties, who grew their hair long and embraced their parents' hippie mind-set, and clean-cut kids who had failed out of Exeter or Andover and retained their preppie mannerisms.

Forbes was neither. The first time Statt met him in English class, Smiley made an indelible impression. Heavyset and sporting a long ponytail like the hippies, he nevertheless dressed conservatively like the preppies. But what caught Statt's attention most was a screwdriver that Smiley was absently but repeatedly throwing up in the air as he sat having a discussion in a circle with the rest of the group. The action seemed unique and at the same time so self-possessed that Statt immediately fell under his spell. Soon the two had become friends.

Statt came from an unhappy family and spent increasing amounts of time at the Smiley household, where he discovered that Smiley had a host of other talents as well. He could do magic tricks and knife tricks, including rapidly stabbing a knife between his outspread fingers without hurting himself. But he was especially articulate in his love of history and literature. While Smiley's weight might have gotten him picked on at other schools, he was tremendously popular at Derryfield, known for a booming voice and wisecracking temperament. He sang baritone in the chorus and went out for chess club and drama club, playing Big Julie in *Guys and Dolls*. But his upright Presbyterianism also made him a natural arbiter of student disputes.

"We both auditioned for the role of a judge in a school play, and he got the role," later recalled Hilary Chaplain, a friend from Bedford and

Derryfield, on whom Smiley developed a crush. "He just had this sense of honesty and sincerity and a strong moral constitution." Despite his popularity, Smiley wasn't the kind of guy girls got crushes on, and what crushes he had went unreturned. He compensated by finding other ways of getting attention. Along with three other friends—one named Peter and two named Paul—he founded the "Literary Guild," a guys-only group of self-styled aesthetes who got together to smoke cigars, drink beer, and discuss philosophy, in that order.

When he got his driver's license, he bought a beat-up Mercedes at a time when his friends' parents were driving hand-me-down Datsuns. "It became kind of a marker for who he was," remembered Statt. "He became that guy who drove the Mercedes." In another instance, he and a few friends planned a trip to Cape Cod to fly kites and hopefully meet girls. Smiley insisted that they make their own kites, spending hours experimenting with construction to make them stay aloft as long as possible. When it came time to actually fly the kites on the beach, Statt recalled, he seemed to lose interest. The act of making them was enough. "He was always very good at sort of narrating his own life, not necessarily in a self-promoting way, but just in a way trying to make whatever he was doing into a bigger story," said Statt, "a better story."

BY COLLEGE, HIS personality was well-formed. Starting in 1974, he attended Hampshire College, a free-form liberal arts school in Amherst, Massachusetts, where students design their own majors. It was, not surprisingly, a school full of eccentric characters. With his strange combination of ponytail and pressed khakis, Smiley managed to stand out without becoming one of them. He confidently bounded across campus, seemingly always in a hurry. In an era of *Blood on the Tracks* and *Born to Run*, he listened exclusively to classical music. And in place of the Mercedes, he began driving an old Checker cab.

To his friends, who were all more or less going through the awkwardness of finding themselves in college, he seemed enviably composed. As with the Literary Guild at Derryfield, he cultivated a group of intellectuals who sat together in the cafeteria debating philosophy and literature. Smiley immersed himself in the classics, studying Greek and Latin and the history of religion and delighting in knowing more than those around him. He started a conversation once by asking his friend Scott Haas which translation of *The Iliad* was his favorite—and fairly howled with protest when Haas said he'd never read any of them.

Another friend, Scott Slater, began taking long walks with him every night after dinner and never failed to be impressed by the way Smiley could stop at an old church steeple and rattle off a half-dozen facts about who had made it and when. Smiley could well engage in the late-night games of intellectual one-upsmanship that characterize college life, but he didn't do it with the insecure caviling of most of his peers. Instead, it quickly became clear to his friends that he simply knew more than they did, and when he stated something, people tended to believe him. No matter how Smiley lorded information over his friends, however, he always did it with a laugh—a great booming laugh that seemed always just below the surface in conversation.

Nor were his talents limited to book smarts. Another close friend, Dick Cantwell, worked on theater sets with him and was routinely impressed at his skill in working with wood. Fred Melamed, who later became an acclaimed actor, remembers him standing outside the dining commons at Hampshire, juggling Indian clubs while reciting Greek classics. At various times, he showed friends how to carve a turkey, cut firewood, and make a campfire. One November when they went camping, he summarily ripped off his clothes and jumped into a freezing-cold lake. No matter what he did, Smiley threw himself into projects he took on with an energy bordering on obsession. When he decided to lose weight after his freshman year, he went on a sudden crash diet, returning to campus in the fall half the size he left it in the spring.

Nothing demonstrates his drive and determination to his friends, however, more than "the dollhouse." Smiley began constructing miniature dollhouse furniture in his dorm room as a hobby, selling items to the local toy store for extra cash. In the summer between his junior and senior years, the owner asked if he'd be interested in building a complete dollhouse for the window. Smiley worked all summer to build a Victorian mansion on a massive scale: four and half feet wide, three feet deep, and two and a half feet tall. On the exterior, he tiled a mansard roof with real slate and added a verandah and widow's walk. Inside, he applied hinges to the walls so they could swing outward and admirers could peer into the rooms, which were furnished with meticulous detail based on research he did on real nineteenth-century homes.

"I took different rooms I liked and fit them into one house," he told the local newspaper, which called the house "more like a work of art" than a child's toy. "I wanted to combine the aesthetic appeal of a Victorian house and the idea of a doll house." He built a tiny grand piano for the living room next to an oriental mural drawn on the wall in pen and ink. In the kitchen, he installed a woodstove and mousetraps smaller than a fingernail on the floor. In the library, he built a pinewood table that could fold out into a ladder that reached the books on the upper shelves. He plastered ceilings, painted walls, and inlaid floors with parquetry.

"It's really carpentry in miniature," he explained. "When I didn't know how to do something, I fell back on the way it's really done." When he'd finished, the owner of the store estimated the price at $10,000—of which Smiley of course received only a fraction. But the owner resolutely refused to sell, keeping it in the window throughout the 1980s and 1990s, a landmark for a generation of local children.

As impressive as his mock mansion was, Smiley illustrated a more grandiose vision to his friends in late-night bull sessions. Among the usual talk of moving in together after college and starting some kind of art commune, Smiley expressed a larger vision. Instead of a house, he told friends that he wanted to start a small village, where they could all move. He spent hours detailing everything it would have—a school where kids could learn through hands-on work, a radio station where they could play all the music they liked. He even had a name for it: Small Hope, which his friends recognized as a typically "Forbesian" touch, at once grandiose and humble. "By calling it small, it was like saying this is such a modest proposal I have here," Statt later said. "But it's going to be a utopian ideal."

WHEN SMILEY FINALLY settled down in New York after college, the place he chose couldn't have been farther from the quaint vision he had outlined. Rather than pick a spot downtown or on the Upper West Side, Smiley decided to make this home in the gritty neighborhood of Washington Heights, finding an apartment on the corner of Fort Washington and 163rd Street. Back in the 1980s, the neighborhood was much more dangerous than it is now. Outside, the building wasn't much to look at—a six-story low-rise apartment house on a desolate stretch of street, with a bodega next door that sold beer through a metal grate. But Smiley saw potential in his apartment, a warren of rooms full of period details—wainscoting, a working fireplace. Smiley put up new molding and refinished the hardwood floors. It was his dollhouse writ large.

Soon he had a partner in the endeavor, a pretty blonde named Lisa who worked in the home furnishings department of B. Altman. Shy where Smiley was outgoing, she looked up to his knowledge and confident personality. The two began dating and eventually moved in together in the Washington Heights apartment, where Lisa's decorator's eye complemented Smiley's own. They began to create a gathering place for friends, who made the exotic trek uptown for dinner parties and late-night gatherings.

After scattering around the country, Smiley's old friends from Derryfield and Hampshire reunited at a series of weddings, and many found their way to New York either as residents or passing through while traveling. Smiley encouraged them to stay as long as they wanted in the roomy apartment. Shortly after college, his oldest friend, Paul Statt, went through a tough time—breaking up with his girlfriend at the same time he lost his job and his truck broke down. "I was feeling like a country music song," Statt later said. Smiley invited him down to the city, telling him, "You are straight, you are not fat, the girls are going to love you in New York." Smiley let him sleep on the couch for six months, never once asking for rent.

In addition to Smiley's friends, Lisa began cultivating a crowd of creative professionals from the fashion and design world. Forbes and Lisa loved playing host—cooking meals and bringing out gourmet cheese and decent wine at a time when most of their friends were drinking cheap beer. Gatherings lasted until three in the morning, with dancing to the Talking Heads and B-52s, while the Hampshire crowd vied to outdo one another in esoteric knowledge, with enormous amounts of beer and red wine to fuel the conversation. Smiley himself was often on the periphery of his own gatherings. He could recount great stories from college with a raconteur's gift for narrative. But even as he created space for others to socialize, he was rarely the one to hold forth in the middle of a gathering, preferring one-on-one conversations with guests in the corners.

AT THE SAME TIME that Smiley was settling into his new life in New York, he was also doing everything he could to learn about the trade into which he had fallen. He had been intrigued by what his boss, Slifer, had told him about maps and those who made them, and he wanted to know more. Slifer encouraged him to visit the New York Public Library. B. Altman was only a half-dozen blocks south of the main branch on Fifth Avenue, which housed the Map Division. That's where Smiley's real cartographic education began.

"I began a twenty-year love affair with the New York Public Library," Smiley told me as we sat talking together on Martha's Vineyard. "It is the greatest institution I know of. There were enormous quantities of maps and atlases there that were not being given attention." By the time Smiley pulled open the brass handles on the Map Division's Room 117, it contained some eleven thousand atlases and 350,000 individual maps—the largest collection of any public library in the world. More than seven thousand visitors passed through each year—real estate lawyers researching property maps for land disputes; news reporters searching for up-to-date maps of Beirut or Grenada; railroad hobbyists searching for old tunnels beneath the city; and plenty of ordinary people just looking for highway maps to help plan their vacations.

The room was particularly conducive to studying antique maps. Called a "Beaux-Art jewelbox," and the NYPL's "holy of holies," Room 117 was forty feet long and nearly as deep, lined with dark-wood bookcases and high arched windows through which sunlight streamed. The ceiling cavorted with plaster dragons and cherubs in gold, green, and vermillion, and golden chandeliers hung over rows of wide walnut tables. Against the far wall, long gray cabinets held thousands of maps in flat drawers, with thousands more maps in the back room.

Lording over it all as an approving mother hen was Alice Hudson, chief of the division since 1981. A big woman with curly blond hair and a playful wit, she had established herself as the map room's guiding spirit by age thirty-five. Originally from Oak Ridge, Tennessee, she had spent her summers vacationing at her great-aunt's big Victorian house in Michigan. There she often visited Greenfield Village, Henry Ford's re-creation of Americana, full of old houses and shops, antique cars, and a historic carousel. Hudson was entranced. "I blame Greenfield Village for my career," she later said. "I wanted to be in the map field because of all that history."

Hudson became captivated by maps during a required geography course at Middle Tennessee State University, and after that she took one geography course after another. When she entered Vanderbilt University to study library science, her professors told her that there was no such thing as a map librarian. But she proved them wrong the year she graduated, when the NYPL offered her a job as a junior map cataloger. She wasted no time learning the collection, climbing quickly to the top post in the division. Her favorite map was the "water map" drawn by a civil engineer named Egbert Viele in 1874 showing the underground courses of the original streams on Manhattan Island. She used to delight in telling journalists how, on more than one occasion, men in waders had come in to consult the map trying to figure out how their construction sites had gotten suddenly soaked.

As much as she appreciated the more modern maps, however, she especially loved the maps from the sixteenth and seventeenth centuries, which were kept separate in their own locked, military-green cases. She delighted in the feel of old cloth and vellum and in the knowledge that these maps had lasted hundreds of years and would someday outlive her. Most researchers came to use the more modern New York–themed maps. A rare atlas might go years in its drawer without being touched.

When Smiley came in telling her he was interested in antique maps, she began pulling them out for him one by one. He sat for hours paging through them, familiarizing himself with names like Dudley, Des Barres, Faden, and Jefferys, mapmakers who soon became central to his career. For even older material, he climbed the marble stairs to the Rare Book Division, which included maps dating back to the fifteenth century. As someone who had always been interested in New England history, he began focusing on maps that illustrated the discovery of North America.

"And I loved the stuff!" he told me, his voice quickening with excitement. "Here was a body of evidence of enormous value for a historian that had never been looked at in a comprehensive, serious way, and it just blew my mind. You don't get handed opportunities like that. You just don't." At the time, the study of cartography was still developing, and the European map dealers who dominated were more interested in studying maps of the world or of their own countries. Smiley ordered up book after book, making connections among them—seeing which cartographers had copied from another, and which had really pushed forth the knowledge of a region with original surveys. Not only was he making findings that no one else had made before, but he was also able to impress his clients at B. Altman by directing them to maps that mattered. He could go to the NYPL and research a particular rare map, and then handle a copy of it a week or a month later at the store.

SMILEY'S ENCYCLOPEDIC MEMORY and enthusiasm for the subject didn't escape the notice of B. Altman's regular clients, who increasingly began to seek him out for advice. He recognized certain customers, calling them in advance when a map that might interest them arrived in the store. One client who was particularly captivated by Smiley was Norman Leventhal, a Boston real estate developer who had turned to map collecting late in life.

The son of Russian and Lithuanian Jews who grew up in the tough Irish neighborhood of Dorchester, Leventhal worked hard enough in his studies to win admission to Massachusetts Institute of Technology at age fifteen. There he earned a degree in civil engineering, eventually working his way into real estate. As with most US cities, Boston's downtown had been gutted by the 1960s, and most developers had turned their focus toward building housing complexes and office parks in the suburbs. Leventhal was committed to urban redevelopment and designed an ambitious downtown project called Center Plaza, the beginning of what pundits called the "New Boston." Other projects followed: Post Office Square, Le Méridien (now Langham) hotel, and finally his crowning achievement, the development of Rowes Wharf and the luxury Boston Harbor Hotel.

Leventhal's contributions to Boston's future made him naturally interested in the city's past. He picked up his first antique map of Boston while visiting London with his wife in the late 1970s, as he was nearing

sixty. Bit by bit, he added to his collection. Then one Sunday morning
in 1982, he was reading *The New York Times* when he saw an ad for B. Altman and Co. that mentioned its antique map division. The next time he
was in town, he visited the eighth floor of the store and was met by a
bespectacled clerk with a similar love of New England. Smiley talked
with contagious enthusiasm about all he was discovering about the early
history of cartography, and he promised to be on the lookout for maps
that might fit in with Leventhal's passions. He called him a short time
later with just such a map, which Leventhal bought over the phone—the
first of several he purchased from Smiley while he worked at B. Altman.

Even as he did, however, the fortunes of Smiley's employer were
changing. Never able to compete with more fashionable department
stores, B. Altman and Co. struggled financially throughout the 1980s.
Finally a change in the tax law in 1984 compelled the owner to sell. The
new buyer announced plans to "modernize" by cutting the store's footprint in half and getting rid of many specialty divisions, including rare
books and maps. Suddenly finding himself faced with the prospect of
losing his job, Smiley made the decision to go out on his own. He
launched his new business as North American Maps & Autographs by
the end of 1984, running it out of his apartment, with his now fiancée,
Lisa. (B. Altman finally closed in 1989 with a fire sale of Waterford
crystal and Christmas decorations.)

His former boss, Slifer, gave him her blessing—and something far
more valuable as well: letters of introduction to some of the most prestigious map dealers in Paris, Amsterdam, and London, where the map
trade was then centered. In a handshake business where personal connections were key, those letters were the closest thing that existed to a ticket
into the business. Because he started his company before B. Altman officially closed, however, she told him it would be unethical to contact any
of his former clients from the store. He would have to wait until they
called him. Smiley spent a nerve-wracking week waiting for the phone
to ring, until Leventhal's call finally came. The two discussed an arrangement wherein Smiley would become Leventhal's main agent in negotiating the purchase of maps overseas. With that, Smiley entered into
the tight-knit but expanding world of map collectors.

Chapter 3

A NEW WORLD

FIGURE 4 MARTIN WALDSEEMÜLLER. "UNIVERSALIS COSMOGRAPHIA SECUNDUM PTHOLOMAEI TRADITIONEM ET AMERICI VESPUCII ALIORU[M]QUE LUSTRATIONES." ST. DIE, 1507.

2300 BC–1670

FLAMES FLICKERED INSIDE silver heat lamps, and potted palms swayed in the breeze atop Miami's Mayfair Hotel on the unseasonably cool February evening that kicked off the 2013 Miami International Map Fair. Cartographic enthusiasts—most men, most gray haired, most wearing blue blazers—jostled their way to the bar as Latin techno-music pulsed through the crowd and what looked like S and M footage played on video screens above. One of the few women in the crowd shouted, "I need a seltzer right now!" as a bartender in a lace minidress stared unmoved. "You're gonna hafta wait, ma'am," she said.

Miami may seem like the least likely place on the map to host an international cartographic conference, much less the world's largest. But in 2013, more than a thousand people were expected to attend—more than the similar map fairs in London or Paris. As the collectors mingled beneath wispy clouds, a mix of accents—southern, British, German— filled the night air. The map community is a small one, with maybe a few dozen serious dealers in the United States and fewer than a hundred worldwide. As they sipped cocktails, dealers, collectors, and tagalong spouses renewed friendships going back decades.

The next morning dawned bright and blue. Bathers had already begun to shed their tops a mile away on South Beach, as collectors filed into the whitewashed stucco building that housed the Museum of HistoryMiami. Inside, several dozen dealers had set up tables in three modest-size rooms, with hundreds of maps displayed on the walls behind them. There were huge maps of tiny stretches of coastline; postcard-size maps of the entire world; colorful eye candy from seventeenth-century Dutch atlases; crude black-and-white woodblocks from fifteenth-century Germany; English sea charts and Italian portolans covered with wind roses and rhumb lines.

Almost all the maps distorted geography in some way—and oftentimes, the more distorted the picture, the higher the price tag affixed to it. California as an island, a surprisingly long-lived fallacy in the seventeenth and eighteenth centuries, is a favorite collector's item. And—at least here in Miami—maps of the Florida peninsula flattened into a saucepan shape were nearly as popular. While some of the maps were framed, most were simply matted and encased in plastic sheets. Even maps worth tens of thousands of dollars hung on the wall with butterfly clips and pushpins. Anyone who had paid $5 admission could flip through the racks and handle maps up to four hundred or even five hundred years old.

At the back of one dealer's bin was a plastic-sheathed map with a slice of coastline in the corner labeled "terra incognita"—Latin for "unknown land." The sliver is the earliest depiction of the American continent a collector could hope to buy. A sticker on the back of the plastic listed the price as $120,000. It's hard to imagine a piece of jewelry worth that much displayed so openly. Yet the map trade is still very much a hand-shake business. Some dealers don't take credit cards; if a buyer doesn't have a check or sufficient cash on hand, it's not uncommon for him to walk out with a map in exchange for an IOU.

Most collectors follow a familiar pattern—they start with one map of their town, city, or state, follow it up with a few more, and then, before they know it, are dropping thousands on geographies halfway around the world. "It's like drugs or alcohol." Collector Neil Outlaw sighed of his habit when we sat down over a brown-bag lunch in the courtyard. "It can make you spend a lot more money than you want to," he continued. "I'm always buying them and not selling them. My wife says that's my problem."

A fifty-one-year-old Alabama peanut farmer, Outlaw started coming to the Miami map fair ten years ago, focusing on buying maps of his area of southern Alabama. "I try to pick maps that have where I'm at on them," he drawled. Over the years, the definition of "where I'm at" had been expanding—from the State of Alabama, to the southeastern United States, to the country, to the world. His most expensive purchase to date was a map of North and South America he bought for $135,000 from the Old Print Shop in New York. "I love the history of it. When I see a map, I like to try and guess when it was made, and whether it was a French map or an English map or a Spanish map—because they all drew the borderlines to their advantage." His neighbors in the farming business, he chuckled, draw their boundaries the same way.

Perhaps the appeal of collecting is seeing the familiar outlines of human nature writ large, and your own little corner of the world participating on the global stage. Arriving at the fair, I vowed to buy my first antique map, and I found it in a map of Boston Harbor that appeared in an English magazine in 1775—three months before the start of the Revolutionary War. By then, it was already clear something major was about to go down in Boston, and the magazine printed the map as a guide for Londoners wanting to follow the action.

I recall similar maps in the newspapers during my own lifetime, remembering how names like Kuwait, Sarajevo, and Fallujah took on sudden geographical significance when conflicts broke out there. I looked for my own hometown of Brookline on the map and found the Muddy River, which still flows a few dozen yards from my house, thinking with a new sense of immediacy about the historic events that took place down the street. The map was listed for $500, which the dealer marked down to $425 with barely a haggle. I left with the map rolled into a cardboard tube, promising to send a check.

MAP COLLECTING IS a recent hobby, emerging only in the past few hundred years. For centuries before that, maps—no matter how beautifully rendered—were tools to settle property disputes or get from point A to point B. That's why, incredibly, we have only a handful of maps from all of ancient civilization. The Babylonians left behind barely enough to count on two hands. The oldest, etched into a clay tablet around 2300 BC, seems to show the estate of a man named Azala as it stood during the reign of Sargon the Great. The first "world" map dates from around 500 BC—glued together from cracked tablets, it looks like a first grader's art project, lines and circles representing the Euphrates River and several neighboring city-states, along with a bridge to the heavenly realm.

The rest of the ancient world fares little better. From Egypt, we have a few maps drawn on scraps of papyrus showing flood stages of the Nile and some Nubian gold mines. From Greece, not a single original map survives. From Rome, only one map of any substance exists, and that is a copy of a copy of a copy made in the eleventh or twelfth century by a South German monk. Called the Peutinger Table, it's a twenty-two-foot-long scroll showing all the roads leading to Rome, mapped out in the style of a AAA strip map, down to the mileages between towns recorded in Roman numerals.

It was the Greeks who put cartography on the map—or rather it was the Hellenized inhabitants of Alexandria, the Egyptian capital that had inherited Greek culture at a time when Rome was still a dirty backwater on the Tiber. Founded by Alexander the Great in 332 BC, it had already become the richest city in the world seventy years later—a city of wide avenues and enormous stone temples sprawling around a harbor bustling with sailors from all over the Mediterranean. With them came scholars who gathered around the Royal Library of Alexandria, then the largest library in the world. Pharaoh Ptolemy III decreed that every traveler entering the city be searched and any manuscripts on his person confiscated and transcribed. A new copy was gifted to its owner, while the original was added to the library's collection. As a result, the library amassed the greatest body of knowledge in the ancient world—the equivalent of a hundred thousand books.

At its head was Eratosthenes, a polymath equally adept at philosophy, astronomy, and mathematics who became the head librarian in 240 BC. His greatest contribution was in geography. From at least Aristotle's time, Greeks had known that the earth was round—otherwise, why would ships' hulls disappear before their masts when sailing out to sea? But they had no idea how large it was. Eratosthenes concocted a formula to measure the circumference by ingeniously noting the angle of the sun simultaneously in two different spots and mathematically extracting the total distance of about twenty-five thousand miles—remarkably close to the actual figure of 24,900.

Eratosthenes and other Greeks of his time made other contributions as well, for example, adding consistent scale and lines of latitude to maps. But it was Eratosthenes's successor at the library a few centuries later, Claudius Ptolemaeus—known to history as simply Ptolemy—who made the greatest strides. Born around AD 100, Ptolemy's fame rests on two books. In the first, the *Almagest*, he famously rejected the popular theory that the earth circled the sun in favor of an earth-centered universe. The Ptolemaic view survived infamously for centuries—until it was finally challenged by the likes of Copernicus and Galileo some fourteen hundred years later.

Despite that cosmic blunder, his second book, the *Geographia*, had a more positive lasting influence. Before Ptolemy, no one had systematically gathered all geographic knowledge in one place. Ptolemy combined historical books by the likes of Herodotus, original observations, and travelers' tales to produce twenty-seven maps showing the entire known world. Just as important, he included a list of some eight thousand place names, each with its presumed latitude and longitude. Theoretically, someone could take that list and faithfully re-create Ptolemy's maps with parchment and a ruler.

That is exactly what happened. Though all of Ptolemy's maps were lost in the fall of Rome, the tables were preserved in Byzantium and the Arab world. After a dreary thousand years of flat-earth religious maps about as useful to navigation as a cartoon, a Greek monk named Maximus Planudes came upon a copy of the *Geographia* in Constantinople and translated it into Latin. In 1397, a Turkish diplomat and scholar named

Manuel Chrysoloras brought a copy to Florence, where the Renaissance was just kicking off.

Just as Alexandria had been the cultural center of the ancient world, Florence was the cultural center of fifteenth-century Europe, attracting "humanist" scholars to debate the great philosophical and scientific questions, looking back to Greece and Rome for inspiration. They seized upon the *Geographia* as a true vision of the world passed down from the ancients—using Ptolemy's tables to faithfully reconstruct his maps. Compared to everything that had come before them, the maps were a revelation. Suddenly the contours of the Mediterranean world emerged in stunning detail, filled with continents and cities only vaguely imagined before (Figure B).

Not surprisingly, Ptolemy's maps contained some errors. He rejected Eratosthenes's calculations of the earth's circumference in favor of those of another Greek mathematician, who wrongly pegged it at just eighteen thousand miles. He also joined a rather indistinct Africa to a huge southern continent, and he vastly extended Asia, shrinking the distance between it and Europe to a mere twenty-five hundred miles. Those errors had profound implications later when Christopher Columbus set off from Spain with a map from the *Geographia* in hand.

Despite them, however, it's difficult to overstate the influence of the *Geographia*, which boldly proposed that the visible world was accessible to the human mind through mathematical precision—a heretical notion in the Middle Ages. As one Florentine described it at the time, the *Geographia* "raises us above the limits of an earth obscured by clouds," demonstrating "how, with true discipline, we can leap up within ourselves, without the aid of wings."

ALTHOUGH PTOLEMY FIRST REENTERED Western Europe in Florence, he didn't stay there long. Scholars meeting at church conferences traded and copied manuscripts, bringing the *Geographia* home to France, Germany, and the Low Countries of Belgium and Holland. At first, they looked at his maps as a way to understand the ancient world—but soon they realized they could use Ptolemy's template to construct their own maps as well.

Mapmaking hadn't totally atrophied in Western Europe during the

Middle Ages. World maps, or *mappaemundi*, were mostly diagrammatical in nature, consisting of a large O with a large T drawn inside separating the three parts of the world (Europe, Asia, and Africa). These T-O maps were, of course, useless for navigation—serving as more of a way to understand cosmology than a practical tool for getting from place to place. But one group of people actually needed maps they could use: sailors. Starting in the 1300s, traders plying the Mediterranean began constructing nautical charts called "portolans," covering small areas of the coast, with virtually no detail of the interior. After a French crusader brought the compass from the Middle East, mapmakers employed two other features as well: strategically placed "wind roses" pointing out the cardinal directions, and spiderwebs of "rhumb lines" showing the bearing needed to sail from one to another.

In the fourteenth century, regional centers consolidated the best mapmakers in Pisa, Genoa, Sicily, Majorca, and Barcelona. Their maps included broader and broader areas, including some attempts at world maps. To fill the blanks in information, they relied on Christian myths and travelers' tales. The kingdoms of the Antichrist, Gog and Magog, were located in Far Eastern Asia, just north of the realm of Cathay, the fabulously wealthy kingdom of Kublai Khan mentioned in the writings of Marco Polo. In the eastern ocean were the island of Zipangu (Japan) and the wealthy islands of the Indies, which Marco Polo had also mentioned. Beyond that was located the earthly paradise of the Garden of Eden, the source for the great rivers of the world.

Another important feature was the kingdom of Prester John, a Christian king who had set up shop somewhere in East Africa and was supposed to unite with the kings of Europe to battle the Antichrist during the "end times." Not content to wait until Armaggedon, European kings made seeking out Prester John a priority. The only problem was a gauntlet of Mongols and Turks that prevented Christian caravans from passing. It was the Portuguese who first searched for a way around the impasse by attempting to sail around Africa instead. Starting in the early 1400s the Portuguese king's third son, Henry the Navigator, began mounting expeditions down the African coast, funding them with gold and slaves acquired in the journeys. In 1488, explorer Bartolomeu Dias rounded the Cape of Good Hope. A decade later, Vasco da Gama kept going, sailing across the sea to the coast of India, which he reached in 1498.

Even as mapmakers were adding incrementally to the knowledge of the coastlines, bigger developments were afoot in Germany that changed the world in more significant ways. An inventor in Strasbourg named Johannes Gutenberg was working on a secretive new technique to cut down on the laborious process of hand-copying manuscripts. His printing press, the world's first, worked by pressing a sheet of paper down on woodblock letters arranged on a form. Gutenberg started small, with handbills and calendars, but after he produced his first Bible in the 1450s, Gutenberg presses began spreading throughout Europe. Humanists began printing their own editions of ancient works, including Ptolemy's *Geographia*.

The first edition of Ptolemy's work, without maps, came out in Venice in 1475. Within two years, an edition was produced in Bologna, maps and all. That edition made use of new copper engraving techniques, which allowed for more precise detail than the clunky woodblock method. Other editions followed, in Rome in 1478 and 1490; Florence in 1482; and Ulm, Germany, in 1482 and 1486. Beginning with the Florence edition, mapmakers began doing something revolutionary: using the latest information from portolan charts to produce modern maps along with reproducing the ancient ones. The Ulm edition went further, altering Ptolemy's maps themselves with new discoveries in Scandinavia. First timidly, then boldy, other mapmakers began redrawing Ptolemy's maps to reflect current learning.

The enormous map on the wall of the Beinecke Library by Henricus Martellus is a good example (Figure C). Dating from 1489 or 1490, it re-creates much of Ptolemy's speculative geography, including a giant island of Ceylon larger than the Indian subcontinent from which it dangles. But it also updates Ptolemy's coastlines in Europe to create a more accurate picture of the known world at the time. Most striking, however, is its depiction of Africa, which incorporates Dias's discoveries to extend the southern coast of the continent through the bottom border of the map, surrounding it with water for the first time. Martellus also added a few speculations of his own, increasing the length of Asia by seven thousand miles and including a sweeping promontory known as the "dragon's tail" that made the trip east to the Indies seem even longer than it was. At the same time, he shrunk the distance between Portugal and Zipangu to less than half its actual eleven thousand miles, making the trip west across the Atlantic seem easy by comparison.

This is the world as it was known on the eve of Columbus's first voyage, in 1492. At the time, no learned person actually believed the world was flat. Nearly a hundred years of Ptolemy had put an end to that misconception. But now as these maps showed the distance around the world growing shorter, a group of Renaissance scholars began speculating that it might be possible to sail west from Europe to all the riches of the Indies, the lost kingdom of Prester John, and even the Garden of Eden itself. If not for these maps, Christopher Columbus never would have set sail with the confidence that he could cross the ocean. His voyage, in turn, forever changed mapmaking in the process.

IN THE SUMMER OF 1901, a Jesuit professor poking around the garret of Wolfegg Castle in the German Alps came across a heavy book with a red beechwood cover and hogskin backing. Looking inside, he made one of the greatest cartographic rediscoveries of all time—the lost map of the world made by Martin Waldseemüller in 1507. Printed on twelve sheets, the map was one of the first to incorporate the new discoveries of Christopher Columbus and Amerigo Vespucci, and the first one to show the New World as its own continent, separate from Asia (Figure 4). But what made it so important to history was a single word printed on the southern continent of the Western Hemisphere: "America" (Figure 5).

Waldseemüller's map was the first map to use the word, and it was more than a decade before it next appeared. The map stayed at Wolfegg for more than a century before the US government purchased it for $10 million—the highest price ever paid for a map. Now it is permanently displayed at the Library of Congress as the "birth certificate of America," an accurate name since Waldseemüller's map is responsible more than any other document for the name of the continent today. And the fact that it is not called Columbia can be summed up in one idea: Sex sells better than God.

Before he made history, Columbus was a Genoan merchant captain based in Portugal, carrying cargo up and down the Atlantic coast. When the printing press took off in Europe, however, he began reading Marco Polo's accounts of gold mines, perfumes, and ivory to be found in the Cathay and made it his mission to see them. He pushed Ptolemy and Martellus to the extremes to estimate a distance of twenty-four hundred

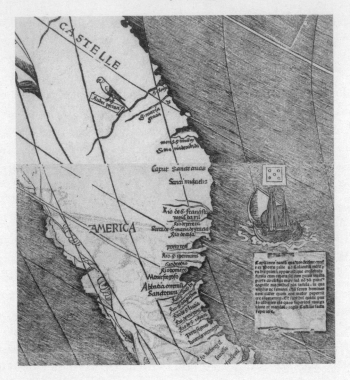

FIGURE 5 MARTIN WALDSEEMÜLLER. "UNIVERSALIS COSMOGRAPHIA" (DETAIL). ST. DIE, 1507.

miles between the Canary Islands and Japan—a quarter of the actual distance. Much of the history is well-known. When his appeals to John II of Portugal were unsuccessful, he turned to King Ferdinand and Queen Isabella of Spain, who agreed to finance his expedition in exchange for sovereignty over any lands he discovered.

A month out to sea, a crewman on the Niña sighted an island, which Columbus naturally assumed must be part of the Indies, a group of islands Marco Polo had described as being in the Sea of Cathay. For the next six months, he traipsed around one island after another, asking every native he met about the location of the gold mines of the Great Khan. Of course, what he'd really found were the Caribbean islands of Cuba and Hispaniola. On three later expeditions, he explored southward to reach the northern coast of Venezuela by 1498, the same year Vasco da Gama reached India.

Eventually, frustrated by his failure to find gold and riches, Columbus began conceiving a more and more grandiose view of himself and his expeditions in order to justify his voyages—eventually believing he had found nothing less than the mythical Garden of Eden. He spread his theories upon his return to Europe in a work called the *Book of Prophecies*, adopting the name "Christ-bearer" and drawing upon biblical passages to prove his voyage had been foretold as a signal for the end of history. All along, he vehemently disputed any hint that he had failed to reach the Orient, making his crew members sign a document attesting that Cuba was part of mainland Asia.

At the same time Columbus was captaining vessels in Portugal, an Italian named Amerigo Vespucci was working as a merchant in Seville, Spain, speculating on goods throughout Europe. He set sail with one of the later expeditions financed by Ferdinand and Isabella—or rather said he set sail, since historians debate whether he actually left land, much less commanded two ships. What seems beyond dispute is that he wrote several letters about his expeditions detailing these new lands. Originally, hitting the coast of South America, he claimed to have discovered the "dragon's tail" on the edge of Asia, but in later letters he wrote that he sailed much farther south than any land existing on current maps—pointing to the existence of a new southern continent.

Much more astonishing, however, were Vespucci's descriptions of the natives of these lands, which are particularly explicit: "Everyone of both sexes goes about naked, covering no part of their bodies, and just as they issued from their mothers' wombs," he said. "The women," he continues, "although they go naked and are exceedingly lustful, still have rather shapely and clean bodies, and are not as revolting as one might think." He adds tantalizingly: "I have deemed it best (in the name of decency) to pass over in silence their many arts to gratify their insatiable lust."

Such details and intimations ensured a hearty reception for the letters back in Europe, where an anonymous printer turned them into a pamphlet distributed throughout the continent. One who read them was a young German humanist named Martin Waldseemüller, who was embarking upon a new edition of Ptolemy's *Geographia* along with a Greek and Latin scholar named Matthias Ringmann. Obtaining an early copy of Vespucci's letters, they realized excitedly that here was "a fourth part of the world" to join the traditional medieval triumvirate of Africa, Europe, and Asia. At the same time, they acquired charts smuggled out of Portugal that showed what the new continent might look like. With this new information, Waldseemüller and Ringmann scrapped their Ptolemy project in favor of a new publication, *Introduction to Cosmology*, which included a map detailing these newly discovered lands. Cobbled together from sources including Ptolemy, Martellus, and the Portuguese charts, the map squeezed a new continent in the far southwest corner. In the accompanying text, Ringmann explained that since all the other continents were named for women, they gave this continent a feminized name, adapting Amerigo to coin "America."

It took only a few years for Waldseemüller to doubt their decision. After Ringmann died in 1511, his partner issued several new maps in which America was no longer surrounded by water, and no longer even called America, but instead labeled "Terra Incognita." Perhaps he felt he'd jumped to conclusions too quickly, or had begun to feel that Vespucci had exaggerated his claims. By that time, however, it was too late. With a thousand copies printed, the map had taken on a life of its own, spawning multiple imitators over the next decade and spreading the name "America" around Europe. Nothing cemented it more, however, than its inclusion on maps of the most successful mapmaker of his time, Gerard Mercator.

LOOKING AT MAPS from the sixteenth century, it's amazing how quickly the details are filled in. The world maps made by German cartographers in the first quarter of the century are grossly misshapen, with a distorted Africa, remnants of the "dragon's tail" in Asia, and barely a suggestion of North and South America. By the time Gerard Mercator published his famous map of the world in 1569, however, Europe, Asia, and Africa have assumed their familiar shapes, and even North and South America have acquired roughly their proper outlines. In 1578, English chronicler George Best wrote with astonishment, "Within the memory of man, within these fourscore years, there hath been more new countries and regions discovered than in five thousand years before."

Around this time, the mapmaking center of Europe shifted again, from Germany to the Low Countries—and there it stayed for a hundred years. From roughly 1570 to 1670, the Netherlands and Belgium ushered in a golden age of mapmaking that coincides roughly with its golden age of painting and still stands as the pinnacle of cartographic beauty (if not accuracy). The shift mirrored political changes at the time: At the start of the century, the region was a soup of gerrymandered counties and duchies sandwiched between France and the Holy Roman Empire. A string of marriages by the ambitious Burgundian dukes, however, gradually unified the area under the Habsburg family. One of them, Philip the Handsome, married Ferdinand and Isabella's daughter Joanna the Mad to inherit the throne of Spain and most of southern Italy.

When Philip died in 1506, he passed down that inheritance to his son Charles, who also acquired a chunk of Germany and Austria from his grandfather, the Holy Roman Emperor Maximilian I. By the time he took the throne as Charles V of Spain, he ruled over nearly all of Western Europe (with the exception of England, France, Portugal, and northern Italy). At the heart of his growing empire were the Netherlands, where he'd spent his childhood and where he continued to focus his patronage as king.

The Portuguese began calling at Antwerp, the closet port to the copper and silver mines of Germany, in order to load up on cash to trade for spices and slaves in Africa and India. As they did, they unloaded cargoes of silk, gold, and gems. Soon Antwerp became a major commercial center, finishing cloth from the woolen mills of England and working leather from Germany. The Jewish quarter filled with gem cutters, and bankers from Germany created the first modern banks. Eventually, Antwerp's merchants started sending their own ships to the Indies, earning ten times what their investors paid to fund the expeditions. Within a generation, it became the richest city in the world, displaying its new confidence with the tallest cathedral in Europe, a four-hundred-foot tiered tower that soared over the city.

The city also had something the Spanish and Portguese didn't: a printing industry that would soon revolutionize the art of mapmaking. Not only did Antwerp have a ready supply of copper for engraving, but it also had a tradition of cultural diversity and religious tolerance, with finely illustrated books and prints in high demand. Engravers organized themselves into guilds, which set rules for working hours and sold licenses, passed down from father to son or transferred through marriage. While that closed entry to newcomers, it also ensured a high quality of craftsmanship. Members increasingly specialized, including some who focused exclusively on maps. Eventually, due to political changes, the Portuguese began bypassing Antwerp for ports in Germany, and Dutch sea captains began competing with the Portuguese for the Indies trade, clamoring for accurate charts that would give them an advantage. Showing the right depth for a channel or a hidden passage between islands could shave days off a trip, translating directly into profit. If the Dutch were going to truly compete, they'd need maps of their own.

INTO THIS WORLD was born the greatest mapmaker of the age—and arguably any age. Gerard Kremer was born outside Antwerp in 1512, the son of a cobbler who died young. But his uncle rescued him and educated him in mathematics and cosmology at one of Europe's most prestigious universities. In the style of humanist scholars, he took a new Latin name, upgrading Kremer, which meant "peddler," to the Latin word for "merchant." Gerard Mercator was born.

Apprenticed to one of the Netherlands' preeminent mathematicians, Mercator showed a gift for map engraving, opening his own business in 1536 to make globes, sundials, and maps under patent from Charles V. His first world map, produced two years later, was an impressive effort, done in a "double coridform" projection with two heart-shaped hemispheres joined at the north pole. The map was both beautiful and influential, the first to name North and South America. But Mercator was dissatisfied with the distortion of the projection. For the rest of his life, he came back to the problem of how to most accurately portray the globe on a flat surface.

Even as his career was on the rise, however, it was derailed by the Counter-Reformation, launched by his patron, Charles V, to stamp out Protestant heresy. Despite the terrible reputation of the Inquisition in Spain, it was even more brutal in the Low Countries. Suspected Lutheran sympathizers were hauled away in the dead of night, imprisoned, tortured, and often burned alive at the stake. Mercator's association with the humanists made him a target, leading to his imprisonment in 1544. For months, he watched as friends were beheaded or buried alive, escaping a similar fate himself only due to a last-minute intercession from connections in high places. Once released, he fled Antwerp for Duisburg,

a university town across the border in Germany, where he lived out the
rest of his days as a professor in self-imposed exile.

Even so, he continued a rich correspondence with other mapmakers,
and his workshop produced some of the most definitive maps of Europe.
By the late 1560s, he fixated on a new project—a different kind of world
map that could actually be used to navigate long distances. It's not clear
where Mercator got the idea for his eponymous projection, but the need
for it had been clear for decades. Rhumb lines on portolans were fine for
sailing short distances but quickly became distorted in the long trip
across the Atlantic, requiring constant correction to maintain a straight
line. Mercator solved the problem with a simple trick: straightening the
lines of longitude and then stretching the distance between the lines of
latitude as they got farther away from the equator. First produced in
1569, the Mercator projection meant that for the first time, sailors could
plot a course on a small-scale map and be assured of a constant bearing
(Figure D). Of course, the technique distorted the shapes of the land-
forms, since the scale of distances lengthened the farther one traveled
from the equator. But these maps were meant to be used, and the overall
distortion seemed a small price to pay.

Mercator's great invention heralded the beginning of the Dutch
golden age—but he wasn't the only innovator at the time. As he worked
in exile in Duisburg, the Antwerp map trade continued to flourish. One
of the greatest workshops was that of Abraham Ortel—better known as
Ortelius—a great friend and confidant of the famous mapmaker despite
being fifteen years his junior. Ortelius got his start in one of the most
influential guilds as a map colorist, serving the new demand of prosper-
ous bourgeois families for maps to hang in their homes as proud sym-
bols of the economic might of their empire. In order to supplement his
income, Ortelius began selling maps on the side. Bringing Dutch maps
to sell at book fairs in France, Italy, and Germany, he returned with maps
from foreign cartographers to sell in the Netherlands—making him one
of the world's first map dealers.

EVENTUALLY, ORTELIUS'S EFFORTS caught the attention of a prosper-
ous Antwerp merchant who'd acquired an edge over his rivals through a
large collection of sea charts of foreign ports. The only problem was,

with so many maps to roll and unroll, it became difficult to find what he wanted. Hearing of Ortelius's business, he asked him to create a single volume containing as much of the world as he could. Ortelius worked hard on the task, reducing dozens of maps to a common scale. When he saw how pleased the merchant was with the results, he reasoned others might find such a book useful as well.

Though other publishers had published corrected versions of Ptolemy or supplemented editions of his maps with their own, Ortelius was one of the first to conceive of creating a Ptolemy without the Ptolemy. For the next ten years, he combed the continent for the most up-to-date maps, submitting them to the inquisitors for careful scrutiny and approval. He wasn't the only one with the idea for a standardized book of maps. Another Antwerp map dealer, named Gerard de Jode, had set himself the same goal. Originally, the two seem to have been collaborators, with de Jode publishing Ortelius's first world map. But at some point the relationship soured, and Ortelius began to use his powerful connections in the guilds to block de Jode's license from the all-important headquarters of the Inquisition.

De Jode watched helplessly as Ortelius published his volume in 1570, calling it *Theatrum Orbis Terrarum*, Latin for "Theater of the world." The world's first true atlas, it was an immediate success, selling out two editions in just a few months. Sources from around Europe began contacting Ortelius to offer him their latest maps, which he then included in future editions. By Ortelius's death in 1598, he'd published at least thirty.

De Jode, meanwhile, wasn't able to come out with his book, *Speculum Orbis Terrarum* (Mirror of the World), until 1578. Unlike the maps in Ortelius's atlas, all of de Jode's maps were engraved by the same pair of brothers, giving the atlas a uniform beauty. By this time, however, Ortelius had cornered the market, and de Jode's volume languished, with only one printing during his lifetime. After he died, his son Cornelius continued his father's work with one more edition in 1593, but he, too, struggled (Figure E). It took five hundred years for the de Jodes to get their due. Since Ortelius flooded the market, his maps are now relatively common today at map auctions and fairs such as the one in Miami. De Jode's maps, however, are extremely scarce, with only a dozen or so copies of the first edition of his atlas in existence. As a result, they command much higher prices than those of his onetime rival.

By the end of the century, Mercator had produced his own book of maps. Clearly his masterpiece, it consisted of three volumes with more than one hundred maps, most reproduced on a Mercator projection. He called the book simply *Atlas*, with the subtitle in Latin: "Cosmographical meditations upon the creation of the universe, and the universe as created." For a few years after Mercator's death in 1594, his son Rumold brought out new editions. Eventually, an Amsterdam-based engraver and printer named Jodocus Hondius bought the plates and began producing new editions of Mercator's *Atlas*—with his name attached to the name of the great cartographer—at the rate of nearly one a year. When he died, the business passed to his son Hendrik Hondius and then to Hendrik's brother-in-law Jan Jansson, who together established an unbroken line of *Atlas* editions through the middle of the next century. They soon supplanted Ortelius entirely, establishing the term "atlas" as the standard name for a bound collection of uniform maps.

With each generation, the maps produced for Mercator's atlas became more elaborate. Maps increasingly became valued as works of art as much as navigational tools. Dutch master Jan Vermeer used recognizable maps of the period to decorate the walls in a half dozen of his paintings. By this time, the Dutch were in open revolt against Spain, and were actively attacking the overseas holdings of Portugal, which remained under the Spanish crown. The demand for maps for both mercantile and military uses increased.

The Mercator-Hondius-Jansson dynasty led the way, eventually beginning its own war against the rival family of Willem Blaeu, a pupil of the astronomer Tycho Brahe who established his own map business in Amsterdam in 1600. For years, the two firms competed to publish the most up-to-date maps, often accusing the other of plagiarism. Because copper plates could be easily reworked, secondhand publishers often sold old plates to buyers, who then changed names and released them as their own. After all, it was impossible to copyright the earth. The temptation to steal another's work often proved irresistible.

Eventually, Blaeu came out on top. After the northern Netherlands rebelled against Spain and acquired its own rights to trade in the East Indies in 1609, the States-General of the provinces favored Blaeu with its commissions. In 1631, he produced his own atlas, name checking both Ortelius and Mercator in his *Appendix Theatri Ortelli et Atlantis*

Mercator. Eventually, Blaeu and his sons Joan and Cornelius established a workshop along one of Amsterdam's canals with fifteen printing presses and a footprint of more than ten thousand square feet. By 1634, the Dutch East India Company, the giant corporation overseeing trade with the Asian colonies, appointed Blaeu its official mapmaker and forbade its merchants from carrying sea charts made by anyone else. In 1648, he created his own twenty-sheet map of the world, drawing from Dutch, Italian, English, Spanish, and French sources to surpass any other map in both beauty and accuracy. Blaeu followed it up in 1664 with his *Atlas Maior*, the crowning achievement of Dutch mapmaking and universally recognized as the most gorgeous atlas ever created (Figure F).

Just as the Dutch mapmakers reached the pinnacle of success, however, they also stood on the brink of decline. Global politics were again changing, and both Spain and the Netherlands began to lose power and influence as England and France began to rise. Along with the dominance of these countries came the dominance of their cartographers, who began to use new techniques that eventually supplanted the Dutch monopolies. It is these mapmakers that E. Forbes Smiley III focused on as he began his own rise in the map business.

Chapter 4

WHO KNOWS THE MOST WINS

FIGURE 6 MOUNT AND PAGE. "A NEW SURVEY OF THE
HARBOUR OF BOSTON IN NEW ENGLAND." LONDON, 1708.
(FACSIMILE REPRODUCTION BY GEORGE GRIERSON, 1749.)

1985–1987

RONALD VERE "R.V." TOOLEY—OR MICK, as he was known to close
friends—was born in London in 1898, "an enchanted world of hansom
cabs and gas lamplighters who came with long poles at dusk," as he later
recalled. The peace of his childhood was shattered with the outbreak of
World War I, during which two-thirds of his regiment was killed in a
single battle. Returning to England after the war, he found security in
the relative quiet of a secondhand bookstore called Francis Edwards.

There, over the next few decades, he became responsible, perhaps more than any other person, for launching the modern map trade.

At the time Tooley began selling books, map collecting was a rare hobby; salesmen at the store used maps that didn't sell to wrap packages. But Tooley gravitated toward the objects, which he found the perfect combination of history and art. In an early map catalog, he wrote, "To hold an ancient atlas of rich and gorgeous coloring, to turn the leaves, to see the quaint fantastic figures adorning their borders, ships riding the seven seas, and towns picked out in red and gold, gleaming as if the sun shone on them, is to have in one's hands the epitome of an age, art and knowledge combined in happy proportions."

In 1930, he left briefly to open Atlas Books, dealing exclusively in maps, atlases, and globes—but unfortunately the market was slow in the making. At the time, Tooley sold a copy of John Speed's famous atlas *The Theatre of the Empire of Great Britaine* for £3; today it would go for more than $100,000.

Tooley soon found himself back at Francis Edwards, where for the next fifty years he held court in a dusty upstairs room, gradually building some of the greatest map collections in history. Every Saturday, he did research in the map room of the British Museum, where he was often the only occupant. But he was just as comfortable in the pub, where he spent most afternoons telling wild stories of his buying trips to the continent. At the annual Antiquarian Booksellers' Association dinner, he was a tireless dancer and a shameless flirt.

Tooley never held maps as sacred. On the job, he wore a linen jacket with pockets crammed with damp paintbrushes, which he'd use on the spot to hand color maps upon request. More controversial was his practice of breaking up atlases and selling maps individually to collectors. As atlases increased in price, only wealthy collectors could afford them. The "breakers," he argued, opened up map collecting to the masses. Of course, the practice was also more lucrative for dealers, who could split up atlases by region—maps of France to the French, Germany to the Germans, and so on—and earn more on each map than for the atlas as a whole.

However eyebrow-raising his practices, there was no disputing his influence. His 1949 book, *Maps and Map-Makers*, was responsible for turning many collectors on to the field. For years, he kept an index file for every map that passed through the shop. Starting in the 1960s, he began publishing a series of books called *The Map Collector's Circle*, each edition focusing on a different geographical region. Even in his eighties, he was still spry and charismatic, overseeing the *The Map Collector* magazine and holding forth at the pub.

That's the man Forbes Smiley met in 1985, when he traveled to London with one of Rosejeanne Slifer's letters of introduction in hand. As he began his search for maps to fill out Leventhal's collection, he had no reference guide upon which to draw. For a city obsessed with its history, Boston was curiously uninterested in its cartographic past; in four hundred years, not one of Boston's many civic institutions and colleges had ever even put on an exhibition of Boston maps. Smiley asked Tooley for advice on where to begin, and Tooley—who had a reputation for unstintingly sharing his knowledge—was only too happy to comply.

Over pints at the local pub, Tooley sprinkled his technical expertise with advice for a career as a successful dealer. "A collection of maps," he told Smiley, "is an attempt to put together a puzzle that's lost many of its pieces. If you can find them, you can learn something about the world that no one has ever seen before." That might seem simple, he said, but it was amazing how many collectors lost sight of that in search of maps that were simply rare or expensive.

"To really succeed at this job," he continued, "you need to understand two things: First, the person who knows the most wins." At the end of the day, a small dealer who knew what pieces to look for could beat out bigger, better-connected dealers. "Second," Tooley said, "if you take care of your clients, they will take care of you." Clients weren't a piggy bank; they were partners in building a legacy. "No dealer is really successful unless he loves his subject," Tooley wrote in one of his books. "And enthusiasm is contagious and spreads from buyer and seller. So many friendships are formed and trust is mutual." Building that trust, he said, was the key to success.

SMILEY TOOK THE LESSONS to heart in his dealings with Leventhal. He began pouring himself into the study of maps of Boston and New England, spending hours at the New York Public Library and traveling farther afield to research the maps at the Boston Public Library and university libraries at Yale and Brown. Every few weeks, he'd get on a plane and fly to London, Amsterdam, or Paris, scouring bookshops and map fairs and bidding in auctions to chase pieces of the puzzle.

Among his first finds for Leventhal was John Smith's 1614 map of New England. The copy he located had been included in the English version of Gerard Mercator's *Atlas*, published in 1635. The last state Smith made before he died, the map included the proper locations of Boston and the neighboring locales of Charlestown, Roxbury, and Newton, which all exist today, alongside many of the fictional town names proposed by Prince Charles. Leventhal was particularly pleased to see his hometown of Dorchester included for only the second time on any map, and bought the map from Smiley for $9,500.

Smiley also found another copy of Smith's map from 1624, and discovered a copy of the map naming both Boston and Dorchester for the *first* time: a crude woodcut made by William Wood in 1634 for his book *New England's Prospect*. He tracked down a beautifully illustrated map of New England and New York made by William Blaeu in 1635, featuring an oversize Lake Champlain taking up most of modern-day New Hampshire and Vermont. Blaeu makes up for the errors, however, with finely drawn pictures of foxes, beavers, and deer cavorting through the woodlands. Smiley also found a map of the same territory created by Blaeu's rival Jan Jansson in 1651 that marks a significant improvement. It includes not only a more accurate survey of the coastline, but also an improved interior, with Lake Champlain shrunk down to almost its proper size (though still on the wrong side of the Connecticut River) and a detailed course of the Hudson River, starting with the bustling city of New Amsterdam and continuing north through Dutch and Indian settlements up into Canada (Figure G).

One of the maps that drew heavily on Jansson's map was by English mapmaker John Speed, found in his book *A Prospect of the Most Famous Parts of the World*, from 1676. The name—"A Map of New England and New York"—speaks volumes. While the Netherlands had been busy establishing its trade empire in the mid-1600s, England had undergone a brutal civil war, which led to neglect of its overseas colonies. During the conflict, Charles I—the king who had founded so many fictitious towns in New England—was beheaded, and his heir sought refuge in Holland but was denied.

Finally restored to the throne in 1660, Charles II wasted little time turning his focus to the English colonies in the New World. Just a few years later, he declared war on Holland—payback, in part, for its refusal to house him during his exile—including the Dutch holdings overseas. He gave the task of taking their American holdings to his brother James, the Duke of York. Hopelessly outnumbered, the Dutch surrendered in 1664 without firing a shot. Speed's map shows to the victors go not only the spoils, but also the geography. His map is almost a perfect copy of Jansson's map, with one major difference: New Amsterdam and New Netherlands have both become New York (Figure H).

The maps Smiley found reflected other changes in the development of cartography as well. As richly illustrated as they were, the Dutch maps were only as accurate as their source maps, which were wildly inconsistent. As the Renaissance became the Enlightenment, however, a more scientific form of mapmaking began in France, where Louis XIV established the first royal academy of science in 1666. One of his first decrees was to make a new topographical map of France, and scientists took up the challenge, dragging a chain from Paris to Amiens to determine the exact length of a degree of latitude, and using the moons of Jupiter to determine longitude. By the time the Académie finished its survey of the coast in 1684, it had determined that even the best current maps were more than thirty miles off the mark.

Using this as a beginning, Gian Domenico Cassini and family triangulated distances from a central meridian to complete the first modern topographical map, a feat that took more than one hundred years and three generations of Cassinis to complete. But the new scientific techniques were used right away. Cartographers including Nicolas Sanson, Guillaume De L'Isle, and J.B. Bourguignon D'Anville led the way in applying the Cassinis' methods to create successively more accurate maps of both Europe and the New World. By the turn of the eighteenth century, the Dutch maps began to feel antiquated.

By then, the new scientific techniques had also crossed the English Channel to the country of Isaac Newton and Roger Bacon. Britain's first great mapmaker, John Speed, used mostly Dutch source material for his maps. But after the Restoration and the ensuing war with the Netherlands, it became a matter of national pride for the English to have their own maps—especially across the Atlantic. How could it fend off encroachments of the Dutch, French, and Native Americans on its territory if it didn't know what that territory was? The same applied at sea. Until the late 1600s, English navigators relied primarily on Dutch sea charts by Lucas Janszoon Waghenaer, whose name became anglicized to the point that all pilot books became known as "waggoners." One cartographer named John Seller, however, envisioned a thoroughly modern, thoroughly English sea atlas, and he fought to make it a reality—even if he personally received little credit for it during his lifetime.

"SO COMPLETELY DID the Dutch mapmakers of the 17th century dominate the sale and distribution of cartographic material, that little attention has been given by the public to efforts made by their English speaking neighbors across the sea," begins a 1986 article in the antiquarian trade magazine *AB Bookman's Weekly*. It continues:

> So beautifully produced are the Dutch atlases, with their lovely engravings, rich color and elegant binding, that we are reluctant to close their covers and open those of a contemporary English volume. But if we do, we are rewarded. We perceive the map trade in its swaddling clothes, intriguing experiments within a wide open market, the efforts of men and women who risked their livelihoods to advance the art and fill the needs of an every expanding empire. And when we turn their pages to the maps and charts of America, we are met by extraordinary records of an empire at work, and documents of England's struggle to settle a continent 200 times her size, and far across a threatening sea.

With such lofty prose, E. Forbes Smiley III began his article "The Origins of the English Map Trade, 1670–1710," his attempt to synthesize the combined knowledge that he'd acquired digging through the New York Public Library's collections and bidding in auctions overseas. As he continued to study, Smiley felt that scholars had passed by English mapmaking at the turn of the eighteenth century—a period that he saw as seminal to the settlement of North America. Smiley focused in on a particular figure whom he saw as key to this development.

John Seller was born around 1632 and apparently had a tumultuous youth, which led to prison time at age thirty for an alleged plot against the Church of England. He began publishing and selling books and maps in an East London shop around 1667, bringing out a well-received navigational treatise. He was appointed hydrographer to the king and awarded a contract to sell compasses and spyglasses to the Royal Navy. But Seller had greater ambitions—nothing less than a complete atlas of all the major sea routes then plied by British ships.

In 1671, he announced his plan: four books, covering the North Seas; the Mediterranean and Western Africa; the Orient; and finally, the Americas. Called *The English Pilot*, it would eventually become, as Smiley wrote, "the earliest sea atlas published in England, and the only guide to foreign waters which England produced for nearly a century." His early efforts fell short of his ambitions. *The First Book* was little more than a compilation of Dutch charts, which Seller had only slightly reworked— sometimes Dutch titles still showed through superimposed English names. No less a wit than Samuel Pepys, the great diarist, derided Seller's atlas as a "pretended new book."

Pepys was probably being unfair. The Dutch plates were as geographically accurate as anything at the time, and Seller did little to hide the fact that he was reworking other sources. Starting with *The Second Book* of *The English Pilot* in 1672, however, Seller began leaning on new original British surveys of the coasts. In *The Third Book* in 1675, the majority of the charts were original, including some of the first maps of Cape Town in South Africa. That same year, Seller produced a kind of compilation atlas of his best maps, called the *Atlas Maritimus*, which he custom built for individual buyers depending upon their needs, so no two copies were the same.

While the atlas succeeded, however, Seller himself did not. By this time, Smiley wrote in *AB Bookman's Weekly*, he "had lost control of the project. About 1675 Seller experienced financial difficulties stemming from his overly ambitious projects, and was forced to seek the help of other booksellers." Seller proposed a consortium, whereby all the partners would enter into a deal together to finish the project, splitting the risk and rewards.

Initially, the plan worked, enough for Seller to start on *The Fourth Book* of *The English Pilot*, covering the Americas, in 1678. A year later, however, the consortium, too, failed. Seller's plates, which he had worked so hard to assemble over a period of nearly a decade, were dispersed to the various members, who took them to make their own sea atlases. "Seller lost most everything," wrote Smiley. For the next two decades, his print shop limped along, but Seller was never able to regain control of his work, and he died poor in 1697.

Despite his individual failure, *The English Pilot* project wasn't entirely dead. One of the members of the consortium, John Thornton, began buying back the original plates one by one from the other dealers and made a deal to publish them with another member, William Fisher, who had retained the naming rights. In 1689, Thornton and Fisher put out the first full edition of *The English Pilot, The Fourth Book.* The preceding decade had changed the fortunes of Great Britain, which by now had begun a lucrative trade with its American colonies. That placed the book in high demand by merchant captains, and Thornton prospered where Seller had failed.

Over the next few years, Thornton began rereleasing editions of the other books of *The English Pilot,* as well as his own *Novus Atlas Maritimus.* Upon his death in 1708, the plates passed to Fisher's son-in-law, Richard Mount, and his apprentice, Thomas Page, who founded the successful firm Mount and Page. Over the next seventy-five years, successive generations of Mounts (William, John) and Pages (Thomas II, Thomas III, Thomas IV) continued to print the books, with at least thirty-four separate editions produced between 1689 and 1794.

Smiley began tracking down these editions, which he realized contained some of the most influential maps in the history of the world—enabling the rise of Great Britain into the sea power it became. As one historian said about *The Fourth Book,* for the "British trading in North America" it "must have been a godsend. . . . To modern eyes the charts are crude and sparse of detail; but to the navigator of American waters in that period, it was his Bible. Whatever its shortcomings, there was really no substitute, no real competitor, for over sixty years."

WHILE HIS SEA atlases were enough to establish John Seller's legacy, he made one more contribution that also particularly interested Smiley. Around 1675, just as his business was collapsing, Seller got his hands on a survey of Massachusetts Bay Colony done by William Reed. The colony's original boundaries were vague, with its northern limit set at the source of the Merrimack River, an east-west-flowing river that spilled into the sea forty miles north of Boston. While it was initially assumed that source would be more or less at the same latitude as the mouth of the river, later explorations found it took a dogleg north a hundred miles into New Hampshire (as Smiley knew well, since he had crossed the river every day from his hometown in Bedford to attend Derryfield School in Manchester).

Eager to increase its landholdings, the colony's commissioners appointed Reed to perform a new survey; however, on the way to London, the ship carrying it was captured by a Dutch privateer and that copy was lost at sea. It wasn't until King Philip's War, an American Indian uprising in 1675 that decimated several New England towns, that King Charles II became concerned about his New England colonies and demanded an update of the situation. The result was a flurry of mapmaking based on Reed's survey, including an exceptional version by Seller that was the first map to include all six New England states (Figure I).

Seller's map reflects a new anxiety about a dark and dangerous continent, with heavy woods and mountains filled with wild animals. Right in the center, a pack of American Indians is pictured doing battle with an outnumbered group of colonists above the town of Deerfield, which had been wiped out in an attack. In addition to its striking artwork, the map corrected long-held errors in Dutch mapping, putting the Connecticut River in its proper place, and drawing the Merrimack accurately up to its source in Lake Winnipesaukee, which was no longer conflated with Lake Champlain. Here, at last, was a map of the area relying on English sources, which was copied over and over for the next seventy-five years. When New England preacher Cotton Mather sat down to write his definitive history of New England, he used Seller's map to produce his own map of the region.

As Smiley continued to research English mapmaking, he focused on Seller as the linchpin, following every lead to new editions of the *Atlas Maritimus* and *The English Pilot, The Fourth Book*. Sea atlases weren't stored in climate-controlled libraries or tucked away in castle garrets for a century; they were meant to be used, taken aboard ships plying the North Atlantic and weathered by sea spray. Often, captains who needed only a handful of charts might break them up and sell the rest off cheaply. As a result, many of the charts were lost over the centuries, such that some of them now existed in only a handful of editions, and some editions existed in only a handful of copies.

Smiley got a bead on one of these rare charts, called "A New Survey of the Harbour of Boston in New England," which had been produced by Mount and Page for their 1708 edition of *The English Pilot*. Prior to this map, Boston had been featured only in small, inset maps, not large-scale maps like this one, measuring more than a foot by nearly two feet in size. According to Smiley's later recollections, he heard of a copy of Mount and Page's *Atlas Maritimus* containing the map coming up for auction in London. He bid hard for it, and after he won it, he broke it up to sell the other charts inside to recoup the cost.

It wasn't until Smiley brought it back to Boston and put it side by side with other maps in Leventhal's collection, however, that he understood how important it was. The two stood together in Leventhal's office as Smiley took a deep breath and set it down next to other maps of the city. Unlike earlier charts, this one included more than twenty of the city's Harbor Islands, drawn in crude but true outlines. More important, it included 132 soundings at low tide throughout the harbor, with a dotted line labeled "Ship Channell," which snaked its way through them to the city—coincidentally landing directly at the location of Leventhal's Boston Harbor Hotel. Viewing it together, Smiley and Leventhal realized they were looking at the first-ever navigable chart of Boston Harbor (Figure 6).

Like a lost puzzle piece that reveals a picture that had only been hinted at before, the map formed a missing link between the earlier sea charts of Seller and Thornton and the next navigable chart, published several decades later. Client and dealer spent the afternoon rearranging maps from Leventhal's collection on the table, determining which mapmakers had traced the lines of this map to create their own maps, and which had drawn from original surveys. It was one of the most pleasurable afternoons of Smiley's life—and there were many more like it, as he and Leventhal together began to understand the mapping of the city in a way that even most historians didn't.

Smiley started to attract other wealthy clients as well. One who contacted him early on was Lawrence Slaughter, then head of computer database operations for the United Nations. Slaughter had grown up an army brat, living all over the country, but spent his formative years at

Georgetown Preparatory School in Bethesda, Maryland, before attending Georgetown University in Washington, DC. He met Smiley at B. Altman, where he bought maps based on places he'd traveled—Paris, Bermuda, the Holy Land. Smiley urged him to focus his attentions on a particular area in order to create a collection that might be important one day. Slaughter took the advice to heart, focusing on Washington and the Chesapeake Bay, eventually expanding to include the entire mid-Atlantic coast. Soon, Smiley was taking regular trips to Slaughter's home in Larchmont, a suburb north of New York City, as well as Boston, with finds from his European trips.

Other clients followed, until Smiley was chasing multiple maps on his trips. "What a thrill for a young man to be handed that responsibility to fly around Europe looking for this stuff," Smiley told me. "And then to bring it back and put it into a collection with a man who was deadly serious about collecting it. At that moment, you have an understanding no one else has."

It was a happy time in Smiley's life, both professionally and personally. On October 12, 1985, Smiley's friends gathered on the rooftop of the Gramercy Park Hotel for Smiley's wedding to his fiancée, Lisa. Drinks in hand, his friends from Hampshire and Derryfield—Paul Statt, Scott Slater, Scott Haas, and Fred Melamed—posed for a photo in mismatched suits with white boutonnieres. In other photos from the day, Smiley looks handsome in a dark suit and silver wire-framed glasses; his new wife wore her blond hair up and a white wedding dress with full lace sleeves. That night, they drove with Slater up to Maine to stay for a night on the Maine seacoast before flying out the next day for a honeymoon on the Canary Islands—the classic embarkation point for generations of explorers setting sail for the New World.

BY NOW, SMILEY was a regular fixture at the New York Public Library, bringing clients there to show them examples of maps he was planning on finding for them. When map chief Alice Hudson put out a call for a "friends' group" to help raise money for the division, he volunteered right away to become one of the five members of the group's planning committee, turning over his Rolodex for the mailing list. The group called itself the Mercator Society and gathered for its first meeting on

March 20, 1986, to celebrate Gerard Mercator's 474th birthday. Each member was required to contribute a minimum of $250—with the money used to conserve the collection and acquire new maps—though many contributed more. In the first year, thirty members together donated more than $10,000.

Guests at the inaugural meeting also found a surprise waiting for them: a pamphlet entitled *English Mapping of America, 1675–1715*. In advance of the meeting, Smiley had contacted nearly two dozen map experts, asking each to pick his or her favorite map from the period and write a short paragraph describing its importance. Smiley served as editor and anonymously donated $4,000 of his own money to print it in a slim gray volume marked as *The Mercator Society: Publication Number One*.

The book's contributors were a who's who of map collecting. Dr. Seymour Schwartz, an avid collector and amateur historian, chose John Seller's map of New England, illustrated with a rare copy of the map from Yale University. University of Wisconsin professor David Woodward picked a 1677 woodcut of New England by John Foster, drawn from the same survey as Seller's map, which had the distinction of being the first map printed in the New World. Tony Campbell, map historian at the British Library, chose Thornton's chart of Long Island from the very first edition of *The English Pilot* in 1689, one of the first maps to accurately depict the contours of the island.

Alice Hudson chose a less accurate map by Thornton, "A New Map of East and West New Jarsey [*sic*]," made in 1700. As she notes in her description, the surveyor "apparently moved mountains in order to conduct his 'Exact Survey'"—transposing the high ground in northern New Jersey into the south. Still, it's a delightful historical artifact, showing the line of partition between the two New Jerseys, which were originally separate colonies. Finally, toward the end of the volume is the "New Survey of Boston Harbor" from the 1708 edition of *The English Pilot*, chosen by "A New England Collector" and identified as the "earliest navigable chart of Boston Harbor." At the end of the book, Smiley closed with a brief paragraph explaining the Mercator Society's role in preserving the map collection, writing that it "considers the maintenance and enrichment of the library's collection its primary concern."

As Smiley began increasing his profile, he and Lisa gave up the

Washington Heights apartment by spring 1987 for a more fashionable address in a Beaux Arts building on East Seventieth Street, a half block from Park Avenue. At the same time, Smiley leased a space around the corner on East Seventy-Ninth Street for a new "gallery," an awkward L-shaped room in a building with several other art galleries and professional offices. He did what he could to make it presentable, installing track lighting and a tile floor in a small front room, where he brought clients by appointment. He also dropped his business's original name, North American Maps & Autographs, to call it simply "E. Forbes Smiley III."

Smiley advertised the move with a full-page advertisement on the inside back cover of *The Map Collector*, the British map-collecting journal founded by his mentor R.V. Tooley. Taking up most of the page was a 1790 chart of Cape Cod by Matthew Clark. Smiley advertised it as "one of nine known copies" and "the only one in private hands." He further described the map as "a rare opportunity to acquire a landmark in the history of American cartography." What he didn't explain, however, was the somewhat disingenuous way he'd acquired the map himself.

BOSTON MAPMAKER MATTHEW CLARK produced the first maritime atlas printed in America, just a few decades after the Revolution. Though the charts themselves are largely derivative of British sources, the book marked a milestone in American publishing, showing that the burgeoning new nation was able to produce its own navigational aids. The copy that Smiley ended up acquiring was originally owned by the Franklin Institute in Pennsylvania, which put it up for auction in a basement room of the library on September 12, 1986.

It was a spectacularly badly conducted auction, thought Bill Reese, a young map dealer who had been in the business for a decade. Reese had made his first sale as a sophomore at Yale, when he bought a map of Mexico at a furniture auction for $800 and sold it to Yale's Beinecke Library for the remainder of his college tuition. After graduating in 1977, he had opened his own business a few blocks down the street in New Haven, featuring old books on Americana as well as maps and atlases. He hoped that the confusing way the lots were laid out at the Franklin Institute auction would work to his advantage, enabling him to get a good deal on the Clark atlas.

He remained calm as the bidding went up past $10,000, then $15,000, then $20,000. The price was just about getting to his threshold of $25,000 when the other bidders dropped out. Reese was elated, knowing that with a bit of restoration work, he could sell the book for more than twice that price. A few days later, he was in his office trying to figure out how to properly restore the atlas when his phone rang.

"Hello, this is Forbes Smiley," the caller intoned in a deep baritone. Reese, who had never heard the name before, listened as Smiley explained he was a dealer in rare maps, atlases, and globes who had just opened a new gallery in New York. Finally, he got to the point, saying, "I'd like to buy the Clark atlas."

"I'm not really interested right now," Reese replied, "but perhaps in the future . . ."

"What if I give you fifty thousand dollars for it?" Smiley asked.

Reese paused. He could probably get more than that after conservation, but not that much more; here was someone offering to double his money with no work at all. "Okay, fine," he said, "I'll sell it to you."

"Great," said Smiley, "I'm taking it up to my client in Boston. I'll be on the next train from New York." In the next hour, Reese made a few calls, confirming that Smiley was a serious dealer with a reputation for knowing a lot about American maps. Picking him up at the train station, he found Smiley brusque almost to the point of rudeness, seemingly in a great hurry to do the deal and get back on the train. At the same time, he admired Smiley's knowledge and was won over by Smiley's enthusiasm for the atlas and its place in American mapmaking.

Smiley wrote him a check and got back on his train, and Reese didn't think much about him for the next few days—until his bank informed him the check had bounced. Reese was stunned. Here he was, left holding the bag for $25,000. Immediately he got on the phone to Smiley in New York.

"Oh yeah, I'm sorry about that," Smiley said when he told him about the check.

"Sorry isn't good enough," Reese sputtered. "I want my money."

"Well, I don't have it right now," he replied.

"Then I want my atlas back," said Reese.

"I'm sorry, I don't have that either," said Smiley.

"Well then, get it back from your customer."

"I can't do that either," Smiley said. "Technically it doesn't exist anymore."

As Smiley explained, he had taken the atlas apart right on the train up to Boston, selling several charts of Boston Harbor to Leventhal and keeping the rest, hoping to sell them to other clients to recoup the cost.

Reese was speechless. As a dealer, he knew he had no control over what a buyer did with a book he sold. Still, he couldn't help but be appalled that Smiley had so cavalierly taken apart a book with less than ten known copies in the world. Smiley promised he'd get him the money in three weeks, which in fact he did. But the experience soured Reese on doing business with Smiley. (He made one other transaction, and again Smiley's check bounced. After that, he vowed, he'd have nothing to do with him again.)

Smiley put the incident out of his mind. To him, the numbers added up—he just wasn't able to complete the deal fast enough. But the truth was, he was overextending himself, chasing too many high-priced maps and atlases before he was able to sell them. He told himself that if he just worked harder, eventually it would pay off with financial success. But the map trade was about to get even more competitive—and some of those competitors were not as understanding.

Chapter 5

CATALOG NUMBER ONE

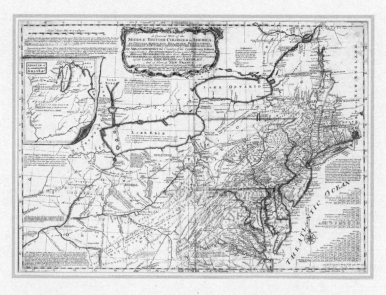

FIGURE 7 LEWIS EVANS. "A GENERAL MAP OF THE MIDDLE BRITISH COLONIES IN AMERICA." LONDON, 1755.

1987–1989

GRAHAM ARADER WANTED to know if I'd read his blog. By his own account the "most successful map dealer in the world," Arader had already mentioned it a half-dozen times on the phone before I ever met him. Now, when I met him in person at his Madison Avenue mansion, it was one of the first things out of his mouth. "It's all in my blog," he assured me. "Everything about Forbes." Six-two, with a thick, athletic build, Arader sat at a computer desk with his back turned, wearing a dark-blue polo shirt, khaki pants, and white athletic socks.

We were in the bedroom of the mansion, which doubles as his office.

A laundry basket blocked the entryway, a four-poster bed filled most of the room, and a squash racket sat under an antique desk sporting elaborate scrollwork. The room's most striking aspect, however, was its walls—every available inch covered in maps, hung so close their frames were touching.

"Want something to drink?" Arader asked, his back still turned. "Want a Coke? Eric, get him a Coke." This last order was directed to his assistant, who went to fetch me a soda. After another long pause, during which he continued to type at his computer, Arader added, "Want something to eat?" I sat for ten minutes eating peanuts and sipping Coke before he turned around to ask where I was from. When I said Boston, that sent him into a headlong monologue on that city's history. "The cool thing about Boston is that after the British got their nipples twisted there, they never went up there again. They realized that messing with the people of Massachusetts was a no-win situation, and you know, they stayed with all the hookers in New York, so the Gage brothers could constantly get laid. I'm sorry, the Howell brothers could get laid. Gage was recalled, I believe in 1776. The Duke of Northumberland, Hugh Percy, said, 'You just got clobbered.'"

Arader had been a champion squash player at Yale, and having a conversation with him is a lot like a squash game: a constant attempt to hit back whatever balls he slams against the wall. I was about to say something when he got up from his desk and sat astride an armchair, legs spread wide. "That is what got Forbes caught," he said casually, pointing to a map in the corner. I got up to inspect it, seeing the portrait of John Smith peering out over the map of New England. "He bid against me for that at Swann," he continued, referring to the New York auction house. "I got the bid, and then he tried to steal one at Yale. I keep it there as a memento."

To hear him tell it, Arader was on to Smiley's thefts before anyone else. "I have been telling people about him for twenty years," he said. Then again, to hear him tell it, everyone in the map-selling business is a thief. He referred to one well-respected map dealer as "the biggest fence in New York." Another, he said, "was stealing from Italian libraries for years. . . . There's me and everyone else. Everyone else is out of morals; they'll do anything to make a buck."

It's not just the crooked dealers—map collectors, too, are at fault for

buying maps at prices too good to be true, knowing the property is stolen. "You go into a massage parlor and you give the girl at the door two
hundred dollars, do you think they knew they were going to get a jerk-
off?" he asked. "These guys feel like the day they were born, God came
down and put a star over their heads, and they could walk around the
planet, and they were going to buy maps for thirty-five percent off what
I had to pay at auction," he continued.

"These are your clients you are talking about?" I tried to break in.

"Yeah, stars over their heads."

W. GRAHAM ARADER III got into the business back in 1972 while he
was still a student at Yale. His father, a management consultant and commerce secretary for the State of Pennsylvania, was also an amateur map
collector. When his son spent a gap year in England after high school, he
used to send him to map dealer Mick Tooley with orders for maps by
Blaeu and Speed. Arader picked up more than a few maps himself—
eventually amassing $8,000 in debt for his collection. His father refused
to bail him out, telling him he'd have to sell off some of his wares. Sell he
did, operating a minigallery out of his dorm room and advertising to the
Yale medical faculty—the only people he could think of who would be
willing to pay for rare maps. Upon Arader's graduation in 1973, his father
advanced him $150,000 to start his own business, and Arader went from
antiques show to antiques show buying and selling maps.

He had a threefold strategy: obtain the best material he could, learn
as much as he could about it, and then sell the hell out of it. Figuring that
when you are dealing with rich people, an expensive map was more desirable than a cheap one, he began marking up prices exponentially. A map
he bought for $1,000, he sold for $5,000. "There was inflation, and then
there was Graham Arader," a London map dealer once remarked. Suddenly, the map trade was thrown into chaos as Arader started asking, and
getting, prices that genteel European dealers never would have imagined.

He was a shameless self-promoter, telling the Associated Press as far
back as 1979, "I am the best in the world at what I do." One of his competitors told *The Wall Street Journal* in 1980 that he was the "Muhammad Ali
of the map world"—not meant as a compliment. By then, Arader was already the most successful dealer in the United States, making $2.5 million

a year. He was thirty years old. Arader used his profits to buy a mansion outside Philadelphia called Ballygomingo for his headquarters, and another mansion on Madison Avenue for his showroom. He worked fourteen-hour days, switching between making phone calls to Europe and barking orders at assistants. His sales tactics were Machiavellian. While people like Tooley invented the concept of "book breaking," Arader began doing it on an industrial scale; on one occasion, Bill Reese remembers, Arader started ripping up a first edition of John Smith's *Generall Historie of Virginia* right at the delivery counter at Sotheby's.

In a fifty-column profile in *The New Yorker* in 1987, one collector tells a story about selling Arader a copy of Samuel de Champlain's 1613 map of New France for $6,500 after Arader told him he wanted it so badly he'd "sleep beneath it the rest of my life." The next morning, Arader called him on the phone to tell him he'd resold it for $27,500. Another collector who called himself a "former friend" was blunt about Arader's tactics. "His most overriding concern in any facet of life is winning," he said. "He's obsessed with the idea of winning, and not being beaten."

He didn't let anyone stand in his way—least of all, other dealers. "He sees competitors as adversaries," Henry Taliaferro, then head of Arader's map department, said in 1987. "He inspires them to jealousy." As much as other dealers might have privately fumed at his brash style, however, they raised their own prices along with his. After an initial run-up in prices in the late 1970s, prices for maps leveled out during the recession of the early 1980s. Now they were poised for resurgence, and once again, it was Arader leading the way.

FOR CENTURIES, there has been one surefire way to let everyone know you have a lot of money—buy some high-priced art and stick it on your wall. In the 1980s, however, that formula started breaking down. As the stock market soared, so did fine-art prices. Suddenly paintings by Monet and Picasso were selling in the millions, and works by even lesser-known American artists were going for hundreds of thousands. Those getting rich on Wall Street—but not rich enough to buy into the art market— needed something else to broadcast their success.

The early 1980s saw a boomlet in the bird and animal prints of Audubon and the botanical prints of Pierre-Joseph Redouté. As prices even on those began to climb, however, some New York interior design-ers began selling their clients on maps, which fit right into the English country aesthetic currently in vogue. For a few thousand dollars, a Wall Street broker or well-off doctor or lawyer could pick up an original piece hundreds of years old that was every bit as much of a conversation starter as a Degas or Monet.

Smiley's wife, Lisa, who had an interior decorating business on the side, alerted him to the trend and urged him to open a public store where buyers could browse without an appointment. In 1987, the Parisian an-tiques market Place des Antiquaires announced it was opening a New York branch in a $20 million subterranean shopping mall on East Fifty-Seventh Street. Smiley became one of the few American vendors amid French furniture, housewares, and jewelry stores. More than twelve hun-dred guests came out for the opening gala that November, featuring New York mayor Ed Koch and French ambassador Emmanuel de Mar-gerie popping the cork on a bottle of Taittinger champagne, while wait-ers circulated through the crowd pouring glasses under towering topiaries of roses and narcissus.

Maps had suddenly become big business. That fall, Smiley pub-lished a list in *The Map Collector* of twenty-four maps for sale, with an average asking price of $2,500. Capitalizing on the burgeoning interest, he took out a full-page ad in the March 1988 issue of *House & Garden*—an upscale home décor magazine edited by *Vogue*'s Anna Wintour—and appeared in a feature article for the same magazine that June. "Maps have a history similar to botanical prints," he told the interviewer. "They were designed, engraved, and colored to impress the eye."

In just a few years, Smiley had succeeded in entering the highest levels of the New York map trade (Figure 8). On his trips to London and Paris, he was now spending tens of thousands of dollars for his clients. Within the map business, different dealers had different business models—some specializing in selling high volumes of inexpensive maps, others selling only to other dealers. Smiley focused on the highest-quality, priciest material, preferring to work one-on-one with clients over time to help build their collections.

He projected the air of a jet-setter, casually telling other bidders at auctions that he'd flown in from Europe the night before. But it was his knowledge of maps and powers of persuasion that truly impressed

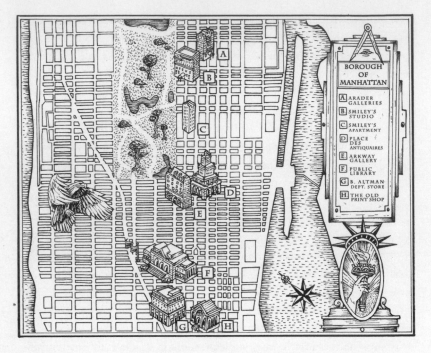

FIGURE 8 SMILEY'S MANHATTAN.

clients. One collector who bought several items from Smiley later said, "He'd talk about the beauty of the design, and if your interest was flagging, he'd talk about the historical importance of it, then if that didn't spark your interest, he'd talk about how it fit into the history of English cartography. He'd find your hot button."

"He was a wonderful salesman," said Paul Cohen, then an up-and-coming dealer with New York dealer Richard Arkway. "He was able to have a lockhold on certain clients who would work exclusively with him. I would often ask him, how do you get these guys? He would look at me and say, you just look them in the eye and blah, blah, blah; he had a very convincing manner." Smiley spoke their language, addressing them with a deferent charm and using his knowledge to explain why certain maps just had to be in their collection.

Some dealers found his superiority arrogant, even as they jealously watched him sew up desirable clients. Graham Arader says he watched him steal away one client—Chicago machine-company magnate Barry

MacLean, whom he described as "one of my dearest friends." After Smiley began courting him, Arader says, "he never spoke to me again." Arader's competitive streak came out, and he vowed to win against Smiley next time.

OTHER DEALERS, HOWEVER, became trusted colleagues and even friends. One of those was Paul Cohen's boss, Dick Arkway, who had been in business fifteen years before Smiley started and was impressed with the knowledge he'd acquired in a short time. Another was Harry Newman, who was just starting out in the business himself and looked up to Smiley as a mentor. Along with his brother Robert, Newman had inherited the Old Print Shop, a rare-book store bought by his grandfather in 1926.

Newman loved maps as a kid—he remembered staring in fascination at a giant sea chart by British cartographer J.F.W. Des Barres on the wall of his grandmother's house—but he was initially scared of dealing in them. There was too much a person could get wrong in a description, and errors could cost thousands. Impressed with Smiley's knowledge, Newman approached him, asking if he'd be willing to write catalog descriptions for him. "How about you let me sell you a few things instead," Smiley replied. That was the beginning of a twenty-year friendship, in which Smiley unstintingly shared what he knew. One time during an auction, Smiley passed him notes on the background of a particular sea chart Newman wanted to buy. On another occasion, he took Newman to the rare-books room at the New York Public Library to show him a copy of a rare sea atlas owned by George Washington.

At the same time, Smiley continued to find top-rate material for his clients. In late 1986 or early 1987, he acquired a rare "proof state" of John Seller's map of New England—sold with a blank coat of arms as an enticement for someone to fund the map's printing (it was later filled in with the arms of Seller's patron Robert Thomson). In an advertisement in *The Map Collector*, he proudly noted that this was "one of only two known copies"—the other being at Yale's Sterling Library. He sold it for $25,000 to Leventhal, who was fast assembling a near-complete record of cartography for New England.

Smiley joked to Leventhal that if he didn't expand his focus, Smiley soon wouldn't have anything left to sell him. The next time they met, he spread out a 1507 world map by Dutch cartographer Johann Ruysch, only the third printed map showing the New World. Unlike Waldseemüller's map printed the same year, Ruysch hedged his bets on whether America was its own continent or part of Asia, covering the west side with a scroll that left it up to the viewer's interpretation. Smiley sketched out a new plan for Leventhal's collection—instead of starting with the discovery of New England, he could backtrack to the discovery of America, gradually focusing in on Boston. Leventhal bought both the map and the project.

Larry Slaughter, meanwhile, became fascinated with *The English Pilot* of John Seller, John Thornton, and Mount and Page. An avid sailor, he became determined to collect as many rare volumes of *The English Pilot* as he could, and with Smiley's help he began amassing a collection of the book to rival that of most libraries. In addition, Smiley helped him focus his collection more closely on the Washington, DC, area, especially its first cartographer, Andrew Ellicott. Congress had passed a law establishing a new capital in 1790. Thomas Jefferson oversaw the work, employing French architect and engineer Pierre Charles L'Enfant, who proposed a grand vision, including fifteen Parisian-style avenues. His imperious attitude, however, alienated the founding fathers—especially when he ran one of his beloved avenues through the property of one of the district's most influential landowners.

L'Enfant was dismissed in 1792, and his assistant, Andrew Ellicott, continued his plan and completed the first survey of the new capital. Before he could print his map, however, two pirated versions appeared in the spring of 1792 in magazines published in Philadelphia and Boston. The official version, engraved by Thackara and Vallance, appeared that June. The public snatched up copies, and more than a dozen more versions were printed over the next decade. The resulting sequence was a map collector's dream, with multiple versions showing subtle variations on the subject. Smiley originally acquired versions of both the rare Boston and the Philadelphia versions of Ellicott's map for Norman Leventhal but persuaded him to sell them to Slaughter and then continued to track down a dozen more editions.

AS SMILEY SPENT more time with clients, appearances began to matter more to him. He started dressing in designer suits by the likes of Karl Lagerfeld and Paul Smith, took taxis everywhere he went, and insisted on picking up the check when he took friends out to expensive restaurants. But underneath the suits and new money was still the same old Forbes, who loved history and once dreamed of buying a New England village with his college friends. Whenever he could, he went back to Bedford to visit his parents and twin sister, Susan, and go on hikes in the surrounding hills.

In the summers, he stayed at a client's cottage in Harpswell on the southern Maine coast, inviting Scott Slater and other Hampshire friends to join him. During one visit in 1988, he was flipping through a real estate circular and came across an ad for an old New England farmhouse. The property was located in Sebec, a fleabite of a town in almost the exact center of the Maine—an hour north of Bangor and eight hours' drive from New York City. The asking price, Slater later recalled, was just $89,000.

When Smiley flew up to take a look along with his father and old friend Paul Statt, it quickly became clear to Statt why it was so cheap. The house was picturesquely situated on a small hill overlooking Sebec Lake—but it was a dump. The floor was full of holes, the bathroom was nonexistent, and there was only a frame where the kitchen should be. He flatly counseled his friend to save his money. To Smiley's father, however, the house reminded him of his own house in Bedford, and with only three hundred people, Sebec reminded him of what Bedford used to be.

Smiley was excited with the potential of both the house and the town. Here at last was the village he'd always dreamed about. After years of studying maps, he knew how small settlements could grow over time. The trick, he told Statt excitedly, was to find a place before it had become gentrified and suburbanized, and play a role in its development to keep those elements in check. He bought the house in cash, paying close to the asking price—even though he later always told friends that he paid $50,000. Slater and other old pals came up with a term for this phenomenon: "Forbes dollars," a personal accounting system in which Smiley always spent less than he had and was always owed more than he was.

He used the same calculus in business. Whenever he saw a map he knew his clients should have, he snapped it up, worrying later how he'd pay for it. At auctions in London he'd walk out with maps, promising to have the money wired, figuring out how to come up with the cash once he got back to New York. He began falling further and further behind in his payments. In 1988, New York State issued warrants for two years of back taxes totaling more than $8,000. He began defaulting on payments to other dealers as well.

In one instance, Smiley walked into the Old Print Shop to see a six-part map of Virginia made in 1807 by James Madison, a first cousin of the president. Harry Newman had spent a fortune to restore it—and when Smiley saw it on the table, he pled with his younger colleague to let him buy it. He wrote a check for $12,000, immediately heading uptown to sell the map to a client. As with the incident with Bill Reese and the Clark atlas, the check bounced a few days later. It took Smiley years to cover what he owed, finally coming in with a check for $15,000 to cover the map plus interest. Newman forgave him and resumed doing business with him, but other dealers, like Reese, stopped, handicapping Smiley's ability to sell.

No one criticized him more than Graham Arader, the reigning king of the map world, who lost no opportunity to disparage his rival. The two were similar in many ways—both projected an air of upscale refinement, down to the "III" at the end of their names; dealt in top-of-the-line material; and touted their superior knowledge as the key to their success. But in many other ways, they were polar opposites. While he could be gregarious in social situations, Smiley retained enough Yankee humility to deflect conversations away from himself. Arader, by contrast, shot from the hip in a stream-of-consciousness patter. He was his favorite topic of conversation.

In one area, he couldn't compete with Smiley. Despite his accumulation of knowledge, he was not the natural scholar Smiley was. Arader never wrote articles in booksellers' magazines about the history of cartography. He'd much rather spend his time on the phone, wheeling and dealing, with three conversations going on at once, than sitting in a library for hours on end taking notes on a sheet of paper. But that's exactly the kind of thing that drove Smiley, as he traveled to library map collections throughout the northeast.

AS HE EXAMINED THEIR MAPS, Smiley began to unravel a complicated web of mapmakers who emerged in London in the late 1600s and early 1700s. This was a time of rampant colonial expansion, in which the newly restored king Charles II pushed colonization as a way to fill England's depleted coffers and hold off encroachment by the French. Like their French rivals, English mapmakers began using modern survey methods to claim the borders of their new territories.

In order to secure the outlays of capital to conduct massive surveys, mapmakers had to please the aristocratic shareholders of the companies that controlled the colonies themselves. One early figure, a Scotsman named John Ogilby, created the first large-scale map of Carolina in 1673, based on a manuscript map provided to him by the wealthy proprietors of the colony. According to their wishes, he attached the names of these investors to rivers, capes, and counties, which still bear them today.

In repayment of a debt, Charles II awarded a no-man's-land between New York and Virginia to William Penn; the only trouble was, the area had already been settled by Swedes and Dutch fur traders. Penn commissioned a map by an Irish surveyor, Thomas Holme, who created "A Map of Ye Improved Part of Pennsylvania" in 1681, cementing the area's ownership by the English lord.

Eventually, mapmakers in London coalesced into a group called the Thames School, a dynasty nearly as influential as the Dutch mapmakers of the previous century. "These, then, were the men who established England's place in the art and business of practical cartography," Smiley wrote in *AB Bookman's Weekly*. "A role in which the English would dominate the world during most of the 18th century." Smiley traced their lineages, as they passed knowledge from master to apprentice, creating maps that not only reflected the New World, but also helped shape it.

By the early eighteenth century, the action in North America had shifted inland. The eclipse of the Netherlands and Spain as colonial powers on the continent left only two countries in the running for control—England and France. While England had a firm grip on the coasts, the French flanked them down from Canada to the west. The stage was set for a brawl over the continent, with the Ohio River—the key passage from the Great Lakes to the Mississippi—as its flashpoint.

Long before the conflict erupted in force of arms, it was fought through maps. The first salvo was fired by Thames School protégé Herman Moll, in "A New and Exact Map of the Dominions of the King of Great Britain on Ye Continent of North America" in 1715 (Figure J) The map is better known as the "Beaver Map," for its inset of beavers chewing through a forest with Niagara Falls in the background. Beaver hats were the rage in London at the time, and Moll was sending a not-so-subtle reminder of the valuable fur trade at stake in America. That was only the beginning of the propaganda contained in the map, which breathtakingly declares nearly all of North America as belonging to England. The land to the west of the St. Lawrence previously known as New France, Moll calls "Part of Canada," granting France only the land north of the river.

Three years later, the French cartographic master Guillaume De L'Isle countered with his own map of North America, in 1718, which splashed "La Louisiane" in a giant font across the entire middle of the continent (Figure K). As outraged as the English were over the cartographical appropriation, they had to concede that the accuracy far outstripped anything England had produced at the time. While England might claim the Ohio, it was clear that France held it. Moll countered in 1720 with a new map of North America that rather brilliantly showed not the boundaries claimed by England, but the boundaries claimed by France, as a way to incite his countrymen to outrage.

For years, the British were forced to use De L'Isle's as the basis for their claim against his countrymen. A 1733 map by Henry Popple used it for his topography, even as he showed the boundaries of Virginia and Carolina stretching west past the Mississippi. Even so, that wasn't good enough for England's powerful Lord Commissioners of Trade, who denounced Popple for conceding the strategically important Niagara Falls to their enemies. His career foundered, and he never made another map.

After the French and Indian War broke out in 1754, the commissioners sent out a call for more accurate maps, and in 1755 John Mitchell delivered with a large-scale map that went beyond Popple's boundaries to claim the Ohio and all of the Great Lakes for England. The same year, Lewis Evans produced "A General Map of the Middle British Colonies," a smaller map that drew from new English sources, including personal expeditions he took to survey up the Ohio. Finally, the British had a map nearly as accurate as the French (Figure 7). In another essay for *AB Bookman's Weekly* on early American mapmakers, Smiley calls it out for special mention, naming it the "greatest effort of American cartography in the 18th century" and an accurate map of the "final theater of war in the English and French struggle."

Maps continued to play a role during the war as well. A crucial flex point in the French defenses was a fort at the spot where the Allegheny and Monongahela Rivers join to form the Ohio, called Fort Duquesne. An officer held captive there smuggled out a map that showed the fort's weaknesses. Using it, British general Edward Braddock boldly marched out to attack with fifteen hundred men—straight into a French ambush. The loss of half of Braddock's troops sent shock waves through the British public, which hotly debated Braddock's tactics, especially after his aide-de-camp published six maps of his battle plan defending his tactics.

That was only the beginning of three years of French victories and British incompetence, as the British lost fort after fort. Eventually the tide turned when British general John Forbes (no relation to Smiley) took back Fort Duquesne after convincing the French's Iroquois allies to defect. In the treaty signed in 1763, John Mitchell's map of North America was used to set the new boundary lines, effectively giving England uncontested control over all the territory east of the Mississippi.

IN ADDITION TO being the definitive conflict for colonial control of North America, the war was also one of the most mapped in history. Surveyors accompanied the troops to battle in every theater, sketching battle plans and mapping forts, which were published after the fact in newspapers and as single-sheet maps to be snapped up by the British populace. After the war, many of these maps were gathered by British cartographer Thomas Jefferys into *A General Topography of North America and the West Indies,* the first great atlas of the American interior. The one hundred maps feature all the seminal maps of the continent, including the first accurate survey of Virginia by Peter Jefferson (the future president's father), the first accurate survey of New York by John Montresor, and all six of the maps of Braddock's disastrous attack on Fort Duquesne.

Though Jefferys died in 1771, his partners brought out another edition, calling it *The American Atlas,* in 1776. It included several more important maps of the colonies, among them a new map of Pennsylvania by Nicholas Scull and a map of North Carolina by John Collet. All these maps were instrumental to the British as they went to war against their own colonists in the American Revolution from 1775 to 1783. Unlike the previous conflict, which was fought on largely uncharted territory, now both sides in the conflict had accurate maps they could call upon to plan strategy.

A partner in Jefferys's firm named William Faden mapped the conflict practically in real time, seeking out surveyors who accompanied British officers. He published thirty-three maps of Revolutionary battles and released them in his own atlas, the most complete record we have of troop movements during the war. Meanwhile, what Faden did on land, Joseph F.W. Des Barres did at sea with *The Atlantic Neptune*—the last of the great English sea atlases. The book was part of an ambitious project by the British Admiralty to scientifically survey its colonial holdings around the world. By the time the three-volume atlas was published in 1775, Des Barres had produced more than a hundred charts of the entire Eastern Seaboard.

The maps are lush and expansive, lavishing just as much detail on the woods and hills as they do on the bays and headlands. Even in Des Barres's lifetime, they were recognized as a superior achievement, with one contemporary reviewer enthusing that it was "one of the most remarkable products of human industry which has been given to the world through the arts of printing and engraving." That assessment has only grown over time. According to map historian Sy Schwartz, "Historical consensus has it that this atlas is the handsomest collection of hydrographic maps ever published."

As the war intensified, Des Barres kept mapping, making charts of several Revolutionary sea battles, including the siege of Charleston Harbor (Figure L). By the time he was done, the territory no longer belonged to the country that employed him. Nonetheless, he pressed on, producing new surveys at his own expense until 1784. His accomplishment is to sea charts what Willem Blaeu's atlas was to land atlases a century earlier, and a direct descendant of the promise made by John Seller in *The English Pilot*. Unlike Seller, however, Des Barres was wildly successful, creating charts superior to anything made in America for another fifty years. Des Barres himself lived almost that long, retiring to Canada as a wealthy landowner and political figure before he finally died at age 103.

BY THE FALL OF 1988, Smiley's fortunes, too, had improved, at least temporarily. Already, his knowledge of English and American mapmakers was among the most extensive in the trade. He put a point on that fact by issuing his very first catalog, *The Early Cartography of North America: A Selection of Maps, Atlases, and Books, 1507–1807.* Up until now, he had produced lists of maps for clients, but this was something different— a scholarly history of the founding of North America told between the lines of sixty-eight maps, along with prices showing the increasing value of historical maps at the time. One map dealer later referred to it as "one of the great rare Americana Catalogues of the last 25 years. . . . It stands head and shoulders above the rest for its combination of rare material and scholarship."

In an editor's note Smiley more modestly called it "our small contri-bution to the history of the discovery and settlement of America, and . . . an indication of our most sincere interest in the cartographic record." The book started with the 1507 Ruysch map of the world Smiley had presented to Leventhal as the basis for his expanded collection ($40,000) and ended with the 1807 map of Virginia made by Reverend James Madison, which Smiley bought from Harry Newman ($17,500). In be-tween, it devoted long blocks of text to explaining the significance of the maps in an academic but readable style.

One page had a sequence of maps derived from John Smith's map of Virginia, the next a full-page description of an incredibly rare map of New France by explorer Samuel de Champlain in 1613. These were fol-lowed by several maps by Blaeu, Hondius, and Jansson; John Foster's map of New England ($30,000), Holme's map of Pennsylvania, and a three-foot-high wall map by John Thornton, which Smiley said was found in only three libraries ($38,000). "We know of no other copies in private hands," he proudly boasted, before describing seven different base maps that Thornton used to create it.

He included many of the maps in the spitting match between En-gland and France over the Ohio, including two by De L'Isle and two by Moll, as well as John Mitchell's map that was used to draw the new boundaries ($28,000). Toward the end of the catalog was a chart of Georgia by Matthew Clark—one of the last pages from the Clark atlas Smiley had bought from Reese several years before. On the following page were three of Andrew Ellicott's maps of Washington, DC, includ-ing the pirated Boston edition, which hadn't appeared on the market for a century.

Taken in total, it was an impressive record of what Smiley had accomplished in just three years of dealing in maps—with a combined asking price of more than a half million dollars. If this "Catalog Number One" was Smiley's official coming out as a dealer, then it was a sign of impressive things to come. As he stated in his introduction, he had the intention of producing more catalogs for the future—and seemed to have the inventory, the clients, and the knowledge to make more than just a "small contribution" to the historical record. Just as he seemed poised for success, however, an event apparently occurred that put his chances for producing a "Catalog Number Two" in jeopardy.

Chapter 6

PLAYING HARDBALL

FIGURE 9 SEBEC VILLAGE, C. 1860.

1989–1995

FOR YEARS AFTER it happened, Smiley told the story the same way: One April morning in 1989, he rushed into his studio on Seventy-Ninth Street in a panic. *No*, he thought, *this can't be happening.* Pushing past police officers, he searched up and down the stairs and on the sidewalk outside, hoping that the thieves had dropped a map or two. *Anything*, he thought. But above all he was hoping to find a rare 1713 edition of *The English Pilot, The Fourth Book* that he had just bought for Slaughter but had yet to deliver. *Maybe they tore out some maps and dropped the atlas*, he told himself as he searched, in vain hope that he could recoup at least part of his investment.

But it was gone, along with all the rest of his inventory. He had been cleaned out in the burglary of his studio, losing hundreds of thousands of dollars in inventory—all of it uninsured. There had been a string of gallery thefts in the neighborhood lately, but he never thought anyone would steal from him. He knew everyone in the business. Where would a thief be able to sell? According to Smiley, police saw the theft as a crime of opportunity. They told him the thieves had robbed several other art galleries in the building, breaking in through a skylight in the roof. In Smiley's case, however, they may have been drawn by the sign on his door that read "Rare Maps, Atlases, and Globes." The maps had probably left the country that night.

Smiley remained hopeful. The thieves would eventually have to sell—and when they did, someone would alert him. He began making calls to other dealers. Some were sympathetic, but by this time Smiley had damaged his reputation so badly that some just shrugged it off. Arkway's Paul Cohen remembers Smiley calling, irate about a John Thornton chart he saw in Cohen's catalog that he was convinced came from *The English Pilot*. But Cohen insisted it came from another volume. Alex Krieger, a Harvard architecture professor who assisted Norman Leventhal with his collection, remembers being questioned by the FBI at the time about the theft, and Ashley Baynton-Williams, a London map dealer who began working for Smiley soon afterward, distinctly remembers seeing pictures of the gallery's bashed-in door.

Other dealers, such as Reese and Arader, doubted the theft had even happened. There is scant evidence in the record to prove that it did. No newspaper stories refer to it, and neither the New York Police Department, nor the FBI, nor Interpol could produce records of any investigation. Smiley himself referred to the incident in court papers several times between 1989 and 1991, putting the loss anywhere between $220,000 and $330,000 depending upon the date. "Though I may be an 'expert' in cartography, I am, admittedly, no businessman," he wrote in one case, "thus no insurance."

The other galleries in the building have long since closed, but I did track down the super, who still works in an office in the basement of the building. He remembered Smiley as a good tenant who paid his rent on time, but as for any burglary in the building at that time, he shook his head. "I can't say it never happened, but there is a one percent chance out of a thousand that it did," he says. Asked if it's possible he was never alerted, he adds, "Usually someone farts in this building, and I hear about it. It's inconceivable to me that I wouldn't hear about something like that."

Whatever the truth of the situation, friends said Smiley grew despondent after the incident. As the weeks went by without a single map surfacing, he hinted darkly that one of his rival dealers might have been behind it. The map world was too small for nothing to turn up. *I get it,* he fumed. *You do this alone.*

"I didn't trust the marketplace after that," he later told me. "I went on to be a loner, and I think it was unnecessary and imprudent." He rubbed his hands together. "It was straight-up foolish to struggle so hard because I insisted on doing everything myself." Smiley stopped advertising and putting out catalogs, relying solely on his network of personal collectors to continue buying and selling maps. Some of his friends and family urged him to cut his losses and get out of the business, but Smiley stayed in. There was no way he was going to allow himself to be beaten.

Rebuilding his collection wasn't as easy as it had been to build it in the first place, however. By now, many of his European contacts had retired or died. To help him, he hired Baynton-Williams, a third-generation map dealer whose father was one of the leading dealers in London, and who called on his connections to help find Smiley material. He was impressed with Smiley's ability to buy and sell but quickly grew frustrated covering for him over his promises to pay. Some of Smiley's best clients were sympathetic toward his plight and told him they'd wait to be reimbursed for items they'd bought but were stolen before he could deliver them.

One person who showed no sympathy was Graham Arader, who had sold Smiley several maps, including a rare 1759 map of Pennsylvania by Nicholas Scull, in May 1989. Smiley signed a note promising to pay him nearly $50,000 for the map by late June. When he failed to do that, Arader sued. The next month, the two settled, agreeing to a new payment plan, but Smiley kept defaulting on payments for nearly a year. It wasn't until the following spring that Arader got his money, along with interest and $5,000 in attorney fees.

In order to make ends meet, Smiley took out a mortgage on the house in Maine for $40,000 and called upon friends for loans. But his debts mounted. Creditors began suing him for unpaid bills, and he defaulted on credit cards, including more than $20,000 owed to American Express for travel expenses. The IRS hit him with liens for nearly $5,000 in unpaid taxes, and ironically, he even failed to pay the bill for $10,000 to a burglar alarm company in April 1990. In another case, he got into a dispute with a Spanish map collector, José Porrúa, who accused Smiley of selling him maps in poor condition. Smiley blamed the gallery theft for his failure to reimburse Porrúa the money for the sales, again defaulting over and over on payments to make up the debt. Eventually, the court ordered him to pay Porrúa $35,000 in April 1991.

As difficult as all these financial problems were for Smiley, nothing hurt him as badly as a falling-out with his first and biggest client—Norman Leventhal.

FOR YEARS, Smiley and Leventhal had a symbiotic relationship. Leventhal worked exclusively with Smiley, who tirelessly tracked down all the pieces of the puzzle he could find to tell the story of the mapping of New England. Together they put together a collection that had never been assembled before—and probably never could be again, given the rarity of some of the maps in the collection. As Leventhal began showing his maps more publicly, however, their relationship became more complicated.

In 1988, Leventhal attended a presentation at the Boston Society of Architects in which Harvard architecture professor Alex Krieger showed slide after slide of old maps of Boston to illustrate how the city had changed over time. After the presentation, Leventhal approached him. "What do you know about maps?" he asked. "Not much," Krieger responded. But he did know about Boston. After visiting Leventhal's collection at the Boston Harbor Hotel, Krieger struck up a friendship with the collector. He introduced him to other local historians and librarians and eventually agreed to become his curator.

When he met with Smiley to discuss the purchase of more maps, Krieger took an immediate dislike to him. He seemed obsequious and too eager to please—the way he called Norman "Mr. Leventhal" and referred to him as "Professor Krieger." "I thought he was slimy," he later told me. "Just the way he was courting Norman in an overdone way—kind of just sucking up, but unduly so," Krieger later said. Until now, Leventhal hadn't been too concerned with how much he paid for the maps Smiley found, writing checks for the prices he quoted without question or negotiation.

But Krieger began to wonder whether the prices Smiley charged were fair. When Smiley brought them a new map, he started calling around to other dealers to ask what they would charge for a similar map. Of course, in a trade with such few players, map prices are a subjective concept, varying dramatically depending on individual taste, condition, and color—to say nothing of the potential motives of Smiley's competition, who continued to be jealous of the way Smiley had sewn up his clients and certainly hoped to sell to Leventhal directly.

According to Krieger, Smiley's prices were close to those of other dealers at first, sometimes higher and sometimes lower. After a year or two, however, Krieger said he began to notice that Smiley's prices were creeping up relative to the competition, frequently coming in highest. When they began to be even higher than Graham Arader's, Krieger really began to become suspicious that he was overcharging them.

Finally, Smiley brought Leventhal a 1785 map of New England by the eighteenth-century mapmaking team of Norman and Coles, which was only the fourth map printed in the United States. Only two copies of the map were known to exist, Smiley told them, with the other at Yale. There would never be another opportunity to buy it, he continued, setting its price at $100,000. Even Leventhal hesitated at that figure, but convinced by Smiley's sales pitch, he agreed to the sale. Afterward, Krieger called Chicago map dealer Ken Nebenzahl to ask how much he'd charge for the map. The Chicago dealer agreed that it was an important map but thought there were several other copies in existence. Based on a photograph, he said a fair price would be $25,000.

Krieger was stunned. He confronted Smiley, bluffing that he had another opportunity to acquire the same map for a quarter of the price. Smiley backtracked, explaining how difficult it was to accurately price maps in the market, but sticking by his initial enthusiasm for the map. He reduced the price to $60,000, which Leventhal paid, and offered several other maps free of charge as well. But Krieger had lost trust in him. By now, other dealers were calling Krieger to offer material for Leventhal's collection, and he began to buy maps from Arkway and others.

Shortly after the incident, Leventhal decided to have the entire collection appraised, and Nebenzahl flew into Boston, staying at the hotel for several nights and removing each map from its frame to price it. Many had appreciated in just a few years and were worth thousands more than he'd paid for them, but some of the more recent ones were worth less than Leventhal had paid, in Nebenzahl's estimation. At the end of the appraisal, Nebenzahl brought out a portfolio of other maps Leventhal might be interested in buying, and soon Leventhal was buying from him too. When I spoke with him, Smiley remembered his falling-out with Leventhal differently. In Smiley's recollection, Krieger and Leventhal were upset not about the high price of a map, but over the cost of an eighteenth-century view of Boston that he'd discovered on wallpaper in a house in France. Due to the cost of cutting it from the plaster and export duties to get it out of the country, the wallpaper became much more expensive than a reproduction of the same view available in the United States. When Krieger and Leventhal discovered that, Smiley said, they balked at the price of the original. "My jaw dropped open," Smiley told me. "We were in the business of collecting originals. If you want to collect facsimiles, go ahead, but it has nothing to do with me."

Whatever the cause, both Krieger and Smiley agreed that the relationship with Leventhal cooled after that. Leventhal bought a few more maps from Smiley, but gradually they parted ways. Smiley felt helpless to retain his client but rationalized the loss with the fact that the collection was practically finished anyway—at least, there was little more he could add to it. But he resented the way he'd been pushed aside and never given credit for the role he'd played in building the first great map collection of such a historically important part of the world.

SMILEY FARED BETTER with his other major client, Larry Slaughter, who became more serious about his map collection after his retirement in 1988. A quiet and private person who rarely spoke about his map collection even to friends, Slaughter appreciated Smiley's diffident formality. Using what Mick Tooley had taught him, Smiley showed Slaughter how he could assemble a collection that could tell stories about how the mid-Atlantic area had been settled. By now, that was easier said than done. A decade of interest in rare maps had dried up the market and driven up prices. By March 1990, *The New York Times* had taken notice, interviewing map dealers, including Smiley, for a feature story on the popularity of maps in home décor. "The problem for dealers is not so much selling as finding the really nice things," Smiley said.

One source Smiley found for new material was Howard Welsh, a New Jersey textile magnate and longtime patron of the New York Public Library, who had assembled a collection of a thousand maps and a hundred globes over forty years. Smiley originally met him at B. Altman; now as he got older, he began using Smiley as his agent to start selling off parts of his collection, with the proceeds going to support his family. When Welsh died suddenly of a heart attack on November 9, 1990, however, his children decided instead to sell the collection through Sotheby's, concluding the deal within a matter of weeks.

Smiley showed up at the auction along with other dealers the following June, acquiring among other maps the John Seller map of New Jersey that Alice Hudson had picked for the Mercator Society book. But he watched as another buyer picked up a group of four books of *The English Pilot*, including *The Fourth Book* from 1713—the same edition Smiley said was stolen from his studio—and the only copy of it sold at auction in decades. He did buy a pair of maps of Washington, DC, by Andrew Ellicott, including a rare map of the original survey of the District of Columbia *before* Washington—printed in an unusual diamond shape rather than the familiar square.

In the following months, he picked up other treasures for Slaughter as well, including a rare 1787 book by President Thomas Jefferson containing a map he'd made of Virginia. Jefferson's father, who'd previously mapped the state, had died when Jefferson was only fourteen, leaving him his surveyor tools. Jefferson taught himself how to use them, becoming an amateur mapmaker—and after becoming president, he updated his father's map for a book he wrote about his state. Smiley purchased a copy in 1991, adding it to three others in Slaughter's collection.

In October 1991, he purchased a beautifully intact first edition of *The English Pilot, The Fourth Book* from 1689 for $45,000 in a sale at Christie's of the map collection of the Du Pont family. In 1993, he bought a first-edition copy of Seller's *Atlas Maritimus* from 1682, the only copy in the United States, at auction at the Christian Brothers Academy for $6,500. And in 1994, he finally acquired a copy of the 1713 edition of *The English Pilot, The Fourth Book* from an auction at Sotheby's London.

At the same time Smiley was helping to build the collection for Larry Slaughter, he was also continuing to work on his scholarship. With the help of his assistant, Ashley Baynton-Williams, he began work on a book, *The Printed Charts of New England 1614–1800: A Carto-bibliography*, that would trace the mapmaking of New England through forty-seven sea charts, starting with John Smith's 1614 map of New England. He approached the curator of the map department at Yale, Barbara Mc-Corkle, who wrote an introduction to the book, and appealed to the Mercator Society to publish the work, which he envisioned as the first in a series that would trace the carto-bibliography of North America. With the enthusiastic support of Slaughter and Alice Hudson, the society solicited bids from printers and tentatively agreed to help raise $8,000 to print it.

According to Alice Hudson, however, Smiley and Baynton-Williams got into a dispute about who deserved credit for the writing. Baynton-Williams had prepared the intial text, but Hudson said later that Smiley thought his descriptions were poor and had to be rewritten; Baynton-Williams, however, believed he'd done the lion's share of the work and Smiley had only come in at the end to polish it. When the two were unable to resolve their differences, Hudson put the manuscript into a file drawer in the NYPL Map Division, where it remained.

Despite the new income from his sales to Slaughter, Smiley's financial difficulties continued. He continued to owe thousands of dollars in back taxes to both the state and federal governments—with the IRS filing a lien for $21,000 in 1992 and another for $25,000 in 1994. Even as he was paying off creditors, however, he was spending lots of money to rebuild the house in Sebec.

BACK IN THE 1800S, logs crowded so thick around the milldam on Sebec Lake that a person could walk across the lake on them. From there, they were floated to the City of Bangor in rafts down the river or, in winter, carried on a special steam train outfitted with skis. At its height in 1870, Sebec was the largest town in Piscataquis County, with a population of more than a thousand people (Figure 9). Since then, however, its fortunes have ebbed as the lumber business has dried up and gone to Canada and the population dropped to only six hundred. Now Piscataquis is the second-poorest county in Maine and one of the most sparsely populated areas east of the Mississippi.

Still, the town has retained a sparse beauty, with wooded hills rising over the lake, and dozens of historic homes clustered around the village center. Among the residents are summer visitors who own homes—still quaintly referred to as "camps"—on the lakeshore. Their children join the local kids jumping off the milldam bridge into the lake and running through the surrounding woods. The house Smiley bought overlooking the dam in 1989 conforms to the New England farmhouse rhyme: "Big house, little house, back house, barn." A five-over-five Colonial saltbox, it features two fireplaces bisected by a central staircase. Attached to it is a smaller carbon copy with kitchen and pantry, servants' quarters that have since been converted into a garage, and finally the big red barn. Smiley put Adirondack chairs on the front lawn and cleared a path through wildflowers and smoke bush down to a grassy area that gave way to a small wooden dock.

He spared no expense on the house itself, digging out a new foundation for the kitchen and installing new cabinets and an antique stove. He put a slate sink in the back pantry, beside ingenious cabinets to hold spices. Downstairs, he laid flagstone tiles and installed a pool table and beer fridge. In the main house, he jacked up the floor and laid new two-by-six stringers to support it, and he rebuilt the chimney.

Lisa's job, meanwhile, was to decorate the home. She chose a rustic, country aesthetic that harkened back a half century. She painted the kitchen bright yellow, installing a long table flanked by rattan chairs. In the dining room was another long wooden table, with matching wooden benches. Off the main hall, a children's playroom was filled with antique toys—a hobbyhorse, a stuffed bear, and a dollhouse. And in the corner was Smiley's office, where he retreated to look at maps and installed shelves for blues records and his father's gardening book collection after he died in 1994. The only map hanging in the house was one that was there when they bought it—a map of Sebec Lake done for the Dover-Foxcroft Chamber of Commerce in 1962 that hung over the dining room table.

Starting the year after he bought it, Smiley and Lisa began coming up to the house every summer as a refuge from the city. Smiley bought two antique wooden speedboats and drove them across the lake to where one of his best friends from college, Bennett Fischer, began renting a home. In the early 1990s, Scott Slater and Paul Statt began bringing their families up as well. A video from August 18, 1993, shows sun streaming through the window as Smiley and Slater sit together at the table beneath the map of Sebec.

"How are your pancakes?" Lisa asks, coming in from the kitchen. Smiley is sitting at the end of the table in a red-checkered shirt. "Oh, very good indeed. We've started our Sebec feeding frenzy," says Smiley. They talk about a house Slater is planning on buying in Harpswell on the Maine coast. "We can . . . visit Forbes and Forbes can visit us on the coast," Slater says. "All summer long, while we're eating." Smiley chimes in: "In between meals. We can have breakfast here and lunch in Harpswell."

The film cuts to a scene later that night, with Smiley coming out of the kitchen with Slater's daughter Felicity, lit by candles on a cake he had made from scratch for Lisa's birthday. "Where did you get this great cake?" Lisa asks. Felicity squeals excitedly, "He didn't get it; he made it." Smiley demurs in his baritone. "Okay, I frosted it, Felicity and I frosted it." Cut to a few minutes later, jazz music playing as Forbes and Lisa slow-dance together by themselves in the dining room.

EVEN BEFORE HE HAD a child of his own, Smiley doted on the children of Fischer, Slater, and the other friends who came to stay with him in Maine. He carried the kids on his shoulders on hikes around the property, and he towed them on inner tubes from the back of his speedboat. As they got older, he began spearheading more elaborate activities for their visits. One night at the dinner table, the kids were lamenting how they couldn't catch the larger frogs in the middle of the lake. The next morning, they awoke to find "Uncle Forbes" constructing a raft out of large logs. He went with them that afternoon, helping maneuver it with a long pole while the kids grabbed up the frogs.

Another time, it was a moose sculpture that the kids built out of spare wood, which graced the back garden for years afterward. Another time, Smiley helped the kids turn the barn into a haunted house, complete with an elaborate maze of booby traps. To the children, Smiley seemed like a magician who could make anything possible. "It was like entering another world," remembered Felicity Slater of the magical summers she spent up in Maine. "Every night we'd go wild with speculation about what we wanted to do the next day."

When Felicity's brother Gordie said he was into King Arthur's knights, Smiley disappeared into the barn for an hour. He emerged with a wooden suit of armor, complete with shield and sword with beveled edges. When Gordie was later stricken with a rare form of cancer that confined him to a wheelchair at age fourteen, Smiley continued to include him in activities, bringing model airplane kits to the cottage and helping him in and out of the speedboat for private rides.

The fantasy world for the kids wasn't without its rules. They couldn't just help themselves to snacks, for instance. When they were hungry, Uncle Forbes or Lisa would prepare platters of cheese or fresh-picked berries with fancy crackers, placing them on the table next to a vase of wildflowers. There were other rules too; for example, no one was allowed to touch Smiley's records or disturb him in his study. "When he was ready to engage with the kids, he was totally there and super-jovial," remembered Felicity. "But if you ran into his study, no way." That just, in her mind, added to his mystique—that this magician had his own private workshop where he performed work they didn't understand.

At night, Smiley held court on the front porch, overlooking the lake, where the rushing sound of the waterfall from the milldam was soon joined by the bass thrum of bullfrogs along the shore. Fireflies winked in and out of the trees while Cassiopeia and the Summer Triangle wheeled overhead. Felicity remembers falling asleep to the sound of blues music while her father and Uncle Forbes continued to sit with big glasses of beer, laughing and telling stories into the night.

IN SEPTEMBER 1993, Smiley invited Slater and Statt to Sebec for the weekend, and the three spent hours drinking beer and whiskey and bullshitting about literature and history, kids and marriage. The next year, they repeated the outing on Columbus Day Weekend, inviting Bennett Fischer as well. After that, the Boys' Weekend became an annual tradition, with the four of them taking long hikes on logging roads, on the lookout for moose, or taking freezing-cold dips in the lake. Smiley brought up special bottles of scotch and cases of craft beer, and eventually their college friend Dick Cantwell, who ran a brewery in Seattle, started sending a special keg for the weekend (though he didn't attend himself). After a few years, Slater's brother-in-law Bob von Elgg began joining them to make it five.

Smiley handled the cooking, pulling out his two favorite French and Italian cookbooks. He started roasting a turkey in the antique stove upon arrival, filling the house with smells of roasting meat and butter and providing pickings throughout the weekend. He'd follow it up with Provençal beef stew, potatoes with poached codfish and cream, smoked ham, or bread and tapenade—sometimes all at once. After dinner on Sunday, the group moved into the living room for annual readings of humorous clippings in front of the fireplace. Sipping scotch and port, they regaled each other with favorites from *The New Yorker*'s "Shouts & Murmurs" or *Harper*'s "Readings," or excerpts from Ian Frazier or Martin Amis. As dawn neared, they'd close with "Auld Lang Syne" led by Fischer, a fan of Robert Burns.

Throughout the weekend, Smiley played music nonstop, bringing obscure 78s of blues musicians he'd had shipped from London. Von Elgg, who counted himself a blues aficionado, had barely heard of most of them. Smiley explained their importance to the genre as if he were describing a rare map, noting records that existed in only five or six copies. Eventually the rest of the guys began teasing Smiley for his newfound love of blues—which they'd been listening to since college.

No matter how much they protested, Smiley insisted on paying for everything whenever his friends came to Maine. He carried around a bankroll in his pocket, peeling off hundred-dollar bills to pay for groceries and liquor. The habit bugged Slater, who continued offering to pay his share, until he eventually just gave up. He started mockingly calling Smiley, "the Squire," envisioning him as an English lord in a manor house, benevolently caring for his village. Something about the way Smiley choreographed their weekends, however, began to bother him.

As much as Smiley worked to create a magical realm for the children, he also worked to conjure a carefree refuge for adults. Having a good time wasn't enough; he wanted his guests' time to be exceptional—always stressing the importance of "becoming relaxed," though he seemed so little capable of it himself. When he wasn't cooking or shopping, he was puttering around the house, building a fence or working on a project in his study or workshop when the others were out taking a hike.

He almost never talked about his work—in fact, none of the men did. Sebec was a place apart from all that, where Smiley could get away from all the stresses of the competitive New York map trade. None of his friends knew just how much he was struggling in that world.

THE TRUTH IS that even as Smiley was working hard to build collections, he was still finding it difficult to keep up with a changing marketplace. As the prices of maps continued to soar, new dealers entered the business, competing with established players to find a small number of rare items for a limited number of high-end clients. "In the old days, you'd go to auctions and pick out diamonds from piles of coal," Harry Newman told me. "It has gotten a lot more cutthroat."

In such a small circle, dealers had to be friendly with one another, since they were often one another's best sources. But as supply tightened, they frequently found themselves squaring off over rare material at auctions in London and New York—the same dozen or two dozen dealers chasing the same items. "At an auction, it's fifty-fifty whether I'm going to bang someone over the head or get out of the way and let you have it," I was told by Barry Ruderman, a San Diego map dealer who entered the trade in the mid-1990s.

In private sales, cooperation was everything. When an estate was broken up, a dealer would often get on his cell phone to call colleagues and competitors, selling off the whole collection on an IOU basis before he'd left the house. "There is a lot of money out there, and it is all based on trust," said Ruderman. Since Smiley had gotten the reputation as a "slow pay or no pay," he was locked out of that circle—not that he wanted to be a part of it anyway. He preferred to go it alone, seeking out auctions in hidden corners of the trade and using his knowledge to beat competitors.

But such tactics began to fail in the face of the new aggressiveness of the trade. While up front auctions may appear democratic, with a set number of bidders fighting one another over prices, behind the scenes deals are being made; alliances are formed and broken before the first blow of the auctioneer's hammer. Some dealers began banding together in mini-syndicates to bid on expensive atlases, breaking them up and dividing the spoils.

"With more people you make less profit, but you take out some of the competition," said Newman, adding that he generally stayed out of such alliances. Other times, dealers made mutually beneficial agreements to stay out of each others' way. "Someone else has a client, and unless I really want it, I'll back off; it's an honorable thing," said Newman. "Unless it's going for absolutely nothing, in which case I'll kick it a couple of times."

While wheeling and dealing on the sidelines had always been a part of auctions, it seemed to Smiley that the gentility and sense of honor that characterized the trade in the early days had completely broken down. "When I was in New York, we played hardball," he told me, sitting at the picnic table in Martha's Vineyard. "You are swimming with sharks, and it is seriously cutthroat." Smiley faulted himself for the go-it-alone attitude that caused him to resist cutting deals with people on the one hand, and then resenting other dealers when they outbid him on the other.

"If I had taken the time to really talk to people and work with people instead of not trusting anyone, I would have done better," he said. "It was business first and maps and atlases second. With the old-timers, they struck a deal and shook hands and stuck to it. In New York, people would do anything, say anything, to win." The new aggressiveness frustrated Smiley, who constantly worried about getting played by fellow dealers.

"You have people approaching you ten minutes before the auction, offering you ten thousand dollars to stay off the lot. I'm pretty savvy about wheeling and dealing, but not savvy about knowing when it's real, or when I'm being screwed, and it's very stressful. There are guys who are good at this, who shook hands with each other and walked away knowing the other guy was full of shit. They just had a feel for it. Now imagine, you've got five good clients depending on you to manage that shark pond; that's why they are paying you all that money, to win.

"I just wanted to do it the old way of targeting certain things and going after them and having a reputation that once this guy goes after something, he can't be bought off. But I'm sure people ran the price up on me all the time, and I didn't know how to get that worked out. I did it because I wanted to build with these clients, I wanted to handle the material, I loved the material, and I wanted to do well and make money—because I wanted to win as much as anyone."

The obsession with "winning" often caused Smiley to overextend himself. In the mid-1990s, he began bidding more on behalf of Barry MacLean, the Chicago collector who had once been Arader's client. By his own admission, Arader began "running" Smiley at auction, bidding up the price to force Smiley to pay out more than he was prepared to pay. "Forbes didn't like going to auctions, because I don't care about the money," he told me. "So I go to an auction and I didn't care what I was paying. So I kicked his ass. And yes, if I saw Forbes bidding, I'd give it an extra two or three." At one auction, he remembers Smiley leaving the room and continuing to bid by phone so Arader wouldn't know it was him. "But I could see him."

Unlike other dealers who had retail businesses and could make up for times they overpaid at auction by charging more to customers, Smiley was usually buying on commission for clients who depended on him to get the best prices. If he went above what they expected, he often had to take the difference out of his own commission or kick in money of his own to keep them happy.

Smiley kept this to himself, even as his resentments against other dealers continued to grow. A certain amount of secrecy was always built into the map profession. Dealers played their cards close to the vest—rarely letting rivals know what maps they had acquired and how much they'd paid. On the one hand, clients could get upset if they knew you'd sold a map they wanted to another collector. On the other, rival dealers could undersell you if they knew how much you'd paid. To some extent, that secrecy was necessary, but it also led to unintended consequences. That became suddenly apparent in 1995, when the profession was rocked by scandal involving one of their own.

Chapter 7

UPWARD DEPARTURE

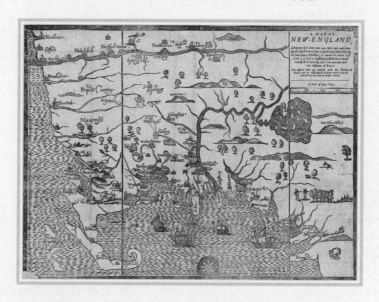

FIGURE 10   JOHN FOSTER. "A MAP OF NEW ENGLAND."
BOSTON, 1677.

1502–2001

GILBERT BLAND WAS no map scholar. A computer programmer from Florida, he got into the map trade in 1994 after apparently stumbling across a cache of antique maps in a storage center. He set up a small-time business out of his home, selling to other dealers, and was surprised by how much he was able to earn. Once he ran out of his initial stash, however, he had no idea how to get more maps.

He soon found a solution: theft. Bland's tool of choice was a single-edged razor blade, which he concealed beneath his fingers and casually ran down the pages of books while he pretended to be scanning text. In reality, he was separating the map from its binding. Bland targeted the libraries of out-of-the-way universities, including the University of Delaware, the University of Florida, and the University of Rochester. Most of his thefts were of fairly common maps by Ortelius, Hondius, and Mercator, and more recent nineteenth-century American maps—the kind that might sell for at most a few thousand apiece.

He got away with the racket for nearly two years, until the day in December 1995 he decided to steal from the George Peabody Library in Baltimore. That day, a bored librarian began watching one of the patrons, a fortyish man with light-brown hair and a slight mustache, when she thought she saw him tear a page out of one of the books he was examining. She called security, who followed him out the door and apprehended him in the doorway of a nearby museum.

Along the way, Bland threw a red spiral-bound notebook into the bushes; when the guards retrieved it, they found two maps from a 1763 book about the French and Indian War folded into its pages. Together they were probably worth around $2,000. Rather than press charges, the library let him off with a payment of $700 in cash for the damage. It was only after they let him go, however, that they noticed that the notebook contained page after page of the names of antique maps along with the libraries where they could be found.

As magazine writer Miles Harvey chronicled in the book *The Island of Lost Maps*, that was just the beginning of a case that eventually included seventeen university libraries around the country and two in Canada. Authorities caught up with Bland again a few months later, when a campus cop at the University of Virginia began investigating the theft of several maps, including those of Herman Moll and Andrew Ellicott. After getting an address for Bland from a local Howard Johnson where he'd stayed, police tracked him to his home in Florida, where he turned himself in. Eventually, he led the FBI to a storage locker in Boca Raton filled with 150 rare maps. Over the next few months, he'd help them recover about a hundred more. All told, the FBI figured their value at around a half million dollars.

Librarians around the country were outraged. "I feel like I was a real victim, like it was a personal assault," one told Harvey. "If Bland gets in front of my car, I'll run over him—but in a nice way," said another. "Oh, and then I'll back over him again." Only four of the affected institutions pressed charges, however. In the end, Bland served just seventeen months in prison and was required to pay $100,000 in restitution. The reason more libraries declined to press charges was simple: embarrassment. By coming forward, they were essentially admitting to the public—and to potential donors—that they couldn't protect their collections. As the FBI began to return maps to libraries, some of them refused to even admit that items had been taken. Some seventy of the maps were never claimed.

In his book, Harvey described Bland as a cipher who had gotten away with his crimes by avoiding notice. "Bland was less of a con man than an un man . . . lulling people into believing he was simply not worth much thought one way or another." Even the dealers who bought from him found him unremarkable: "Mr. Bland was bland," one said. "He looked bland, he sounded bland, he acted bland. There was no personality: nothing there."

The scope of his crimes put the map community on notice— warning that they would have to be more wary about whom they bought from. But Bland was hardly the first person to ever steal a map.

MAP THEFT HAS always been a shadowy twin to the map trade. As John Smith knew when he named New England, and the French and English learned when they played out their coming war on paper, mapping an area is tantamount to possessing it. From cartography's earliest days, maps were closely guarded secrets. The Roman emperor Augustus locked his maps in the most protected chambers of his palace. A Carthaginian general purportedly ran his ship aground and drowned his crew to keep sea charts from falling into Roman hands.

During the Age of Exploration, the kings of Portugal decreed that copying that country's charts would be punishable by death. That didn't stop Alberto Cantino, an ersatz horse trader in the secret employ of an Italian duke, from smuggling one out of Lisbon in 1502. The Cantino chart, beautifully illustrated on vellum, is now the oldest surviving Portuguese sea chart. Among other features, it shows a colossal new southern continent in the Western Hemisphere that had recently been "discovered" by Amerigo Vespucci. The map eventually came into the hands of German mapmaker Martin Waldseemüller, who used it in part to create his famous 1507 map naming America.

Theft continued to be important to the history of mapmaking for centuries. When the Dutch supplanted the Portuguese as the dominant trading power with the East, they did so with the help of the Dutch East India Company's "Secret Atlas"—a volume containing 180 maps showing the quickest passage to the East. Throughout the sixteenth and seventeenth centuries, the French and English Crowns handsomely rewarded privateers for capturing maps held by Dutch, Portuguese, or Spanish sea captains. One of the reasons few Spanish charts remain today is that ships' captains frequently weighted them with lead and threw them overboard when captured, lest they fall into enemy hands.

Mapmakers and map dealers stole from one another as well—often without attribution or shame, reworking one another's copper plates and passing them off as their own. Blaeu stole from Mercator, Jansson stole from Blaeu, Seller stole from Jansson, and so on. As the French and English fought over North America, Moll, De L'Isle, and Popple all stole from one another's geography to create their propaganda. And after the outbreak of the American Revolution, it was the theft of a map from West Point that exposed Benedict Arnold as a traitor.

In modern times, libraries have been targeted by map thieves at least since 1972, the same year Graham Arader began dealing out of his Yale dorm room. Another dealer offered Yale's Sterling Memorial Library a copy of a rare Dutch Atlas the library thought it already had. But when curators checked, they discovered it had actually gone missing—and that in fact, the atlas offered for sale had been taken from its shelves. The FBI traced it back to an unlikely pair of thieves—two Byzantine priests named Michael Huback and Stephen Chapo, who had apparently smuggled that book and others out of the library under their robes. When authorities searched their monastery in Queens, they found hundreds of other rare books taken from not only Yale, but also Dartmouth, Harvard, Notre Dame, and other universities. The priests were defrocked and sentenced to a year and a half in prison.

New to the business, Arader was angered by the injustice done to the Sterling, where he'd first learned about maps. He took it upon himself to police the trade, keeping a lookout for other thieves. He soon found one in Charles Lynn Glaser, a map dealer based in Arader's hometown of Philadelphia. In 1974, security guards at Dartmouth College had found eight antique atlases, including a rare copy of Thomas Jefferys's *American Atlas*, in the trunk of his car. Convicted of stealing the books from the Dartmouth library map room, he was sentenced to three to seven years in prison but was paroled after serving only seven months.

A few years later, in 1978, he called Arader offering to sell him two maps of New France by Samuel de Champlain. Knowing how rare those maps were, Arader called the FBI and then wore a wire to negotiate the deal. The evidence he gathered, in part, led authorities to determine that Glaser had stolen the maps from the James Ford Bell Library at the University of Minnesota. Glaser pled guilty and spent six months in prison. But that wasn't enough to stop him—in 1992, he again pled guilty to stealing a map from the Free Library of Philadelphia. This time, he received only probation.

Arader also played a role in apprehending another thief, Andy Antippas, a thirty-seven-year-old Tulane English professor. Arader bought five maps from Antippas at a New Orleans antiques fair in 1978, including a copy of John Seller's seminal 1675 map of New England. As he was cleaning the maps for resale, he noticed that one had a faint Yale University stamp of ownership on it. When he called the college, it turned out that all five were missing from the Sterling.

Faced with the evidence, Antippas pled guilty to charges carrying a maximum sentence of ten years. "I can only ask for compassion," Antippas said at sentencing, and the judge showed it, giving him only one year in prison. "We were amazed he got so little," Yale assistant librarian Margit Kaye said at the time. "Everyone seemed shocked." (Though Antippas lost his job at Tulane, he was soon back on his feet, opening a folk art gallery in New Orleans; later he was suspected of but never prosecuted for taking part in a bizarre grave-robbing ring.)

As part of the case, Yale completed an inventory of its collection in April 1978, finding that sixteen sheet maps and seventy-one maps from books were missing in addition to the five that Antippas had admitted stealing. Even so, it declined to release a list of the missing maps. Writing that June in *AB Bookman's Weekly*, the president of the Antiquarian Booksellers' Association of America and Yale alumnus, Laurence Witten, blasted Yale for not reporting the theft earlier. "The stolen items can be moved very quickly to remote places where they may not be recognized; and booksellers are likely to be deceived," he wrote. After the case, the library did report to *The New York Times* that it was tightening its security procedures and moving most of its precious atlases to the Beinecke. The flat sheet maps, including Seller's map of New England, however, stayed at the Sterling.

ARADER FELT VINDICATED by his work bringing down two thieves, and he vowed to bring down more. "What I have always practiced is relentless, unyielding due diligence," he told me in New York. "It's almost a giveaway if someone says, 'I got this from my grandmother.' I mean, the direct translation of 'I got this from my grandmother' is they stole it." The difficulty in prosecuting map theft, however, is that it is so hard to prove provenance. It's not like dealing with art theft, where each item is a one-of-a-kind work or numbered edition that can usually be easily identified.

A common myth about theft of paintings is that they are taken on behalf of eccentric billionaires, who put them privately on display—an urban legend first popularized by the James Bond film *Dr. No.* (In one scene, Bond passes a recently stolen portrait by Goya in the titular villain's underground lair and shrugs, saying, "So that's where that went.") In reality, most art thieves steal with only a vague idea of where they'll sell their paintings and are unable to fence them. That's why many art thieves are either caught within days of their crimes, or else their stolen artworks go underground for decades.

Maps are different. No one can know with certainty how many copies of a particular map have survived over the centuries. Like the Waldseemüller map found in Wolfegg Castle, extremely valuable maps in fact do turn up in strange places. At the Miami map fair, Harry Newman told the story of how in the 1950s or 1960s his grandfather took a house call in Brooklyn from Newman's Sunday school teacher that led to the discovery of the original manuscript maps from Lewis and Clark's expedition in a trunk in the attic. He had them authenticated and then sold them to Yale for $7,500. "They'd be worth millions today," he said.

And those are very rare maps with only a few copies—plenty of maps worth thousands still exist in dozens or even hundreds of copies. Forget *Dr. No.* Someone could hang a stolen map in his house without anyone—including himself—knowing it was stolen. Outside of a giveaway such as a library marking stamp, it's very difficult to tell which copy of a given map has come from where. And unlike art, maps aren't hung in galleries or museums, off-limits to inspection. They are mostly kept in libraries, where they are meant to be handled. Gilbert Bland used a razor to slice out maps, but others have used a wet string, balled up in their mouths and then placed in the binding of a book, to take maps. In a few minutes, saliva deteriorates the ancient paper to the point where the page can be easily removed.

No profile exists for those who steal maps. In most cases, the motive is simply the hope for a quick payday with little risk; in some cases, however, possession itself is the goal. In 1986, the curator of University of Georgia's rare-books library, Robert "Skeet" Willingham, was discovered with at least seventeen maps from the collection framed in his home. Arader helped in that case as well, providing the initial tip that led police to suspect Willingham. (Sentenced to fifteen years in prison, he was paroled in two and a half.) Such "insider" theft accounts for some 75 percent of thefts from libraries and museums. The Beinecke Library had its own brush with it in 2001, when curators discovered that a twenty-two-year-old student volunteer named Benjamin Johnson was stealing from the stacks. In all, he stole $2 million worth of rare books and letters—though most were recovered from his dorm room, among other locations, before he could sell them.

"It's the same old story, a person recognizes libraries have the best material and don't have the money to protect these things," Travis Mc-Dade, a University of Illinois librarian and lawyer who has written extensively about map theft told me. "So people cut out two or three maps, go to a dealer, and say my uncle died or my grandfather died, are they worth anything?" The secrecy and competition among dealers, said McDade, aid thieves, who find the deals simply too good to pass up. "If they don't buy it, he'll sell it to a competitor. It's a cutthroat business where ultimately it pays not to be as discerning a buyer as everyone else is," he said. "If you have been in the business long enough, you have dealt in stolen items."

No library is immune. Even the Library of Congress was vandalized by a sixty-two-year-old Alexandria bookstore owner named Fitzhugh Lee Opie, who raided the library's stacks for ten years before he was finally caught in 1992 with two Pacific Railroad survey maps under his sweater. He received six months in prison. For years, such lenient prison sentences were the norm in book and map theft, with none of the thieves serving more than two and a half years. That was probably a combination of *who* was doing the stealing—mostly middle-aged white men without any criminal past—and *what* they stole—mere pieces of paper. Prosecutors and judges often failed to appreciate the inherent value of items known to only a small community of specialists. With another case that hit the courts the same time as Bland's, however, that was about to change.

DANIEL SPIEGELMAN WAS both cautious and daring in his thefts. Cautious, because unlike most map thieves, he didn't try to sneak material out in front of onlooking guards. Daring, because instead he broke in to commit crimes at night, after the Rare Book and Manuscript Library at Columbia University had closed. Spiegelman started stealing at the same time as Bland—the spring of 1994—by shimmying up an abandoned dumbwaiter from below the locked stacks where the rare books were kept.

He visited night after night for months, stealing hundreds of medieval and Renaissance manuscripts and dozens of letters written by US presidents from George Washington to Woodrow Wilson. Among his targets was one of Columbia's gems: a nine-volume German edition of Blaeu's *Atlas Maior* from 1667—one of only a few copies in the world. One by one, Spiegelman razored more than two hundred maps out of the volumes. When he was done, one volume had only three maps left.

The library didn't discover the thefts until Fourth of July weekend, when a librarian realized a sixteenth-century liturgical manuscript was missing from its case. After a wider search revealed a dozen empty manuscript boxes, director Jean Ashton called in the FBI. Columbia broke with the discretion embraced by most libraries victimized by thieves, privately circulating a list of stolen items. It caught the attention of a Dutch dealer the following spring, when a man approached to sell books and manuscripts, all of which were on the list.

Police set up a sting, surrounding Spiegelman at a Holiday Inn in

Utrecht as he tried to make the sale. Later they raided a storage locker in New York, where they found dozens of letters, manuscripts, and, in the last locker, many of the maps severed from the Blaeu atlas. The ensuing legal case took years to unfold. Spiegelman successfully fought extradition from the Netherlands for more than a year—in part, bizarrely, because he was for a time falsely rumored to be a suspect in the April 1995 Oklahoma City terrorist bombing, and the Dutch wouldn't extradite him if he was facing the death penalty. He returned to the United States in November 1996 and made a plea bargain in April 1997, a month before Bland left prison.

As Travis McDade described in *The Book Thief*, the plea bargain started routinely. Spiegelman detailed his crimes, and prosecutors agreed to follow the sentencing guidelines. Since the 1980s, the federal system has followed a fairly straightforward table to calculate sentences, with the level of severity of the offense on the horizontal access, and the degree of defendant's criminal history on the vertical. To find the sentencing range, all the judge has to do is identify where they intersect.

The guidelines also give judges some leeway to take into account the particular details of the case and the defendant's level of cooperation, allowing them in some circumstances to opt for a "downward departure" to decrease the sentence or an "upward departure" to increase it. Downward departures were actually quite common in the Southern District of New York, where Spiegelman was prosecuted, used in 34 percent of cases at the time. Upward departures, meanwhile, were rare, used in only 1 percent of cases.

In Spiegelman's case, the guidelines put the sentencing range at between thirty and thirty-seven months, or about a year more than the twenty-two months he'd already served. When library director Jean Ashton heard about that range, she was appalled. Here was a man who had systematically desecrated Columbia's rare-book holdings, forever altering and destroying documents that had survived for hundreds of years.

"The very existence of rare books and manuscripts provides the basis for new discovery and interpretation in almost every area of study," she wrote the judge. "[T]he destructive acts of one person can cause a piece of history to be lost to all future generations." The argument had its effect. When the parties met again for the sentencing hearing in June, Judge Lewis Kaplan surprised the court by announcing he was considering an upward departure. Spiegelman's defense attorneys protested, demanding hearing after hearing to argue against the move.

If anything, the strategy hurt their client by giving the library a forum in which to present its case. In the final hearing in March 1998, Ashton brought several items, including two volumes of the Blaeu atlas. "They are considered the great glory of the golden age," she began, as she held one of them up with a pair of white gloves. Opening the cover, she displayed row after row of page stubs that had once held maps. That afternoon, Kaplan granted an upward departure of five levels, increasing the sentence to sixty months in prison.

Since Spiegelman had now been in prison for three years, that added another two. But he had no intention of serving out the entire sentence. A year and a half into it, in September 1999, Spiegelman escaped from a halfway house in Manhattan. Rather than go into hiding, he recovered a cache of stolen items and offered them to a rare-book dealer in Connecticut. Police caught him in a sting almost identical to the one in the Netherlands, and the judge added another two years to his sentence. He finally left prison on July 19, 2001, after serving more than six years.

The hefty sentence for Spiegelman in comparison to those given to other convicted map thieves was a victory for Columbia. But it was also a victory for the idea that the value of rare maps and books went beyond the dollar amount they commanded on the market. After the Supreme Court affirmed this idea in another case, the US Sentencing Commission revised its guidelines in November 2002 to add a new category for "Theft of . . . Cultural Heritage Resources," with a base level two steps higher than simple larceny, and even more steps added if the object was stolen from a library or museum or if it was taken for monetary gain.

THE BLAND AND SPIEGELMAN thefts were a wake-up call to the cartographic community. Maps had never been stolen this brazenly, or on such a large scale. Conference panels were called, best practices shared on library Listservs. Starting in the late 1990s, some libraries began installing security cameras in their reading rooms; others began to make digital images of their most valuable maps in order to identify them in case of theft. There was only so much they could do, however. When a recession hit a few years later, funds for additional security dried up, and many efforts were put on hold.

On the other side, map dealers started becoming more wary about where they bought material. One strident advocate of self-policing was Tony Campbell, a London map dealer and former librarian at the British Library, who sent out a call for dealers to band together against theft in 2001. "It is essential that formal, international networks are established, to circulate immediately news about thefts and about the suspects involved," he wrote. His pleas to set up a centralized list of stolen maps fell on deaf ears. But individual dealers began more closely scrutinizing where they got material and became more suspicious about those who sold them maps—if only to protect their own reputations.

One person who came under increasing attention was Forbes Smiley. His reputation for slow payment and bounced checks was well-known, but at least one dealer suspected him of worse. Bill Reese, the New Haven dealer who'd been burned in the purchase of the Matthew Clark atlas, became suspicious of some of Smiley's goods. As he told me the story, he was doing some research on the map of New England made by John Foster, the first map printed in America. Produced in Boston in 1677, the map is incredibly rare, with almost no private copies in existence. A slightly more common version, however, was printed in London the same year; it's notable for a typo designating the White Hills of New Hampshire as the "Wine Hills" (Figure 10).

At some time in the 1990s, Reese acquired a London Foster and thought it would be fun to compare it to the Boston version, a copy of which was held down the block at the Beinecke Library. When he requested the book in which it ordinarily appeared, William Hubbard's *Narrative of the Troubles with the Indians in New-England,* he found the map was missing. Immediately, Reese thought of Smiley—whom he remembered boasting of handling a Boston Foster a few years before. He shared his suspicions with the library and was later told the FBI investigated but nothing came of the tip.

He wasn't the only one, however, who distrusted Smiley. Reese told Norman Fiering, the head of the John Carter Brown Library at Brown University, and he in turn told his map department curator, Susan Danforth. The Brown library had lost several maps to Gilbert Bland, and

Danforth vowed not to lose any more. After hearing about Smiley's poor reputation, she always made sure to sit next to him whenever he visited the library. "To be honest, I looked forward to it," Danforth later told me. "He had great stories, and I learned a lot about maps from him."

Eventually the rumors about Smiley subsided—and even started seeming foolish. Announcements came back to back that the two great collections Smiley had helped assemble were finding permanent homes. Rather than taking maps out of libraries, he was helping put maps into them.

Chapter 8

THE BATTLE OF SEBEC

FIGURE 11 ANDREW ELLICOTT. "PLAN OF THE CITY
OF WASHINGTON IN THE TERRITORY OF COLUMBIA."
PHILADELPHIA, 1792.

1996–2002

WHEN LARRY SLAUGHTER became sick with lung cancer and passed away on June 2, 1996, even his own family was astounded by the map collection he'd left behind. In the end, Smiley and Slaughter had together assembled some six hundred maps, one hundred atlases, and fifty books. They included four of the earliest editions of *The English Pilot, The Fourth Book*—from 1689, 1706, 1713, and 1732; four copies of Thomas Jefferson's *Notes on Virginia*; one of only a handful of copies of Ellicott's original map of Washington, DC (Figure 11); two rare wooden globes that were the oldest English globes in the country; and countless other rarities. Twenty-three maps in the collection were unique, with no other known copies in the world.

But the collection was much more than the sum of its parts—like Leventhal's collection of New England, Slaughter's assemblage of maps of the mid-Atlantic states was as close to a complete chronicle of the region as it was possible to make. "This collection was built as a study collection so that the materials as a whole could be examined for comparative purposes and aid scholars in various historical fields," Smiley explained to a Westchester County newspaper at the time.

Smiley and Slaughter had had many conversations about the value of keeping the collection together. After Slaughter's death, his wife, Susan, agreed to donate the collection to an institution where it could honor his memory. The obvious repository was the New York Public Library, where Slaughter had served as a devoted member of the Mercator Society. But the Library of Congress would be equally fitting given the collection's heavy emphasis on Washington and the surrounding area.

Together Smiley and Susan Slaughter decided to tell both libraries of the potential donation and have them both make their case. Alice Hudson was thrilled to learn the news. "That suits us perfectly!" she wrote Smiley in a letter. "This gift would be extraordinarily exciting for the Library." Hudson arranged a meeting with Smiley and the New York Public Library's president, Paul LeClerc, to show that the library was serious. LeClerc told him the library was in the process of renovating its reading rooms, including Room 117, and starting a new scholar-in-residence program. This collection would be a perfect contender for more study.

He layered on other perks as well, including a major exhibition and a professional catalog of the collection. Smiley told him he would personally love to see the collection go to New York, but the library would have to show Slaughter's widow that it could protect it and make it accessible to future generations. In a follow-up letter, Hudson assured him the library would do that, writing that "we are committed to protecting the collections" and that it would be "made secure in locked cases, away from the reading room, in our own adjacent air conditioned, locked, non-public stack area."

Of course, that would take money, and Smiley pointed out that the donation wouldn't come with an endowment. That wouldn't be a problem, LeClerc assured him, since in addition to contributions from the library's general fund, it would conduct a separate fund drive around the gift. That would be terrific, Smiley told them, but would they consider another idea: selling off maps in their collection that overlapped with Slaughter's? If so, he'd be happy to facilitate the process—in exchange for his standard commission, of course.

A few days later, Smiley was impressed to receive a letter from LeClerc reiterating many of Hudson's points, and adding a few new ones including the one he'd suggested. "To provide financial support for the maintenance of the Collection, the library will consider the sale of duplicates from the Map Division collections which are in poorer condition than the Collection's equivalents," LeClerc wrote. He added more personally: "Perhaps you and the donor would have tea with me one afternoon so that we can review the steps that must be taken to bring this great collection to the New York Public Library."

SMILEY WAS THRILLED. Just fifteen years earlier, he was sitting in the map room struggling to learn the names and dates of the major mapmakers. Now he would be sipping tea with the library's president, discussing how to enshrine a decade of work. Though the collection would have Slaughter's name on it, it would be covered with Smiley's fingerprints. This was his legacy—and how fitting to think it might be permanently displayed in the very temple where he'd first fallen in love with maps. Then there was the fact that he could personally profit from the deal by earning a commission on the sale of the duplicates—no small consideration given the precarious state of his finances.

In addition to meeting with Hudson and LeClerc, he traveled to the Library of Congress and the John Carter Brown Library at Brown to hear them make their cases. In February 1997, Smiley met again with Hudson and LeClerc as well as the director of the NYPL's research libraries, Bill Walker, who promised in another letter to catalog the collection within twelve months and dedicating "in excess of $100K" to make it happen. Eventually, Brown dropped out of the running, and it was down to the two libraries. Smiley produced an "analysis of need," detailing the number of duplicate maps, atlases, and books in each of the collections, to show which library could benefit more.

New York's collection overlapped with seven out of the forty-nine atlases in Slaughter's collection, while the Library of Congress's overlapped with twenty-two. As far as loose maps, New York had duplicates of 63 percent of Slaughter's maps, while the Library of Congress had 74 percent. Clearly, Smiley concluded, the New York Public Library would benefit most from the collection. By March 14, 1997, the decision had been made. Smiley wrote Hudson a letter on his letterhead informing her that Slaughter's heirs had decided the collection would go to New York.

Two months later, on May 28, 1997, the agreement was signed. About half the collection was donated as an outright gift, while the other half was given as an indefinite loan (a common way for donors to spread out their tax liability). The agreement included a passage stating that as an "inducement to the donor" LeClerc and Walker had "made certain commitments," attaching the letters from the administrators with their promises of swift cataloging and an exhibition to be funded in part by the sale of duplicates from the collection.

As promised, LeClerc invited Smiley and Susan Slaughter, along with Walker and Hudson, to tea in the president's office to celebrate the acquisition. Soon after the acquisition, the library publicized the gift with a front-page article on the library's newsletter, mailed to the library's many supporters. "The items that Mr. Slaughter assembled in this collection cannot be found together in any other repository in the world," Hudson said. Smiley added what he had realized years ago in private moments with Leventhal and Slaughter. "A scholar can line up ten maps on one table and suddenly see a new connection," Smiley said; "literally 100 new stories that have never been told will be told here."

When the celebrations subsided, Hudson turned to the gargantuan task of cataloging and conserving the materials in time for an exhibition the following year. The maps needed to be sorted into two groups— those donated directly and those on loan—before they could be cataloged for the collection. She drew up a plan estimating the cost at $88,422, including $43,638 for the cataloger. Nothing was included for

Smiley, despite the fact that he was the only one with the knowledge necessary to sort through Slaughter's sixty ring-bound notebooks in order to identify the hundreds of maps that needed to be cataloged.

SMILEY SAID NOTHING to protest the arrangement, even as he spent the fall organizing the notes from Slaughter's binders and matching them to maps in the collection. He set up materials at the long table farthest from the reference desk, coming in day after day to perform the work. Sometimes, Hudson and Smiley were the only ones left at the end of the day after all the patrons had left. They chatted about the various maps as they worked and shared frustrations over having to figure out which of the hundreds of maps belonged in the gift and which belonged in the loan.

Over time, Hudson began thinking of him less as a patron and more as a professional colleague—one who had done more in her tenure to improve the quality of the map collections than anyone else. She watched him diligently work to tease out discrepancies between the maps listed in the donation and those actually present in the collection. In some cases, maps were mistakenly listed twice, but in other cases, they were just entirely absent from where they were supposed to be. At one point, Slaughter's widow, Susan, called Hudson to privately express her frustration over several dozen missing maps that didn't seem to be present with others. "So where are they?" Hudson remembers her complaining. "I want this all to be in order."

For Smiley, business was finally looking up after a decade of trouble. In January 1997, he had paid off a federal tax lien for more than $25,000, and in February a state tax warrant for more than $6,700. Now he and Lisa began scoping out real estate outside the city. They had lived in New York for nearly two decades and had lately begun to tire of the fast pace of life there. Practically speaking, Smiley could work anywhere with a post office and a phone, and Lisa could practice interior decorating anywhere there were people rich and stylish enough to hire her. Recently, they had also been considering having a child and didn't want to raise one in the city.

For a time, they considered settling in the Boston area, close to research libraries and plenty of educated clients. But Boston seemed like a defeat to Smiley, looking as if he wasn't able to play the game in New York. After exploring the Connecticut coast and Cape Cod, they finally settled on Martha's Vineyard, an island off the south coast of Massachusetts that came alive every summer with vacationing celebrities. It was the perfect combination for the two of them—with enough history and New England charm to satisfy Forbes, and enough style and cachet to please his wife.

It would also be a perfect place to raise a child, with a small-town vibe Smiley had experienced in his own childhood. Moreover, no one could see this as a defeat for Smiley. In fact, it was quite the opposite. Dozens of wealthy businessmen and celebrities had homes there— including actors Ted Danson and Mary Steenburgen, newsmen Mike Wallace and Walter Cronkite, singers James Taylor and Carly Simon, and *Washington Post* publisher Katharine Graham. For the past several years, even President Bill Clinton himself had chosen the Vineyard for his annual summer vacations.

Yet, the prevailing attitude of islanders toward all the fame in their midst was a collective shrug. Locals were so used to running into faces they'd seen on TV while picking up butter at the local market that they seemed to barely notice. That sensibility fit perfectly with Smiley's own peculiar mix of New York flash and New England reserve. The Smileys rented the summer home of Scott Slater's sister Wendy for two weeks in October before finding a home on the quieter, western side of the island—"up island" as the locals call it. The location on a road wooded with scrub oak was away from the summer tourists who crowded the population centers of Vineyard Haven and Edgartown.

The house itself wasn't anything special—an ugly, oval-shaped cabin they nicknamed the "spaceship." But the price was cheap for the Vineyard, and with the demand from summer visitors they could rent it out during summers while they lived in Sebec, and then in a few years tear it down to build a new home. In December 1997, Smiley signed the purchase agreement for $265,000, putting 20 percent down as he and Lisa made preparations to move in the following summer.

BEFORE THEY DID, however, Smiley was in for a disappointment. When he presented Hudson with his list of duplicates the library could sell, she passed it up the chain to Walker, who dismissed it out of hand. These weren't duplicates, he argued—differences in condition, color, paper, and a dozen other attributes made every one of Slaughter's maps unique. Hudson contacted Smiley apologetically to tell him the news, but she had to agree with her boss. In fact, she was embarrassed she hadn't seen the obvious differences herself.

It took a few more conversations before it became clear to him what she was saying: The library wouldn't be selling *any* maps from its collection. Hurt, and then angry, he called Hudson in early March 1998 to express what she later called "deep concern" about the decision. Hadn't LeClerc told him in person that they would consider it, and hadn't he included it in a letter that had become part of the offical agreement? He ended the conversation brusquely, demanding that Walker send him a letter clarifying the library's position.

Hudson felt caught in the middle, wanting to keep Smiley happy, but also not wanting to create problems with her superiors. In a long memo to Walker, she suggested sending Smiley a letter expressing "our immediate inability to deal with the issue of duplicates, and our long-term desire to live up to our multifaceted agreement." Only after the whole collection had been cataloged could any question of duplicates be considered. "We have not forgotten the issue of duplicates, but we must accomplish the exhibit, the scanning, the cataloging, in order to meet our highest priority, which is to make the [Slaughter] collection as accessible as possible to scholars and researchers," she concluded. Smiley calmed down enough to continue his work cataloging the collection and helping to prepare for the exhibition that fall, and the topic of selling duplicates was tabled for the time being.

In early March, patrons of the library who had donated $250 or more to the Map Division filed in to Room 117 to be among the first to view the maps from Slaughter's collection, laid out on the long table where Smiley had worked. A few weeks later, several dozen donors and library administrators gathered at the Williams Club for a dinner to celebrate the acquisition of the collection. Susan Slaughter, who had suffered a recent heart attack, did not attend, but eight members of Slaughter's family did. Smiley got up to address them, offering kind words about Slaughter's vision in putting the collection together.

By this time, however, Smiley was dealing with his own health problems. Inclined to be overweight since childhood, he also had dealt with years of high cholesterol. Now, at age forty-three, he was informed by his doctor that his arteries were occluded and he would need to have open heart surgery to unblock them or he would almost certainly have a heart attack. Smiley took the news like a bullet. "I was told if I didn't have bypass surgery, I would drop dead," he told me. "When you are grandiose and in your forties, you just don't think that way. And then to be told you are not only mortal but you've got a problem, you are sick, changes the way you look at things, and I did not deal with that very well."

What was worse, the doctor told him he wouldn't be able to fly for a time, keeping him away from map fairs and auctions in London, Amsterdam, and other European destinations where he searched for material for his clients. Shortly after moving to the Vineyard permanently in the summer of 1998, he traveled to Boston for the quadruple bypass surgery. He spent the fall recuperating, gradually gaining back his strength, all the while barely pausing in his work cataloging the Slaughter collection in preparation for display.

On October 24, 1998, the New York Public Library opened the exhibit, *In Thy Map Securely Saile*, coinciding with the one hundredth anniversary of the Map Division and sponsored by *Condé Nast Traveler* and Jaguar. For the title, Hudson had chosen a line written by English poet Robert Herrick in 1610—just after John Smith had published his map of Virginia and before he published his map of New England. It was a time when the inhabitants of Great Britain were beginning to see new colonies appear on paper that most of them would never see in person. As a *New York Times* article said about the exhibit: "Envy, Conquest, Revenge: It's All in the Maps." Smiley helped Hudson choose one hundred examples from Slaughter's collection that traced the rise to dominance of the English over the North American continent. They put similar maps side by side—for example, the same maps from *The English Pilot* by John Seller, John Thornton, and Mount and Page—so viewers could compare them and see the progression of colonization and conquest, with lands being discovered, cities being founded and changing hands, and coastlines and boundaries swimming into focus with increasingly sharper detail.

In the accompanying brochure, Hudson devoted a paragraph to Smiley, whose "advice and counsel were instrumental in the Map Division's acquisition of the Lawrence H. Slaughter Collection and whose research is found between the lines of much of the exhibition text." The following March, Paul Statt and Scott Slater drove down from Massachusetts to see the work their friend had put together. They arrived in the afternoon, walking through Central Park and down Fifth Avenue to meet Smiley in the library. "He took us, after much embracing and too-loud-for-the-library enthusing, to the gallery where the Slaugther exhibition was," Slater later wrote in his journal. Among friends, Smiley rarely talked about his work—now, Slater and Statt listened raptly as he held forth about the significance of the maps he'd collected. For the first time, Slater saw how Smiley had turned his love of history, and his love of New England, into a successful career.

It was "extremely illuminating as to what Forbes actually does in life," wrote Slater. "The insights we gathered were as much about him as about cartography or history." Afterward, Smiley met them for drinks along with Bennett Fischer, and the four raised pints of Guinness and glasses of Jameson to Smiley's success.

As proud as Smiley was of his accomplishment, however, the perks he expected from the library never came to pass. A year came and went, and no professional catalog for the collection ever emerged. No sale of duplicates was authorized. And no new book about the collection ever appeared. It was with some chagrin, then, that he heard about the publication of a new book based on the other collection he had helped put together—the one for Norman Leventhal.

NOW IN HIS EIGHTIES, Leventhal had begun to seriously think about his legacy, contemplating the best way to preserve the knowledge embedded in his growing collection of maps of Boston and New England. Back in 1990, a conference in Boston organized by John Carter Brown Library head Norman Fiering examined the mapping of New England for the first time. During the event, Fiering proposed a definitive carto-bibliography listing all the known maps of the region and tapped Yale map collection head curator Barbara McCorkle to write it.

Leventhal, however, had a different vision—he was less interested in a scholarly work than he was in a popular book that would appeal to a wide audience interested in Boston's history. The idea was galvanized by the arrival in 1992 of a new map curator at Harvard University named David Cobb. Cobb had come from Chicago, which had an active map society sponsoring cartographic lectures and events, and was struck by the lack of a similar organization in Boston. "What this town needs is a map society!" he told colleagues over a few glasses of wine one day, and they immediately nominated him to start one.

The Boston Map Society began meeting soon afterward, with its official headquarters at Harvard and Leventhal as an enthusiastic patron. By this time, Smiley had stopped working on Leventhal's collection, so Cobb had few dealings with him. In fact, he met Smiley only twice—in the 1980s at B. Altman and years later when he briefly visited the Harvard collection. He did, however, get to know Norman Leventhal and his curator, Alex Krieger. At the time, Cobb knew as much about the early mapping of America as anyone in the city, and Leventhal and Krieger began relying on him for advice on buying new maps for their collection.

Eventually, they asked him if he'd like to cowrite a book with Krieger using the collection as the basis to look at the mapping of Boston and New England. Over a series of meetings at Leventhal's office at the Boston Harbor Hotel, they fleshed out a work that would straddle the line between generalist and specialist, providing scholarly information about the maps interspersed with stories, anecdotes, and photos that would appeal to a coffee table audience.

MIT Press, the university press at Leventhal's alma mater, agreed to publish the book, *Mapping Boston*, which appeared in August 1999. According to Cobb's later recollection, the publisher originally set a print run of several thousand copies. Cobb urged more. "This is Boston," he told them, a city obsessed with its own history. "This is going to fly off the shelves." He was right. The publisher upped the run to ten thousand, all of which sold out within a few months of the book's appearance. The publisher hastily printed another ten thousand. Eventually, the book sold well over twenty-five thousand copies, making it one of the most popular cartography books ever written.

That October, Krieger and Leventhal commissioned a multivenue exhibition based on the book at the Boston Public Library, the New England Aquarium, and the Boston Harbor Hotel. The exhibit was the most popular in the library's history, drawing two hundred thousand visitors in six months. Smiley brought his friends Scott Slater, Bob von Elgg, and Scott Haas through the exhibit, explaining each map in detail. At one point, Haas remembers Smiley proudly telling hotel staff he was the one who helped "Mr. Leventhal" put the collection together. Apart from a thank-you by Leventhal in the foreword of the book, Smiley received no credit for his contribution.

In fact, over the course of a year, Smiley had seen back-to-back exhibitions of much of his life's work—and yet he'd received little recognition, and no money, for all of his contributions. At the same time, another event later that fall put even more pressure on his career. On November 28, 1999, Smiley's wife, Lisa, gave birth to their son, Edward Forbes Smiley IV—Ned for short. Smiley called his friend Slater to brag about how "big, robust, and strapping" a child he was. He'd always been good with kids—he doted on his friends' children when they came up to Maine, and now he became determined to give Ned as idyllic a childhood as his own. Their home base would be on Martha's Vineyard, but they'd spend every summer at the house in Sebec, which Smiley now set about turning into even more of a refuge for his family—even to the point of transforming the town itself.

SMILEY'S VISION FOR SEBEC went beyond his restored farmhouse. In fact, slowly but surely he began to construct the Small Hope of his college imagination, despite some objections from his neighbors. I arrived in Sebec in 2013 for the Fourth of July parade, the annual highlight of the town calendar. A hot July sun shone down on more than a hundred people lining both sides of the bridge crossing the narrow outlet where Sebec Lake turns into the Sebec River. They were all dressed in red, white, and blue, waving American flags as shiny muscle cars and fire engines drove past. Children scrambled for Blow Pops thrown from cars, while older folks in lawn chairs held their hands over their ears when a zealous logging-truck driver laid on the air horn.

Across the lake, Smiley's old farmhouse sat at the top of the hill, the perfect backdrop for the occasion, complete with a red barn topped by a white cupola. When I mentioned Smiley's name to the locals, however, it garnered an immediate negative reaction. "He came in here and divided the town," said Louisa Finnemore, taking a pause from swinging a hammer on last-minute repairs. "He came in with all these rules. But they were all his rules."

"Yeah, rules 'from away,'" chimed in another woman sitting in a folding chair nearby. That phrase, "from away," conveys special meaning to Mainers. On its face, it means anyone from out of state, but more broadly, it refers to anyone who doesn't "get" the Maine way of life. Flatlanders from New York and Boston have been coming up here since the nineteenth century telling people what to do and putting strictures on traditional pursuits like hunting, fishing, and lumbering. Tensions continue between those trying to save the land and those trying to use it.

But northern Maine isn't easy to stereotype. For every beer-drinking redneck, there's a hippie back-to-the-lander. They might not agree on politics or land use, but generally they agree to stay out of each other's way, united by the cardinal rule of "live and let live." That's the rule some locals accuse Smiley of breaking. "He just thought he was better than everyone else," said one old-timer, sitting down to an after-parade chicken barbecue plate. "He had a lot of ideas, and some of them were good ideas," said another, "but he went about them the wrong way."

In October 1997, a gregarious computer programmer named Glen Fariel moved with his family into the house next door to the Smileys and soon became a frequent guest. Fariel wasted little time getting involved in town politics, soon being elected one of the town's three selectmen as well as president of the Big Bear Snowmobile Club—an essential institution during the long Maine winters. Smiley donated money to the group and helped with trail maintenance, but Fariel urged him to do more for the town. Along with the local historical society president, David Mallett, he encouraged Smiley to buy a piece of land across the lake from his home and to help restore it. The land was then choked with smoke bush, a fast-growing shrub that grows a feathery top to give it a "smoky" appearance. Smiley purchased it in October 2001 and donated it to the historical society to be used as a park.

Mallett—a local folk singer nationally famous for writing "Garden Song" ("Inch by inch . . . ")—spearheaded fund-raising to clear the property, build an octagonal gazebo, and plant rosebushes. Sebec Community Park opened in time for the July Fourth celebration the following year, with a ceremony dedicating it to the children of the village. Smiley paid to help sponsor kids' crafts in the park to coincide with the annual parade. But that was only a small part of the plans he and his friends had for the village.

Smiley also purchased land across from the park that was home to the old Sebec post office, now a rotted shell of a building with an old goat pen and chicken coop out back. Smiley announced plans to restore it as a new centerpiece of the village. Other crumbling mill towns throughout New England had leveraged their natural beauty and charm to become tourist meccas, sprouting artist studios and restaurants serving local food. Why couldn't Sebec do the same? It was just the kind of grandiose plan that excited Smiley.

"Largely encouraged by many local residents of Sebec, I have taken on this project in the hope that its success will add in a small way to the health and prosperity of the town as a whole," Smiley modestly told *The Piscataquis Observer*, detailing his plans to include a renovated post office and shops. "We're trying to fish around and see what people need. The key is to listen and keep asking questions—and to meet local needs first."

He spent tens of thousands of dollars over the winter renovating the post office, installing terrazzo floors and restoring rows of brass post office boxes. It officially opened in the spring of 2002, managed by Mallett's wife, Jayne Lello. By late summer, Smiley had added a general store complete with candy counter and farmers' market selling local produce. "Hey, neighbor! The old-fashioned general store of your childhood is alive and well—here in Sebec, Maine," warmly greeted the Sebec Village Shops' website. The store catered both to local needs and to the more upscale tastes of Sebec's summer visitors, stocking gourmet Rao's Coffee next to Maxwell House. The homewares section featured a $120 hand-carved children's rocking horse, a $50 earthenware mixing bowl set, and a $35 beaded "wine skirt."

The following year, in the fall of 2002, Smiley opened a restaurant with the same sensibility, hiring a local chef to make simple food with quality, organic ingredients. Affectionately dubbed the "chatterbox café," it quickly became a neighborhood hub where locals sat in spindle-back chairs and gossiped about fishing, the logging business, the Red Sox, and their neighbors. In the morning, the café served home-baked bread and biscuits, truck-stop egg breakfasts, and stacks of pancakes with local maple syrup. For lunch, it offered sandwiches and hamburgers. And three nights a week, it opened for dinner with entrées of roast chicken and local trout.

The businesses were a godsend to the town economy, employing between fifteen and thirty people depending upon the season. Smiley ran the business as a nonprofit, paying above-prevailing wages for the area and earning a steady stream of supporters for his largesse. "He was Robin Hood," Mallett later remembered. "He came up here with a vision to revitalize the town, and he employed practically everyone in it."

From the beginning, the project bled money. By local estimates, Smiley spent $600,000 on the renovations alone, and thousands more every week on payroll during the summer. Now when Smiley's friends came to Sebec for summer visits or Boys' Weekends, they ate all of their meals there—leaving generous tips for the waitresses, but otherwise paying nothing. Smiley sat back proudly, reveling in how he had nearly single-handedly revitalized a town that badly needed it (Figure 12).

NOT EVERYONE SHARED Smiley's vision, however. As he went around trying to gain support to turn the village into a historic district, he met resistance from property owners who refused based on the cost it would take to restore their properties. "Sometimes he went by my house and I swear I caught him looking up at the molding on the porch like he owned it," one of his neighbors later remembered.

Next door to Smiley's shops was a community center called the Sebec Reading Room, a lending library that hosted events including the annual Fourth of July festivities. Smiley tried to convince them to restore the façade and increase the setbacks from the road. The association's president at the time, Louisa Finnemore, flat-out refused. Smiley had broken Maine's most important, if unstated rule—stay the hell out of your neighbors' business. "Who is this flatlander who has come to town to tell everyone what to do?" some of his neighbors began to complain.

No one clashed with him more than Bill and Charlene Moriarty, who had moved to Sebec from Sanbornville in New Hampshire's Lakes Region, an hour and a half drive north of where Smiley grew up. There the couple had operated a boat repair and storage facility amid a family vacationland of speedboats, fried food, and video arcades. Bill Moriarty knew Sebec from hunting trips in Maine and was enamored of both its natural beauty and its unique educational system—which allowed students to attend nearby private prep school Foxcroft Academy free of charge.

The Moriartys purchased a home and general store in Sebec in January 2001, across the lake from Smiley's house and directly across the street from the Sebec Village Shops. They planned to turn the property into a marina that would include an ice cream shop and docking for local boat owners. As they began construction in the spring of 2002, Smiley and his friends were dismayed. It was exactly the kind of business they didn't want in the village; they could only imagine the loud and rowdy boaters it would attract.

Examining the permit the Moriartys had been issued the previous April, however, he and his friends thought they saw a way to stop it: The couple had never included the word "marina" in their application. In fact, the permit for the property specified "that it stays as it is, dry storage to sell," and the chairman of the planning board had written the Moriartys a letter confirming the permit "pertains only to the use of the buildings, not to include an exterior marina." She also said, however, that the planning board was "investigating further the proper procedures for issuing a permit for a marina" and would let them know if it needed any more information.

The preservationists filed a complaint with the town, and on June 5, 2002, the town's code enforcement officer, Bill Murphy, issued a "stop work" order to close down construction. Until now, most local disputes had been ironed out over coffee at the local diner or at town meetings, where members of the same families had filled the seats of the selectmen and planning board for generations. Now the marina issue became a lightning rod, dividing the town and raising the heat at town meetings.

Post office manager Jayne Lello remembered standing up to insist that the permit include the word "marina" and being told to "stick it up your ass." Another burly man asked if she wanted to take it outside. She stopped going to meetings after that. The battle continued in letters and newspaper editorials. "I am ashamed that what should have been a simple permit request by a business entrepreneur was allowed to remain 'unclear' for over a year because the nature of the business wasn't spelled out on the request," selectman Susan Dow wrote to a local paper. "I, for one, don't want more regulations telling me what to do with my property."

A few days later, Mallett fired back in another editorial. "I am very concerned that local and state environmental laws have been publicly disregarded," he wrote. "Indeed, I feel as if we do not have a town government at all, but have resorted to a more tribal approach." While Mallett seemed to be leading the charge, however, it was Smiley who

FIGURE 12 SMILEY'S SEBEC.

became the public target of the opposition. At the annual town meeting in August, residents approved every one of forty-two articles on the agenda, except one—a proposal by residents to pave Cove Road, the road where Smiley and Fariel had their homes. Soon after, Charlene Moriarty wrote a letter to the town enforcement officer with a list of alleged violations at Smiley's shops, including the percentage of parking and vegetative growth, and permits to serve food.

Privately, she and her husband began bad-mouthing Smiley, saying he was spending money "like it wasn't his own." It was idle speculation on their part, since they had no evidence that he'd done anything wrong in the way he had acquired his money. At the same time they were spreading their rumors, however, a librarian at Yale University's Sterling Memorial Library had begun to suspect the same thing. And she thought she had proof.

Chapter 9

MISSING MAPS, MISSING CARDS

FIGURE 13 ROBERT DUDLEY. "CARTA PARTICOLARE DELLA
VIRGINIA VECCHIA E NUOUA." FLORENCE, 1646.

2002–2004

YALE'S STERLING MEMORIAL LIBRARY looks more like a cathedral than a library. Two heavy wooden doors open onto a long aisle with a four-story vaulted ceiling lined with stained-glass depictions of thinkers, explorers, and saints. It takes a half minute to walk across the flagstones to the main desk at the end of the hall, where a row of elevators take visitors up to the Map Collection on the seventh floor.

Compared to the rest of the library—or for that matter, the state-of-the-art Beinecke a few blocks away—the map department is underwhelming. Cramped and cluttered, its three rooms are stuffed to capacity. On one side, giant flat files hold modern maps (that is, anything more recent than 1850). Past them, a locked door leads to a room where the old maps are stored. To the other side is the reading room, half of it occupied by a large wooden table, the rest with file cabinets and shelves filled with reference books and globes.

On a recent visit, I was greeted at the door by assistant librarian Margit Kaye, who is tall and blond and was wearing a light black sweater and slim gray slacks. "I've been working here twenty-plus years," she told me in a German accent. Actually, the number is more like forty-five. She worked with the first curator of the map department, Alexander O. Vietor, and mentored generations of students. "You know Graham Arader? He calls me his mentor," she continued. Few people know more about antiquarian maps than she does—and no one knows Yale's collection better.

"We've got everything ready for you," she said, leading me inside and opening the top of a metal storage box in the corner. Pulling out a plastic-encased map, she slid John Seller's 1675 "Mapp of New England" onto the table. This was the same copy that Andy Antippas stole from Yale back in 1978, before Graham Arader bought it from him and alerted authorities. It was also the same map that, in another copy, Smiley advertised in one of his very first ads before selling it to Norman Leventhal in the mid-1980s.

Printed on rough gray paper, it is just a foot and a half high and about as long. But it holds an impressive amount of detail. The interior teems with woods and hills, British soldiers fighting off a skirmish of American Indians, and animals. Kaye pointed out a turkey west of Boston she said is the earliest image of the animal ever depicted on a map. The map is surprisingly full of color; pinks, yellows, and greens trace the borders of counties and colonies and fill in the clothing of the two Native Americans on either side of the cartouche.

All in all, it is a fine copy of the map—though not without a few stains, or "foxing," as it's called by collectors. One dark smudge below and to the left of a ship sailing past Martha's Vineyard always gave Kaye a twinge of guilt, since she suspected she was the one who made it during her many handlings of the map over the years. She knew that smudge so well, she did a double-take one day in July 2002 when she saw it on Forbes Smiley's website.

Smiley had just launched the site a month before, advertising Seller's map as one of the first he offered for sale. As Kaye examined the picture on the site, she immediately noticed the smudge in the corner. *Oh my God,* she thought. *That's our map.* The listing referred to it as "a fine dark impression, carefully colored in an original hand," going on for several paragraphs about the history of the map and the later maps it inspired. At the end of the listing, the description noted, "Yale University is home to an uncolored copy of the first state, bound with four pages of printed text comprising a brief history of New England."

Except that wasn't true. The library's curators had long ago separated the map from the pages of text, storing it separately. And now as Kaye went to look for the map to prove she wasn't imagining things, she couldn't find it in the drawer where it was supposed to be filed. She searched methodically through other drawers, flipping through map after map without success. That wasn't unusual—with a quarter-million maps in the collection, it was impossible to keep all of them filed correctly. But this was a special map, one of only a handful of its kind in the world—and it shouldn't have been missing.

Kaye printed out the page from Smiley's site and took it to the head curator of the department, Fred Musto, to share her concerns. "What do you want me to do?" he said, according to her later recollection. "Call the police and arrest the guy?" Kaye had to admit the evidence was circumstantial. Since the Sterling didn't keep records of maps checked out by patrons, there was nothing to prove Smiley had even looked at it, much less taken it.

All Kaye had was the smudge. But as Smiley made clear, his copy was colored, while Yale's wasn't. And why would he mention Yale's copy on the site if he himself had taken it? Most important, Smiley was a respected map dealer, and Kaye was a loyal employee. Yale had paid for her master's of library science degree at Southern Connecticut State University, where her teachers had taught her that to go over the head of superiors was "worse than the kiss of death." She let the matter drop. But from then on, she resolved to keep a closer eye on Smiley whenever he visited.

SMILEY WAS IN the Sterling often in those days. At least once a month, he took a plane from his home on the Vineyard to Tweed Airport in

New Haven, invariably wearing an olive-colored tweed jacket and appearing at the library full of jokes and good humor. He installed himself in the reading room and filled out slip after slip for maps he wanted to research. Sometimes, he took whole drawers out of the card catalog into the reading room to flip through.

Oftentimes the catalog listed only the drawer and folder where a map appeared along with other maps from the same time period. At his request, Musto and Kaye brought him whole folders containing dozens of maps at once. Musto had been trained as a general reference librarian and knew little about maps. According to staff who worked with him, he often took long lunches and was away from the map department for hours at a time. Even when he was there, he sometimes spent long minutes in the back room, searching for or cataloging maps.

It was during one of those times that Smiley sat in the reading room, brooding. *Sebec worked,* he thought. For all the problems he'd had in the map business, he'd watched family after family come up to Sebec and be happy. And now he had the opportunity to extend that happiness to others in the community—if he could see the project through. With the marina standoff brewing, his whole vision was now at risk. And he was struggling as it was to find the money to pay the workers at Sebec Village Shops. He glanced over at the circulation desk, empty again. Then he glanced at the map on the table. How many people would even know if it disappeared? Almost without thinking, he folded the map into a rectangle the size of a credit card and slipped it into his blazer pocket. He looked around again. The desk was still empty. The rest of the maps were still on the table as if nothing had happened.

He gathered them up and returned them to their folder. A few minutes later, he walked out of the room with his heart pounding, taking the elevator downstairs and walking across the flagstone floor. As he pushed open the heavy wooden door to head back outside, no one gave him a second look.

That's the way Smiley described the first map he stole. "The Sterling Library is the first place I realized I had access to material that was not well catalogued," he later told me, "and it wasn't clear it would be missed." When combined with the financial pressures he faced, that opportunity to walk out with the map became impossible for him to resist. "I am looking at a piece of paper that I can fold and put in my pocket, that people in New York expect me to show up with because I've been doing this for twenty-five years legitimately. And I can get thirty thousand dollars wired up to Maine that afternoon," he explained.

Smiley told me he didn't remember exactly which map he stole first, though in court records he claimed that his thefts started in the spring of 2002. If that is true, then the John Seller map of New England may have been among his first. After taking the map, he carefully colored parts of it to obscure its origins, dabbing paint onto the three-hundred-year-old paper just as he'd seen Mick Tooley do in London years earlier. He filled the blank shield to the left of the cartouche with a shade of salmon pink and painted the skirts of the Indians holding up the cartouche a pale green.

When it was ready, he brought the map to his friend Harry Newman, knowing it was just the kind of map he loved—crudely drawn and primitive, with lots of stories written into its blank spaces of exploration and American Indian wars. He offered the map at $75,000—easily half of what it was worth on the market. Since Smiley's costs were zero, however, he could afford to sell on the cheap. But this wasn't a map Newman would want to sell; this was one he'd want to frame and keep, and having recently bought a house, he was in no position to buy it. After he turned it down, Smiley called another client, Harold Osher, a doctor and map collector from Portland, Maine, who had turned his collection into a map library based at the University of Southern Maine. Osher was thrilled to see such a rarity at such a good price and gladly bought it from him.

The stealing became easier after that. He was at the Sterling and other libraries all the time doing research. It was easy enough when he saw an opportunity to slip a map into his pocket and walk out undetected. For all the ease with which he stole the maps, however, he was mistaken in thinking that no one noticed.

AFTER THAT FIRST INCIDENT with the John Seller map, Margit Kaye began to carefully watch the maps that Smiley requested on his visits to the Sterling. Over the years, she had gotten to know him well—and had always been impressed with how well dressed and full of knowledge he seemed. She'd even found herself wishing her daughter could meet a nice man like that.

Now, however, she noticed a change in him. He always seemed to be in a rush, arriving late on a Friday with excuses of plane delays, and then hastily requesting dozens of map folders. As Kaye went to collect them one by one from the back room, she often had to leave him unattended in the reading room. She tried to keep an eye on him, but all she saw was a harried map scholar, eagerly turning over pages.

When Smiley wasn't at the library, Kaye continued to monitor his website for any other maps that Yale might be missing. That October, she discovered four maps on the site that Yale had in its catalogs but weren't in the drawers. Three of them were important early state maps—of Pennsylvania, Louisiana, and South Carolina from the late eighteenth and early nineteenth centuries—while the last was a sea chart of the Pacific Ocean by Samuel Thornton, John Thornton's son and successor in producing *The English Pilot*. Again she printed out the pages and brought them to Musto's attention—but once again, he told her there was nothing he could do without proof.

As she continued to look at the website, another image continued to bother her: a map of Boston that Henry Pelham made in 1777, just after the Revolutionary War had broken out. She was sure that she'd seen that map in Yale's collection, but there was no card in the catalog to indicate it. Finally, in February 2003, it suddenly occurred to her that there was another source she could check. Back when the library began digitizing its card catalog some twenty-five years earlier, staff made a microfilm copy of it, exactly as it appeared on June 30, 1978.

Kaye spooled through the roll to the place where the maps of Boston were catalogued, and there she found the image of the card: "A plan of Boston in New England with its environs . . . Henry Pelham . . . 1777." She went back to the card catalog, but the card definitely wasn't there. As she looked at the evidence, she suddenly realized: If someone could steal maps, they could also steal cards. That meant the library could be missing maps of which it had no record at all.

ONE SUCH MAP, in fact, had gone missing along with its card the previous spring—and Kaye failed to realize it. It was the most valuable of all of the maps Smiley had stolen so far, a plan of Boston made by John

FIGURE A. GERARD DE JODE. "UNIVERSI ORBIS SEV TERRINI GLOBI," FROM *SPECULUM ORBIS TERRARUM*. ANTWERP, 1578.

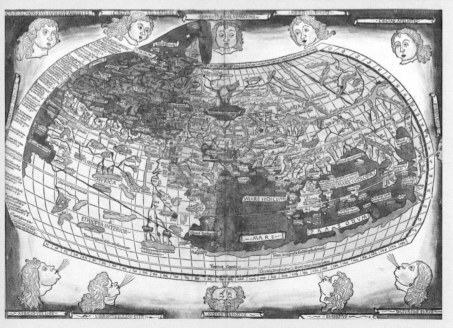

FIGURE B. CLADIUS PTOLEMY. "UNTITLED (MAP OF THE WORLD)." ULM, 1482.

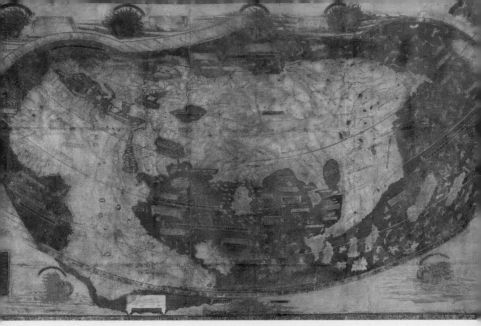

FIGURE C. HENRICUS MARTELLUS GERMANUS.
"UNTITLED (MAP OF THE WORLD OF CHRISTOPHER COLUMBUS)."
MANUSCRIPT MAP, C. 1489.

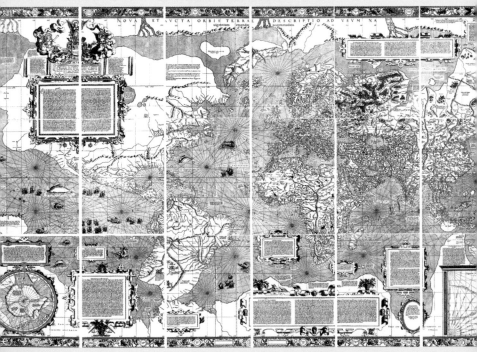

FIGURE D. GERARD MERCATOR.
"NOVA ET AUCTA ORBIS TERRAE DESCRIPTIO." DUISBURG, 1569.

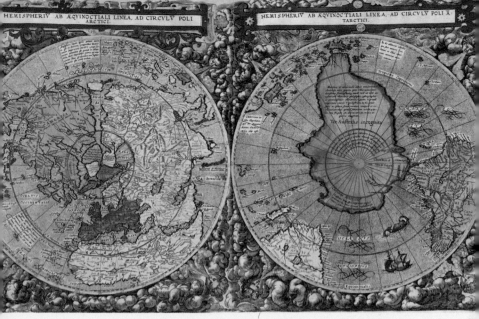

FIGURE E. CORNELIUS DE JODE. "HEMISPHERIU[M] AB
AEQUINOCTIALI LINEA, AD CIRCULU[M] POLI ARCTICI . . .
AD CIRCULU[M] POLI ATARCTICI." ANTWERP, 1593.

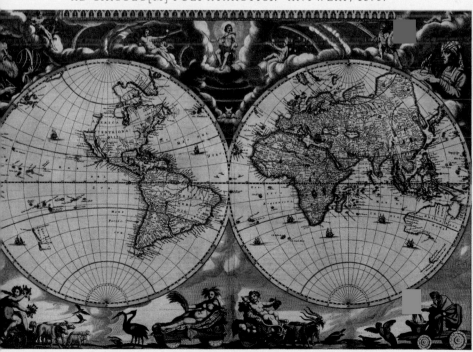

FIGURE F. JOAN BLAEU. "NOVA ET ACCURATISSIMA TOTIUS
TERRARUM ORBIS TABULA." AMSTERDAM, 1664.

FIGURE G. JAN JANSSON. "BELGII NOVI, ANGLIAE NOVAE,
ET PARTIS VIRGINIAE NOVISSIMA DELINEATIO."
AMSTERDAM, 1651.

FIGURE H. JOHN SPEED.
"A MAP OF NEW ENGLAND AND NEW YORK." LONDON, 1676.

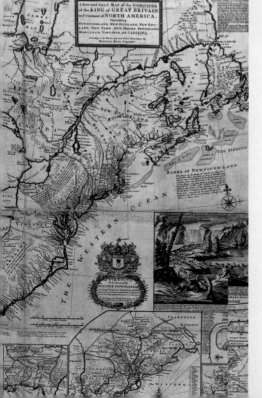

ABOVE: FIGURE I. JOHN SELLER.
"A MAPP OF NEW ENGLAND."
LONDON, C. 1675.

LEFT: FIGURE J. HERMAN MOLL.
"A NEW AND EXACT MAP OF
THE DOMINIONS OF THE KING
OF GREAT BRITAIN ON YE
CONTINENT OF NORTH
AMERICA." LONDON, 1715.

ABOVE: FIGURE K. GUILLIAME DE L'ISLE. "CARTE DE LA LOUISIANE ET DU COURS DU MISSISSIPI." PARIS, 1718.

RIGHT : FIGURE L. JOSEPH F. W. DES BARRES. "A SKETCH OF THE OPERATIONS BEFORE CHARLESTOWN, SOUTH CAROLINA." LONDON, 1780.

FIGURE M. SHIPYARD BREWERY
SUMMER ALE,
LIMITED EDITION LABEL
SHOWING JOHN SELLER'S
"A MAPP OF NEW ENGLAND,"
2003.

FIGURE N. HENRY BRIGGS. "THE NORTH PART OF AMERICA
CONTEYNING . . . THE LARGE AND GOODLY ILAND OF
CALIFORNIA." LONDON, 1625.

FIGURE O. E. FORBES SMILEY III, MUGSHOT.
JULY 8, 2005.

FIGURE P. SMILEY LEAVING COURT AFTER HIS SENTENCE
HEARING. SEPTEMBER 28, 2006.

Bonner in 1743, which Smiley listed on his site for $185,000. A sea captain in the Indies trade, Bonner first made the plan in 1722 at the age of seventy-seven, the only map he'd ever made. At the time, it was the first city plan ever engraved and printed in America, and it's the only map of Boston that survives from the period when the capital of New England was growing in prosperity.

After Bonner's death, map seller William Price acquired the plates and revised it eight times. Yale owned the fifth state, which featured some of the most significant changes, such as the addition of Faneuil Hall, where the Sons of Liberty met a few decades later to plan the Boston Tea Party. Only five copies of this state were known to exist—and only three copies of *any* state of Bonner's plan were now in private hands. Even Norman Leventhal, the great Boston collector, owned it only in facsimile.

Smiley brought the map to Harry Newman, who'd never held an original copy of Bonner's map in all of his years as a map dealer. This one was in rough shape, folded into six sections and nearly falling apart. Knowing what it would go for in good condition, however, Newman bought the map and sent it out to his restorer, who painstakingly recon nected the pieces in time for it to appear in the Old Print Shop's 2002 summer catalog, which was shipped—among other places—to the Sterling's map room.

The following summer, one of the maps Smiley stole ended up in an even stranger place. Every two years, the prestigious International Conference on the History of Cartography took place in a different part of the world. In 2003, the conference chose the Harvard Map Library in Cambridge and the Osher Library in Portland, Maine, to host the get-together. Hundreds of map scholars, dealers, and collectors were set to attend. To celebrate the honor, Osher arranged with the Portland-based Shipyard Brewing Company to produce a special label of beer to be sold at the conference.

Attendees arrived to find a limited-run edition of Shipyard's 2003 Summer Ale in large-format bottles, described as a "2-row British Pale Ale" with a "mellow malted wheat flavor" that was "great with seafood." Wrapping around the label was the library's newly acquired John Seller map of New England, with "ICHC 2003" replacing the title in the cartouche. On either side were the Native Americans whose loincloths Smiley had painted green (Figure M).

A HUNDRED MILES farther north, the feud in Sebec was escalating. Charlene Moriarty's list of complaints about Smiley's shops had been mostly dismissed by Sebec's code enforcement officer, Bill Murphy. But he did "withhold final judgment" in the issue of parking. Smiley's project had been "grandfathered" to allow parking space to take up 20 percent of the property, while the rest had to remain vegetated land. If Smiley went over that amount, he would be in violation of his permit. The planning board, which included several of the Moriartys' supporters, also filed a complaint with the selectmen, charging that Smiley's parking took up 32 percent and demanding that Smiley submit new plans. "We have an obligation to uphold the laws of the town and the state," planning board member Walt Emmons said at the selectmen's meeting that November.

Smiley countered with a formal appeal of the Moriartys' marina permit, which earned an angry response from the Moriartys' lawyer. "Consider this a shot across Mr. Smiley's bow," he wrote. "If he continues to engage in meritless meddling into the Moriartys' affairs, we will respond in a very aggressive manner, putting Mr. Smiley and Mr. Fariel at considerable legal risk." Glen Fariel resigned from the board of selectmen nine days later, citing "increased responsibilities and demands" at his work. Smiley refused to withdraw his appeal, which was denied by the remaining two selectmen in short order.

On December 2, 2002, the selectmen finalized a new agreement with the Moriartys, stating that the original permit was "ambiguous" and granting the Moriartys permission to operate the marina so long as they obeyed all state and local environmental laws. The same day, the town's code enforcement officer, Bill Murphy, opened a formal investigation into the alleged violations at Smiley's shops.

Smiley was furious. He had spent hundreds of thousands of dollars to help his neighbors, and now instead of being thanked, he was being persecuted. Put on the defensive, he gave an interview to the local paper, *The Piscataquis Observer*, saying the town had simply been "overwhelmed with all of our plans and details." His lawyer, Greg Cunningham, however, was more forceful, alleging the investigation into Smiley's property was nothing but payback for his opposition to the Moriartys' permit. The town's response was "to have our property investigated and put under the microscope," he said. "I think that's a unique way of handling local land-use issues."

Backing down wasn't in Smiley's nature. Concluding that fairness was impossible to find in Sebec, he filed a new appeal—this time against the town as well as the Moriartys—in the county superior court a week before Christmas. The town had "exceeded its authority" in signing the deal with the Moriartys, he charged, engaging in actions that were "arbitrary, contrary to law, and not supported by evidence in the record."

Of course, not everyone saw the situation that way. The town's two selectmen, Buzz Small and Susan Dow, publicly contended that they were simply trying to forge a compromise that would allow everyone the freedom to pursue their projects. With the help of one of Smiley's friends, they each arranged to meet with him separately to plead with him to withdraw the lawsuit. Smiley refused, telling them, "I don't like to lose."

The town continued to pursue its investigation into the parking at Smiley's shops, with the code officer declaring in February 2003 that he was in violation of exceeding the permitted amount. Smiley's lawyer insisted that the property lines Murphy used were incorrect and that by his calculations, Smiley had been grandfathered parking on 41 percent of his property. At a meeting that April, the Portland attorney stood over a desk in a jacket and tie while selectman Small reviewed the plans in a red-checkered flannel shirt. By his calculations, he said, Smiley was allowed 35 percent—but he might be willing to concede another 3 percent, to bring the total to 38. Smiley had until October to correct the problem, the selectmen said.

Still no word had come from the superior court on the Moriartys' permit. The town was now solidly split into two camps, one that ate at Smiley's café in Sebec Village Shops and mailed their letters from his post office, and another that ate at the diner down the street and drove a dozen miles to the next town to send mail. In February 2003, some residents charged the Big Bear Snowmobile Club, where Glen Fariel was president, with discrimination because it had two tiers of dues, one for long-term members and one for newer members. They formed their own snowmobile club called the Sebec Freedom Riders, unsuccessfully petitioning the town for a share of Big Bear's state funds for trail maintenance.

When the Moriartys finally built their boat dock and moorings in the summer of 2003, they put up a sign prohibiting any boater from docking there in order to visit Sebec Village Shops. According to Smiley and his friends, speedboats began buzzing Smiley's house, drawing figure eights in the water with their outboards, while riders waved American flags and screamed obscenities. Finally, one summer night, Smiley and his family were woken up by the sound of a gunshot followed by breaking glass. Smiley panicked and threw on the outside lights to find that one of his barn windows had been shattered.

SMILEY'S LEGAL BATTLES in Sebec put new pressure on his finances. In order to pay his bills, he expanded his list of targets. By 2003, they included the Boston Public Library (BPL), which had exhibited the Norman Leventhal collection a few years earlier. Unlike the New York Public Library, the BPL didn't have a dedicated map room, or even a map curator to look after its collection. Maps were included as part of the rare-books and manuscript department, housed in a nearly forgotten room on the library's third floor.

To get there, Smiley climbed a marble stairway from the main reading room and threaded his way through a warren of rooms with random, almost bizarre exhibits—including a room full of dioramas depicting three-dimensional versions of classical paintings and another re-creating the office of a former Boston Symphony Orchestra conductor. He checked his coat and briefcase—but left on his blazer—and greeted the librarians warmly, asking about their families and telling them about the trips he took to Europe and the stores he was building in Maine. Often, he dropped references to the collection he'd helped build for "Mr. Leventhal." Few people ever requested the maps in the department, much less dealers of Smiley's stature, so they were eager to help. Once inside, Smiley filled out call slip after call slip. He was so well-known by staff, he barely included his name and address, writing only "SMILEY MA" in all capital letters.

The BPL's rare-books reading room wasn't large, but it did have one drawback for efficient monitoring—a series of several pillars that blocked some tables from the view of the curator's desk. And it was attractive to Smiley for another reason. Unlike the Sterling, which carried mostly single-sheet maps, many of the BPL's maps were contained in books, which were often poorly cataloged, with little indication of the specific maps they contained. Twice in 2003—once on January 14 and once on May 12—he checked out a copy of the *Speculum Orbis Terrarum* by Cornelius de Jode, whose father, Gerard, had fruitlessly battled rival Abraham Ortelius to produce the first atlas. Cornelius had carried on his father's legacy with a new edition of his atlas in 1593 but was ultimately no more successful at breaking Ortelius's monopoly, making the book extremely rare.

On one of those two days, Smiley opened the book's stiff, bone-colored parchment cover, which had been bowed and warped by centuries of moisture. He flipped to the book's highlight, a double-hemisphere world map, showing the Northern and Southern Hemispheres in conjoined circles as viewed from both poles (Figure E). Most double-hemisphere maps depict the Eastern and Western Hemispheres, making the map as unusual as it was beautiful. Perhaps de Jode was responding to the interest in searching for a Northwest Passage to hasten travel to Asia. His map shows a clear open sea route above North America, only a couple of inches from Holland to China, tantalizingly short compared to the vast distances shown on a Mercator projection.

Smiley took in the map's coastlines and calligraphy, waiting for his moment. Perhaps he sat at a table behind one of the pillars; or perhaps he stood at the card catalog with his back to the monitor; or maybe he just waited for a time when the desk was left unattended. Whatever the case, he found a moment to separate the map from its binding. The next map in the atlas, one of the earliest views of North America, was nearly as spectacular. It showed a rugged continent with tall, shaded mountains, again with a clear blue passage at its top. Smiley took that one too.

In the winter and spring of 2003, Smiley made at least a half-dozen trips to the BPL to view the maps in its books. While the Dutch were producing their gorgeous seventeenth-century world atlases, the French and English were still in the infancy of their exploration of North America. The main form of propaganda they used to stake their claims were travel narratives that detailed the adventures of explorers and the natural resources of the land. John Smith excelled at the genre with his books about Virginia and New England, but he was not the only explorer writing travelogues.

The most successful explorer of his time was Samuel de Champlain, a Frenchman who first ventured into American waters in 1603. He returned for twenty voyages in all, the "single most important factor" in the establishment of a French foothold in North America, according to map dealer and historian Philip Burden. Like many explorers, Champlain set out initially to find a Northwest Passage—but stumbled across the densely forested wilderness of lakes and rivers along the St. Lawrence instead. He founded Quebec and set about exploiting the land for lumber and furs.

Champlain was also the first person to use scientific survey methods to map the New World. His first map appears in his 1613 book *Les Voyages du Sieur de Champlain,* which details the riches he found. His "Carte de Nouvelle France" is considered the mother map of Canada, preparing the region for colonization. Like John Smith, he used artistic license in forecasting the future, depicting Quebec as a castle flying the French flag, even though no more than two hundred people lived there in his lifetime.

Champlain also included another, smaller map of New France in the book, showing the most recent expeditions by English explorers. Both maps exist now in only a handful of copies, making them extremely valuable. At the time Smiley looked at Boston's copy of *Les Voyages* on January 20, 2003, Champlain's book had only rarely come up for auction in past decades. When one finally did appear at Sotheby's five years later in 2008, it sold for $250,000. A year later, a copy sold at a Bloomsbury auction for a staggering $750,000.

A WEEK AFTER examining the Champlain book, on January 28, 2003, Smiley requested a thirteen-volume set of writings by Theodor de Bry, a Flemish cartographer who worked in Antwerp, London, and Frankfurt in the late sixteenth century. De Bry's work catalogs nothing less than all the voyages of discovery around the world. While in London, he acquired a manuscript map drawn by a French protestant named Jacques Le Moyne, who was one of the only survivors of a Spanish massacre of an early French settlement in Florida. De Bry reproduced the map in his work, depicting a flattened peninsula in the shape of a saucepan, beneath the edge of a vast inland lake that was supposed to cover the area around the modern-day Carolinas. The image became the dominant depiction of Florida for a century after Jodocus Hondius used the map in his editions of Mercator's atlas (and much later, a favorite for collectors at the Miami International Map Fair).

Another seminal map de Bry included was a map of Virginia by English settler John White, governor of the ill-fated Roanoke colony. The colony was founded by Sir Walter Raleigh before the settlement of Jamestown; during White's time there, he produced an accurate map of the area, bringing it back to London in 1587 just as de Bry was looking for material. No sooner did he arrive, however, than the Spanish Armada blockaded the English coast. England's eventual defeat of the Spanish fleet helped ensure English dominance of the oceans for centuries. But for White it was little consolation. By the time he returned to his colony in 1590, all traces of it had disappeared, an enduring mystery to this day. Only the map, now included in de Bry's book, survived.

De Bry worked in London during a feverish time for English exploration. Interest in the New World had been sparked by the writings of Richard Hakluyt, a geographer whose two books, *Divers Voyages Touching the Discoverie of America and the Islands Adjacent* (1582) and *The Principall Navigations: Voiages and Discoveries of the English Nation* (1589), recounted the travels of early explorers such as John Cabot. Hakluyt's books, in turn, inspired and supported a generation of Elizabethan sea dogs including Sir Francis Drake and Sir Walter Raleigh to set sail in search of adventure and fame.

Hakluyt's papers were inherited by Samuel Purchas, a minister from a seaside vicarage with an insatiable appetite for collecting stories of captains and explorers. In 1625, he combined them with his own research into a book entitled *Hakluytus Posthumus, or Purchas His Pilgrimes*. Smiley requested the BPL's copy of the work three times: on July 27, 2003; January 14, 2004; and September 14, 2004. Inside, Purchas included a number of important maps, including a reprint of John Smith's map of Virginia; a map of New Scotland by Sir William Alexander, an English lord granted the rights to colonize the region north of New England; and a map of North America by Henry Briggs (Figure N).

Briggs's map was the first to accurately illustrate the discoveries of explorer Henry Hudson, including Hudson's Bay. But it is better known for its role in propagating one of the most notorious myths in cartography: the island of California. For a century after its discovery in the early 1500s, the West Coast of North America appeared on maps by Mercator, Ortelius, and others much as it does now. Almost out of nowhere, Henry Briggs's map shows a dramatically different image—a triangular wedge broken off from the edge of the continent, in almost the same size and shape as the modern-day state. To modern eyes, it's as if the Big One has finally arrived—breaking the land along the San Andreas Fault to be cast adrift in the Pacific.

The error most likely has its origins in a Spanish expedition in the 1590s in which a friar boldly combined the Gulf of California with a purported inland sea to the north. Soon after, a Dutch ship supposedly captured the map, bringing it to Amsterdam. It's unclear how Briggs, a prominent English astronomer, acquired it, but he apparently used it to create his own manuscript map in 1622, which became the basis for the map in Purchas's book.

After that, the misrepresentation spread like a virus. Prominent English cartographer John Speed picked up the change in 1626, and from there it crossed the channel to all the Dutch giants, including Hondius, Jansson, and Blaeu. English and French mapmakers followed suit; John Seller reproduced the mistake in at least a half dozen of his sea charts. The difficulty of exploring the area perpetuated the myth. Spanish galleons bypassed the fog-shrouded cliffs on their way from the Philippines to South America, uninterested in risking their cargoes in pointless cartographic surveys.

Finally, in 1698, the inaccuracy was corrected when Jesuit friar Eusebio Kino traveled overland from California to Mexico, charting the terrain. But mapmakers persisted in creating an islanded California for another half century. Finally, Spanish king Ferdinand VI had to outlaw the practice with a royal decree in 1747 that stated simply, "California is not an island."

Of course, the persistence of the mistake has made maps showing the island of California a favorite among state residents. Depending on whether you are a California sympathizer or a California detractor, it can be seen as either a cheeky celebration of the state's proud otherness, or a punishment for its profligate ways. The sheer number of maps that feature the error—more than 150 different maps with thousands of individual copies—ensure plenty of examples to satisfy even casual Californian map lovers. But for the serious collector, the original Briggs map is most coveted, commanding prices of up to $25,000—a fact Smiley well knew when he ripped the BPL's copy out of Purchas's book.

SMILEY SOLD HIS MAPS to his network of dealers, including Newman, Arkway, and London map dealer Philip Burden. Burden literally wrote the book on North American exploration, *The Mapping of North America*, in the mid-1990s, and he had consulted with Smiley during his research. Burden started buying from him after Smiley bounced a check for something he purchased. "Let me make it up to you," Smiley told him. "Let me sell you a few things." In February 2003, Smiley sold Burden a copy of the Le Moyne map of Florida from the de Bry book. The following year, he sold Arkway a copy of the White map of Virginia from the same volume, along with a copy of the John Smith map of Virginia from *Purchas His Pilgrimes*. Smiley sold other maps directly to collectors, including a sea chart of Chesepeake Bay by English mapmaker Sir Robert Dudley, which he sold to New York bond trader Bob Gordon for $19,000 (Figure 13).

Dudley is one of the most colorful characters in all of cartography. Born in 1574, he was the son of Robert Dudley, the Earl of Leicester, and Douglas, Lady Sheffield. His father was the favorite courtier of Queen Elizabeth and the subject of endless "did they or didn't they" rumors from Elizabethan times to the present. Perhaps out of fear of the queen's jealousy, he hid his relationship with Douglas, revealing it only when she gave birth to their child. Elizabeth forgave his dalliance, but he knew naming Robert his heir would be too much.

Instead, Dudley was sent to live with his cousin. He grew up with all the trappings of a young English lord but, as an illegitimate child, had none of the prestige. Dudley sought to prove himself, studying at Oxford and excelling in geography and nautical science. The sea was to young men in sixteenth-century England what space was for boys and girls in twentieth-century America—the new frontier, full of possibility and the promise of adventure. In 1594, Dudley set out to win glory for himself, planning a joint expedition with Walter Raleigh in search of El Dorado, the mythical city of gold.

When Raleigh couldn't get his ships together in time, Dudley went alone, earning a lifelong enemy in the process. On the voyage, Dudley explored the mouth of the Orinoco River and claimed Trinidad for the queen. Two years later, when England attacked Spain, he commanded a ship in the successful sacking of Cádiz, for which he received a knighthood.

His promising career came to an abrupt halt, however, after Elizabeth died in 1603. Taking advantage of the opportunity, Dudley sued to have his father's titles reinstated by proving his father and mother had been legally married when he was born. The trial went badly, however, when his mother and other witnesses gave conflicting testimony. Dudley's rivals, including Raleigh, pressed their advantage, accusing Dudley of bribery. The new king, James I, meanwhile, came out publicly favoring Dudley's cousin, Sir Philip Sidney, for his father's titles. It was no surprise to anyone when the verdict came out against Dudley.

Dejected and outraged, Dudley left England on July 2, 1605, ostensibly for a three-month trip to the continent. Soon after he'd gone, however, news broke that he had left his wife and four daughters to run away with a nineteen-year-old handmaiden to the queen who had been disguised as a pageboy. Once in France, they scandalized English society by declaring themselves Catholics to avoid extradition. Finally, the celebrity couple arrived at their real destination: Florence.

The city had declined since its days as the center of the humanist revolution. But the Medici grand duke Ferdinando I still presided over a city famed for art and culture and had bigger plans to consolidate his control over the Tuscan coast. Dudley went to work in his service, applying his knowledge of shipbuilding and navigation to build a new navy to defeat the pirates of the Barbary Coast, and developing the coastal city of Livorno (Leghorn) into a modern port.

But he never gave up his fight to see his titles restored. As his fame grew, so did the calls back home to restore his earldom. Finally, in 1644, James's son Charles I wrote a proclamation declaring that the truth of Dudley's birth had been hidden from his father, and restoring Dudley's titles. The gesture was enough for Dudley, who never returned to claim them, dying in his adopted city of Florence in 1649.

Before his death, however, he bestowed one last honor on his native country: a sea atlas called the *Dell'Arcano del Mare*. Dudley's ambitions exceeded his experiences; he had taken only one voyage of exploration himself. The book, whose title means "Secrets of the sea," was nothing short of a comprehensive atlas of every known coastline on the planet, a feat not even the Dutch had attempted. At the time, the English hadn't even produced a sea atlas of England.

As Dudley collected charts from explorers and navigators, he applied another revolutionary twist: He rendered each of them on a Mercator projection—something that wasn't consistently applied by cartographers for another fifty years. Though the English didn't realize it for years, the book is a valuable missing link between the early maps in books by the likes of Hakluyt, Purchas, and Smith, and the later sea charts of Seller, Thornton, and other cartographers of the Thames School.

Despite some inaccuracies in Dudley's maps due to faulty source material, the atlas is a stunning work of art. Dudley gave his manuscripts to a young Florentine engraver who spent twelve years and used five thousand pounds of copper to reproduce them. He copied them in a delicate, spidery hand, transcribing the Italian words with a fine calligraphy adorned with loops and pirouettes. The overall effect is breathtaking, making Dudley's charts highly desired collector's items today.

Smiley checked out the BPL's copy, a two-foot-high tome with a brown leather cover, on January 14, 2003, May 12, 2003, and again on July 19, 2004. On one of those dates, he flipped through the feather-light pages until he came to the maps of the Americas. In addition to several general charts of the East Coast, Dudley had produced several larger-scale charts: one chart of New England and the New Netherlands based largely on Dutch maps of Blaeu; one of Chesapeake Bay; and one of southern Virginia, both drawn from the maps of John White and John Smith. Smiley slipped a razor down the length of the binding, the blade curving slightly along the grain of the paper as it sliced through all three sheets at once.

Chapter 10

CAUGHT!

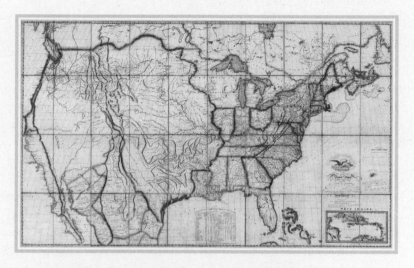

FIGURE 14 JOHN MELISH. "MAP OF THE UNITED STATES OF AMERICA." PHILADELPHIA, 1816.

2004–2005

EVENTUALLY FOR SMILEY the stealing just became habitual. "I know this stuff really, really well," he told me. "I know it without having to think about it which maps would be easy to sell. I didn't go looking for these things, but I saw the opportunities, and I couldn't walk away from it." Strangely, he never felt much anxiety about walking out with maps in his pockets. If anyone asked, it was perfectly reasonable for him to be carrying old maps. How could anyone know that he didn't walk in with them?

When he wasn't in the libraries, he rarely thought about what he was doing. Somehow, he could compartmentalize and rationalize the thefts. "The libraries weren't using these things, and I'm building collections where they are going to be used," he told me. People were going to look at them every day on their walls; they were going to compare maps and make new connections about the world. Besides, hadn't he been invaluable in helping libraries build their collections?

That conviction became stronger in 2003, when Norman Leventhal announced that he was donating money to create a new center at the BPL to house the library's map collection—and was looking for a new home for his own collection too, with the library as the presumed beneficiary. A celebration that November drew six hundred of the city's businessmen and socialites, who ate at private dinner parties around Back Bay and Beacon Hill and then walked to the library for a reception of drinks, dessert, and dancing. Leventhal insisted Smiley be invited to the most important dinner, held at the library for a select group of map scholars and donors. Smiley sat at a table in the back, looking miserable. "He did not exhibit the old kind of arrogance," remembered Alex Krieger.

His friends noticed the changes too. Whereas before Smiley would always be gracious and generous, he now seemed secretive and controlling. During the annual Columbus Day Boys' Weekends in Sebec, he arranged every meal and activity, getting upset when anyone deviated from the schedule. The "Squire" nickname Slater had given him now seemed to apply in earnest. By the fall of 2002, the weekends didn't seem the same anymore. The men divided into factions, with Slater, Fischer, and von Elgg hanging out together and only Paul Statt sticking by his oldest friend.

But even Statt noticed a change, especially since Smiley's heart surgery in 1998. Smiley had become difficult, more guarded in conversations and less forthcoming with details about his life. The one thing Statt had always loved about Smiley was his ability to turn his life into a fascinating story—even if that meant straining a bit at the truth. Now he just seemed like he had something to hide. Sometimes he would hint darkly that if he told Statt the whole truth about his business, he'd never believe it—but Statt took that to refer to the crooked dealings of the trade, not anything criminal on Smiley's part.

He became increasingly stubborn in his dealings in Sebec as well, putting more pressure on himself to "win." Despite letter after letter from the town's board of selectmen, Smiley refused to respond to requests to deal with the parking issue at his shops. The October deadline set by the town came and went, and another site visit by Murphy found that Smiley still hadn't gotten rid of the extra parking spaces. In February 2004, he was issued an official violation. By March, selectman Buzz Small was visibly frustrated, sputtering at a meeting, "What can we do? Do we put them in jail for noncompliance? Can we shut them down?"

Even as the town waited for Smiley to act, he and his supporters were waiting to be vindicated by the ruling of the county court. Finally, on March 25, 2004, Superior Court Justice Nancy Mills handed down her decision. The Moriartys' permit, she wrote, was "legal, supported by substantial evidence on the record and does not indicate any abuse of discretion." Furthermore, she said, "there is no evidence of bad faith on the part of the Moriartys." It was a complete victory for the town—and the Moriartys. "I would just like to express how pleased I am with the outcome," Charlene Moriarty said publicly at the next selectmen's meeting. "I hope that we can now try to work toward a positive goal in the village."

The situation now was worse than ever for Smiley and his supporters. Not only would the Moriartys be able to operate their business, but the Sebec Village Shops were in danger of being shut down. Several of Smiley's employees wrote an open letter to the local paper in his defense. "Through the vision of our employer and his countless dollars of investment, a little oasis has been created," they wrote. "We are lucky to have one of the few folks in our midst that wants to do something right 'just because.' He thought that central Maine would be a good place for this venture because we are in need of jobs, and a sense of community spirit."

Whatever his intentions in establishing that spirit, he'd done the opposite, turning the community into a morass of feuding neighbors and legal complaints. Smiley returned to Sebec for the summer of 2004 dejected, knowing he'd ruined the very paradise he'd hoped to protect. He spent the season struggling to find a way to win in what was clearly a hopeless cause, continuing to ignore the calls from selectmen to bring his property in line. They began issuing fines but allowed the stores to stay open out of respect for the jobs they created.

As for the Moriartys, despite their victory, they continued to look for ways to punish Smiley. They put plans in place to build a new garage on their property by the lake. When finished, it would perfectly block the view of the lake from the Sebec Village Café. Later, Charlene

Moriarty joined the garden club, and one day in the middle of summer Smiley woke to the sounds of a bulldozer in front of his house. By rights, the town owned the boat landing in front of his property, which for years had been overgrown with smoke bush that screened Smiley's house from the lake.

Now the town had voted to "beautify" the area, allowing the Sebec Garden Club to remove the shrubbery, plant new grass, and erect an American flag at the landing. Smiley stood at his kitchen window helplessly watching the bulldozers tear through the vegetation, knowing there was nothing he could do to stop it. He grabbed a digital camera and took pictures through the window, one after another, all capturing the same image: the bulldozer by the lake, tearing up his land.

As soon as it was gone, Smiley packed his family into their car and drove away, leaving Sebec behind.

THOUGH HIS FIGHT in Maine was over, he only increased his pace of stealing in order to pay for his continuing debts. Among his targets now was the building where he'd first become a map lover, the New York Public Library. If he had any qualms about ransacking his onetime temple, he suppressed them. Access couldn't have been easier. Readers in the map room were required to fill out a separate call slip for each item they wanted to view. But after all the hours Smiley had spent organizing the Slaughter Collection, Hudson and the other staff gave him the leeway they'd give a colleague.

As at Yale, Smiley requested an entire folder on one call slip, saying he had to compare several maps at once. Invariably, he took them to the same table he used to work on the Slaughter maps—the one farthest from the circulation desk. It was easy enough to find a moment when a staff member was answering the phone or helping another patron to fold up a sheet. No one asked him to present his belongings for inspection on the way out. Here he could easily fold up a map and put it in his briefcase with others he'd brought with him, and then walk out without suspicion.

He became increasingly brazen in the maps he stole, including some of enormous size. One, John Melish's 1816 map of the United States, was nearly three feet high and five feet wide. The map shows the outline of a country recognizable as the United States, but with the West left practically blank, waiting for manifest destiny to fill in the details (Figure I4). It's the kind of map that even a non–map lover might covet for his living room. The map is backed on linen squares, each one measuring about half the size of an eight-and-a-half by eleven-inch piece of paper, with small folds between them. Smiley could fold the map into a tight packet and conceal it in a stack of papers or his briefcase.

Another map—of North Carolina by John Collet—was nearly as large, but it was printed on two sheets without folds. Smiley must have had to create folds for himself, then iron them out later for mounting and sale. The library's staff never suspected such large materials were missing. Smiley sold the Collet map to a dealer, who resold it to San Diego map dealer Barry Ruderman. At the Miami map fair that year, Ruderman displayed it framed in his booth, and Smiley and Alice Hudson stood admiring it together. Ruderman listened in as the two discussed how it was one of the rarest and most important maps of the region, done just before the Revolutionary War. "We have an excellent copy of that in our collection," Hudson said, as Smiley nodded.

Unbeknownst to Hudson at the time, Smiley had also taken another map she treasured—the John Thornton map of "East and West New Jarsey" she had chosen for her contribution to the Mercator Society's first book nearly two decades earlier. At the same time, he defaced some of the atlases he had used to learn about antiquarian mapmaking, tearing pages from Des Barres's maritime atlas and William Faden's Revolutionary War atlas. Not content with just stealing from the map room, he also made his way upstairs to the rare-books collection on the library's third floor, where, among other books, he ransacked two editions of Samuel de Champlain's *Voyages* for their maps.

Even as he was stealing, Smiley continued to compete on the auction floor. At one auction at Swann Galleries in New York on December 9, 2004, a rare copy of John Smith's map of New England came up for sale. The copy was the fifth state of the map, circa I626, and was expected to fetch between $15,000 and $25,000. Smiley bid hard for it, watching as the price climbed above $30,000. Eventually, there were two bidders left, Smiley and a phone bidder. Finally, Smiley dropped out of the running, and the other bidder purchased the map for $36,000 plus 15 percent commission, for a total of $41,400. Though he didn't know it at the time, the other bidder was Graham Arader—who had beaten him once again.

The victory was particularly sweet for Arader when he found out about it. Lately, he'd become strident in his criticisms of Smiley. In an e-mail to a client in January 2005, he railed against his rival. "Forbes doesn't advertise, do shows, issue a catalogue, his checks bounce, he rarely buys at auction, no collectors I know will have anything to do with him," he wrote. "He is a crook. A very bright guy with knowledge, but there is NO WAY that he can be getting these maps legally. He stinks." The collector defended his decision to continue doing business with Smiley. "You need to get beyond your own ego on this and see that it is possible that every other dealer is not a crook or a thief and only you the safe harbor of true value."

EVEN WHILE SMILEY was struggling to succeed, both legally and illegally, in the map business, he was looking for his own "safe harbor" to replace the one he'd lost in Sebec—a new statement project that could demonstrate his success and provide a refuge for his family. Lisa had long wanted to tear down their dark Vineyard cottage and build a modern home, and Smiley finally gave her his blessing. The Smileys demolished the home in the summer of 2004, moving into a small one-room studio on the property. That November, they signed a contract with local contractor David Pizzano to build a house designed by Resolution: 4 Architecture, a New York–based architectural firm that specializes in stylish modular homes.

Watching from afar, his friends Paul Statt and Scott Slater thought it seemed foolish, even for Smiley, to embark on such a big project so soon after the bruising fight in Sebec. But he threw himself into creating a new home on the Vineyard with all the energy he'd put into Maine. The up-island town of Chilmark was wealthy, but it also retained enough small-town atmosphere to make it feel like a real community, with a quaint general store on the corner and a clam shack down by the water for a local hangout.

One thing it lacked was other families with young children. Now that Smiley's son was approaching school age, Smiley took new interest in the school, which was designed for one hundred students but had an enrollment of only forty-six. To increase enrollment, a group of residents proposed building a private preschool to act as a feeder into the elementary school and make the town more welcoming to young families. Smiley helped organize the group and signed on as its business agent and secretary, raising money for the school and contributing some himself.

Though he was only forty-eight years old, he began looking for an exit strategy from the high-stress world of map dealing. But he had to hold on a little longer, to finish the new home and establish himself in the community before planning his next move. He'd gotten too used to high-end living, too used to projecting the image of himself as a successful map dealer, to give it all up now. The pressure of maintaining that life, however, was taking its toll on his body. His back began seizing up on him, making it painful to move or even stand for long periods of time. He had trouble sleeping too, waking up with nightmares and finding himself unable to go back to bed.

Smiley's new modular home arrived in nine parts in February 2005, hauled on a barge from Port Elizabeth, New Jersey, to Chilmark harbor. It was such an unusual sight, one of the local papers featured a photo on the front page. As construction began, Smiley wrote a letter to the editor apologizing for the unsightliness in a strangely passive voice. "Due to certain delays in the construction process, our new residence . . . has been left naked to the scrutiny of all passersby," he wrote. "Please be assured that, as soon as possible, our plans to face this building in old stone and screen it heavily to the road will be accomplished."

The truth was, however, that Smiley was overextended again. According to their contractor, Pizzano, the Smileys had ordered a $105,000 kitchen from Italy and spent $20,000 on flooring alone. When Pizzano suggested they cover the outside with fake stone, Smiley told him there was no way he was going to have imitation materials on his house—it would have to be real stone, a decision that added $250,000 to the construction cost. "Money was no object," Pizzano later remembered. "I was billing him monthly for forty, eighty, ninety thousand dollars." As Smiley struggled to keep up with the cost, the home remained a mess of tar-paper siding, with pallets full of construction materials strewn about the dirt driveway.

And even though he'd left Sebec, planning never to return, he was still supporting payroll up in Maine through the slow winter months, all the while paying tens of thousands for the new home on the Vineyard. That January, the government filed a tax lien for $57,063 on his property. The only way he could see to get out from under was to increase the pace of his thefts.

THAT PREVIOUS SUMMER, the Boston Public Library had officially launched the new Norman B. Leventhal Map Center. As its first curator, it appointed Ron Grim, who was previously a map history specialist at the Library of Congress. Short and genial with owlish spectacles, Grim was the perfect person for the job, displaying an infectious enthusiasm for cartographic history. When he first arrived in Boston, he began going through the shelves to familiarize himself with the collection, noting the call slips that provided a record of who had used each item. Smiley's name came up over and over. *Smiley knows this collection better than I do,* he thought.

He had no idea at the time that Smiley had been using his knowledge to systematically dismantle it. Among the rarest of all the treasures in the new map center were several copies of *The American Pilot,* a collection of sea charts by John Norman and his son William that was the American answer to the *The English Pilot, The Fourth Book.* The sea atlas was continually updated in the decades after the Revolution, guiding the clipper ships from Boston and New York that finally led to the American dominance of Atlantic trade. As with any maritime atlas, however, the books were in constant use aboard the rolling decks of merchant vessels, leading to their rapid deterioration.

Only ten copies of *The American Pilot* were known to have survived, and Boston had four of them—one from 1794, two from 1798, and one from 1816. Smiley examined the last copy multiple times, including in December 2004 and January 2005. On one of those occasions, he tore out a chart of Florida and the Bahamas and took it down to New York to show his friend Harry Newman at the Old Print Shop. Even by 1816, Florida was still relatively uncharted territory. Smiley showed Newman where the mapmaker had copied from other English charts and where he had added new information from an American ship captain. Newman was happy to purchase it.

That fall, he went to Boston to view another sea atlas, *The Atlantic*

Neptune of J.F.W. Des Barres. A few months later, in February 2005, he sold a chart of Charleston, South Carolina, from the book to Burden. Later that spring, Grim met Smiley for the first and only time. When one of his colleagues mentioned that Smiley was in the rare-book room, Grim went over to say hello and the two got into a spirited discussion about a map Smiley was viewing. Around the same time, Smiley sent Grim a check for $1,000 to preserve another map from the Des Barres volume, this one of Chesapeake Bay. Perhaps he sent it out of guilt, or simply to keep up the impression that he was a wealthy map dealer and benefactor—or maybe he was planning his next theft. Whatever his motive, the check bounced.

While he was up in Boston that spring, Smiley also headed across the Charles River to Harvard University. He avoided the Harvard Map Collection, the basement repository where *Mapping Boston* author David Cobb served as curator, and targeted Harvard's rare-book library, Houghton Library, instead. Perhaps he felt the curators there would be less likely to know which maps they had tucked inside their books. Sitting beneath portraits of past Harvard presidents, he requested a copy of Champlain's *Voyages*, along with travelogues from several other French explorers that also contained maps of New France.

During one of his visits there, he took out a copy of Hubbard's book about the New England Indian wars, containing John Foster's map of New England. It's this map that, in its London printing, famously includes the "Wine Hills" typo. Harvard, however, had two copies of the book with the rare Boston printing of the map with the correctly labeled "White Hills." The library's catalog, however, listed the map in only one of them, erroneously listing the other as missing. When Smiley found the map inside, he slipped it out, making the listing accurate. It was the same map that Bill Reese had suspected Smiley of stealing from the Beinecke back in the 1990s. It's ironic then, that it was in his briefcase when he visited the Beinecke that spring.

Smiley had avoided going to the Beinecke for years—perhaps due to the bad taste left in his mouth after that incident with Reese. That May, however, he visited twice. On one trip, he requested a rare book by German geographer Johann Huttich dating all the way back to 1532. He opened the white vellum cover and turned stiff, crinkly pages filled with Latin text until he came to what he was looking for: an unusual "double-cordiform" map of the world by French cartographer Oronce Fine that represented each hemisphere in a unusual heart-shaped projection.

Shortly after looking at it in the library, he brought it to Paul Cohen at the Arkway in New York, but Cohen wasn't interested in buying it. Smiley then called Harry Newman, telling him he was up the street and asking if he was interested in taking a look. Newman was excited—he'd never seen a copy of Fine's map. "I'm going to take a cab," said Smiley. "I'll be there in a few minutes." When he got to the Old Print Shop and opened his portfolio, however, it was empty. In a panic, Smiley ran back outside to the street to see if the map had fallen out. It had started raining outside, and water sloshed in the gutter of Lexington Avenue as he searched, but there was no map to be found. He called Arkway, but Cohen told him the map wasn't there either. Newman put out a call on the Internet for the map, asking anyone to contact him if it turned up somewhere at another dealer's shop, but it never did. The map, valued at more than $40,000, was simply lost.

On his second trip to the Beinecke, he requested an even older book, by Hernán Cortés, the Spanish explorer who had led the conquest of Mexico. The book, published in 1524, had a map of the Aztec capital of Tenochtitlán, which has the distinction of being the first map made of any North American city. It is also the *last* map of Tenochtitlán. After Cortés completed his sketch, he burned the city to the ground. (The location is now the site of Mexico City.) Again, Smiley called Newman, who agreed to purchase the map. Even as Newman marveled over the rare find, he couldn't help but notice the change that had come over Smiley. Gone was the enthusiastic, bombastic Smiley he had known. Now he seemed tired, beaten down, and distracted. Newman was concerned for his friend, but he never put together his appearance with the rare finds he was coming up with on a regular basis—assuming he was suffering from stress and poor health.

The truth was, no matter how much Smiley stole, he never seemed to have enough to cover his debts or alleviate the stress he felt. When he arrived at the Beinecke on June 8, 2005, he was in a virtual state of panic. He had already paid out more than $500,000 on the Vineyard house and owed at least $200,000 more. In order to make up that kind of money, he'd need a big score. The John Smith map of New England was an obvious choice. He could sell it easily and make up for the one he'd missed out on at Swann a few months before. But that map was probably worth only $50,000 to $60,000 at most.

To make a real dent in his debts, he'd need something truly rare. A few years earlier, Arkway had sold a copy of the world map from *Speculum Orbis Terrarum* by Gerard de Jode for $85,000. A pristine copy like the one in the Beinecke's collection could fetch as much as $125,000. The day Smiley decided to take it, however, was also the day he dropped his razor on the floor—and the Beinecke's staff already had him under surveillance.

WHEN I VISITED the Beinecke eight years later, in the summer of 2013, the guard opened a door labeled "Staff Only" and led me through a maze of corridors. This was the side of the library few patrons see—gone were the polished tables and glass cases full of books, replaced with metal lockers and drab walls. The guard led me into a control room outfitted with five huge flat-screen TVs on one wall, and a half-dozen computers beneath them. The screens were split into multiple camera shots; each table had a feed from directly overhead, and the guard showed me how she could zoom in close enough to practically read over a patron's shoulder.

"None of this was here back then," she said, referring to the day Smiley was caught stealing the de Jode map. "If it weren't for him, we wouldn't have this nice control room and we all wouldn't have jobs," she said jokingly. At that time, the library's security cameras were pretty basic, pointed from a fixed position with no capacity to zoom. The guard cued up a tape on one of the monitors—the only one that will still play the old format—and there was Forbes Smiley sitting at the end of the table farthest from the circulation desk, with light streaming in through the courtyard windows. His white hair was cut short and thinning on top, and he was wearing a white shirt, skinny black tie, and silver wire-rimmed glasses.

As the tape started, Smiley was flipping rapidly through a weather-beaten atlas propped on a foam support. After a few minutes, he closed the book and tied it up quickly and almost carelessly with string. He left for a few minutes before returning with another large book in a case. As the counter on the monitor read 50:00, he unfolded the case to reveal a heavy brown leather volume. He put both case and book down on the foam and flipped the pages one by one for twenty-seven seconds.

Finally, he arrived at the page he was looking for. In the corner was a "wind face"—one of the puffy-faced cherubs de Jode placed around the margins of his world map to label the names and directions of the winds. Smiley paused a moment, and then, so quickly as to be nearly imperceptible, he flicked his wrist to fold two pages of the map down in half. He closed the book immediately, holding it tight with one hand as he placed it spine-down on the table. With the other hand, he took the case off the foam supports.

For nearly a minute, the camera's view was obscured by the back of a blond woman wearing a white tank top who seemed barely aware of Smiley. Then, at 51:06, he sighed and opened the book again to the title page, staring at it intently. At 51:21, his right hand slowly slipped under the pages to find the ones he had folded down before. At 51:36, he began to look around and make notes with his left hand, all the while his right was working beneath the page. This activity went on for nearly a minute, before, at 52:20, his right hand suddenly darted from beneath the page.

"See that! He's got it now!" shouted one of several security guards who had gathered around the monitor to watch with me. But I had to rewind and play the tape several times to even see his hand move—never mind see the map, which was presumably now in his lap. At 52:45, he reached back over with his right hand as if to put his pencil in his blazer pocket. It was at that moment, perhaps, that he transferred the map to his pocket—though it remained invisible on the monitor.

From there, he only had to clean up. At 52:57, he began to intently pull little pieces of paper out of the center of the binding, making no attempt to hide his actions. He put a small pile of the paper pieces to the left side of the book, his hand shaking slightly. By this time, the curators and guards who had been watching him from the reader services desk must have seen his suspicious actions. At 54:00, a staff member walked by, and Smiley glanced up at her, then down again. After she passed, he furtively glanced back again before blowing his nose on his handkerchief and coughing.

At 54:27, his eyes darted again to the staff member, before he again wiped his nose with the handkerchief. Finally, at 55:05, he began turning the pages rapidly for several minutes as his hands continued to shake. At

57:10, he took the little pile of paper and put it in his left outside blazer pocket. Another staff member walked by; then at 1:00:00, he looked around, unfolded the case, and put the book back inside. He folded it up, then unfolded it again, checking again to make sure all remnants of paper were gone. He folded it again, then at 1:00:58, unfolded it one last time to check, before finally walking out of the monitor frame to return the book and leave the library.

Of course, he didn't leave alone. Following close behind, Yale policeman Martin Buonfiglio was on his tail, finally catching up with him at the Yale Center for British Art and bringing him back to the Beinecke. Within a few hours, it was all over. Library staff had identified its map, and the Yale police had led Smiley off in handcuffs to be processed.

After feeling numb throughout the arrest, thoughts finally began to filter back into Smiley's consciousness as he sat in the cell that night. He could still get away with it, they said. Even if they found the one map, he could talk his way out of the others. He'd get a warning, maybe probation. And then he'd get out of the map business for good. Even as he considered those possibilities, however, darker thoughts crashed in. This could be very bad, they said. He could go to jail for a long time. He could owe people a lot of money. He could lose his reputation, his family, all the work he'd put into growing his business for twenty years. Then his mind would go numb again, and he'd stop thinking of anything at all.

Chapter 11

THE PLEA

FIGURE 15 SAMUEL DE CHAMPLAIN. "CARTE GÉOGRAPHIQUE DE LA NOUVELLE FRANSE." PARIS, 1613.

2005–2006

THE DIRECTORY ON the building across from Boston's City Hall had no listing to indicate it was home to the Boston Division of the Federal Bureau of Investigation, overseeing agency operations in four states. I rode the elevator up to the sixth floor, where two bored-looking officers led me through a metal detector, and a woman behind glass made me surrender my driver's license and cell phone. Another agent took me into a cramped law library, where I met Special Agent Stephen J. Kelleher. He hardly seemed movie-stock G-man material. Short and gangly, with a shaved head, he wore jeans and a black polo with a shamrock-shaped badge reading "Boston FBI SWAT" on the chest.

"My supervisor came over one day and dropped a file on my

desk—Yale has this thing and this guy stole some maps," he recounted in a Boston accent. "Can you go check it out?"

The case hardly excited him. Prior to joining the FBI, Kelleher had worked as a patrolman in a working-class suburb of Providence, Rhode Island. He had his share of war stories—like the time a guy high on coke had gunned a Ford Explorer into him during a traffic stop and he had to fire a bullet at his assailant, hitting the hood of the car instead. Or the time during a domestic disturbance call, when he tackled a man holding a woman down on the ground with a knife at her throat—he earned a special award for that one.

Compared to those cases, this seemed routine. He drove from the New Haven field office to the Yale Police Department headquarters, and from there walked over to the Beinecke with Detective Martin Buonfiglio. There, they watched the videotape showing Smiley stealing the de Jode map, and looked at the maps Buonfiglio had recovered.

Despite the persuasive evidence, Kelleher saw a problem—there was a difference between Smiley having copies of maps the library was missing and proving Smiley had *the* missing maps. "You know, they weren't cars with VIN numbers," he told me. "Who knows how many copies there were, and when the last time was someone saw it in a book." He couldn't even use fingerprints from the crime scene, since Smiley had been given permission to handle the books. He explained all this to library staff as they looked together at de Jode's world map and his atlas spread out on the table. "Is there anything you can show me to prove that this map came from this book?" he asked.

There was one thing, said dealer Bill Reese, who had also been called to attend the meeting: wormholes. For centuries libraries had been plagued with wood-boring insects that laid their eggs in the stacks. When the larvae hatched, they used the digestive enzymes in their alimentary canals to chew through wood and paper, leaving behind a tiny trail. Somewhere in its 427-year history, the Beinecke's copy of the *Speculum* had contracted its own case of pests. In the front of the book, a dozen pages sported a small constellation of three pin-sized holes near the bottom and another hole three inches up. Now, as the librarians laid the map carefully back into the volume, those holes matched identical holes in the edge of the map where it had been held in place (Figure 16).

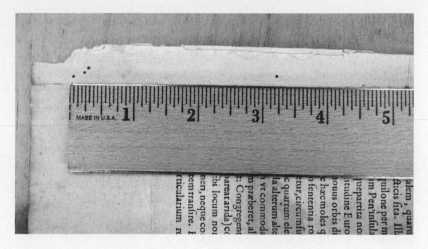

FIGURE 16   WORMHOLES IN GERARD DE JODE'S
SPECULUM ORBIS TERRARUM.

"That's the first time I realized there were actually bookworms," Kelleher told me. "Because I was never called a bookworm as a kid."

Those wormholes were as good as a fingerprint to Kelleher, proving the map came from that volume and making the theft a federal offense. Under the Theft of Major Artwork Act, passed a decade earlier, any cultural item stolen from a museum that was more than one hundred years old or worth more than $100,000 was a felony. The definition of "museum" was intentionally kept vague; with its display of a Gutenberg Bible in the mezzanine, the Beinecke qualified.

But the de Jode map was only one of eight maps recovered from Smiley that day—and the Beinecke claimed only four. Where did the other maps come from? Kelleher swore the staff to secrecy as he began to work the case, asking them to involve only those they needed to to identify the other maps. The librarians had already introduced him to dealer Bill Reese, who knew as much about the Beinecke's collection as anyone. As Kelleher sat down to talk with him, Reese told him about his suspicions about Smiley dating back more than a decade.

Kelleher listened with rising concern. There was no telling how long Smiley had been stealing—and eight years as a beat cop had taught him that an offender rarely stopped after one crime. If Smiley stole from the Beinecke, he probably stole from other libraries too. On July 6, a month after Smiley's arrest, Kelleher wrote a post to ExLibris, an e-mail List-serv dedicated to rare books, requesting that librarians examine their collections to determine if Smiley had been there and whether they were missing maps. If so, he wrote, they should contact him.

TWO DAYS LATER, on July 8, Smiley showed up at New Haven Superior Court for his first appearance, wearing khaki pants, a yellow tie, and his olive-checked blazer. On his way into the court, police surrounded him and announced that he was under arrest again. They took him to the station and formally charged him with larceny in the first degree for the theft of three of the four maps the Beinecke had identified as its own: the John Smith map of New England, a world map from Hakluyt's *Principall Navigations,* and a 1635 map of the Northwest Passage by Luke Foxe. Noticeably absent was the most valuable map stolen from the Beinecke that day, the de Jode map of the world. Kelleher was saving that for the feds.

After taking Smiley's mug shot (Figure O), they brought him back to the courthouse, where Connecticut judge Richard Damiani set his bail at $175,000 and ordered his passport confiscated. Reporting a story a half hour from the courthouse, *Hartford Courant* reporter Kim Martineau got a call from her editor—a map collector himself who had heard about Smiley's arrest from one of his dealers—sending her to the courthouse. She arrived just as Smiley was being led into the room, and filed an article that appeared in dozens of papers around the country.

Map dealers throughout the profession weighed in on the revelations. "You're talking about Da Vinci with a carving knife," said San Diego dealer Barry Ruderman. "You're talking about a person who defiled the institutions that defined his existence." Graham Arader gloated, telling the paper that he'd been warning people about Smiley since he started undercutting his prices in the early 1990s. "It made me crazy," he said. "How can I compete with map dealers whose costs are zero?"

Smiley's friend Scott Slater heard the news on National Public Radio. He was shocked by the allegations—but at least there was an explanation for his friend's strange and controlling behavior of late. He began making calls to rally old friends from Derryfield and Hampshire, many of whom asked what they could do to help. Finally, he told his daughter Felicity. Now fifteen, she was hard hit by the truth about those magical summers in Sebec—that the gauzy fantasy "Uncle Forbes" created had been supported by crime.

Many of the residents in Sebec were similarly sent reeling by the unmasking of their Robin Hood; the employees of his shops began worrying what would happen to their jobs and the community he'd helped create. The Moriartys, on the other hand, celebrated—buying extra copies of the *Hartford Courant* to distribute to their neighbors and posting a copy of the article in the window of their marina, along with a copy of Smiley's mug shot.

Alice Hudson was at her desk at the New York Public Library when she got a call with the news. She sat stunned, unable to breathe. If he was stealing from Yale, then she knew he must have also stolen from New York—from *her*. She thought of all the late nights he'd spent in the division organizing the Slaughter material. At the time, the long-planned renovations to Room 117 had finally begun, and for the past nine months Hudson's division had been temporarily located in the genealogy department. Maps were everywhere, filed in unfamiliar cabinets and piled on unfamiliar shelves—Smiley could have easily taken advantage of their vulnerabilities to steal any number of maps. She was going to have to resign, she thought. Either that, or any day she would get the call from her supervisor asking her to gather her things and leave the building.

At the Boston Public Library, the Leventhal Map Center's new curator, Ron Grim, thought back to his experience when he had first arrived and seen so many call slips with Smiley's name on the shelves. He called Kelleher immediately, speaking to him on July 8 as Smiley was appearing in court. Kelleher told him that it would be up to the libraries to determine what he stole—the bureau didn't have the manpower. "Was he allowed to wear a sports jacket?" Kelleher asked. "Yes," said Grim. Kelleher tried to console him. "He was just as friendly with the staff at other libraries as he was with you," he said. "You shouldn't consider yourself at fault."

Kelleher began fielding calls from other libraries—including the New York Public Library, Yale's Sterling Memorial Library, Harvard's Houghton Library, and the Newberry Library in Chicago. As he spoke with each librarian, he began to realize how difficult the case could be.

Some of the libraries, like the Beinecke, had electronic records of every item viewed. Others, like the Sterling, kept no records at all. To each curator, Kelleher explained that prosecutors would need hard evidence to prove their case—including catalog records, digital images, distinguishing marks—anything that could be used to prove that a specific copy of a map had come from their collection.

He wondered how many hours he'd have to spend in the next few months chasing leads that went nowhere. Just as he'd begun to worry, he got an unexpected call from Smiley's attorney: Smiley, he said, wanted to cooperate.

WHEN SMILEY WAS first charged with theft, he was appointed a public defender, who optimistically told him he might be able to beat the charges. His friend Paul Statt, however, insisted he hire a private attorney—referring him to New Haven lawyer Dick Reeve. At their first meeting, according to Smiley, Reeve sat him down in his office and said two words: "You're cooked." The evidence against him was overwhelming, Reeve continued—maps in his briefcase, a surveillance tape of him stealing—and now the FBI was poking around with the probability of federal charges. "Now, what do you want me to do?" Reeve asked.

He laid out the options: Smiley could plead not guilty and make the FBI and US attorney prove each theft beyond a reasaonble doubt. They'd miss many of them, to be sure, but they were also sure to succeed in proving some of them. Or he could cooperate fully and hope that cooperation would win him some leniency from the feds at sentencing. "I want to make good on the harm that I've caused, and I don't care what happens to me," Smiley said, according to his later recollection. "I want the least possible harm to come to my family."

That meant cooperating fully and completely, warned his lawyer. If he held back any information, it could invalidate the entire deal. "Each and every time you talk to them, listen very carefully to what they are asking," Reeve told him. "And try your best to answer." The advice made Smiley nervous. For years, he'd been lying out of habit to nearly everyone, telling them what he thought they wanted to hear. How could he tell the truth now?

For Kelleher, sitting down with Smiley was a devil's bargain, but one he was willing to accept. He discussed it with the assistant US attorney on the case, Christopher "Kit" Schmeisser, who agreed that getting back more maps at the end of the day would be better than putting Smiley in prison for a long sentence while maps disappeared forever in some collection overseas. Schmeisser and Reeve drew up the outlines of a cooperation agreement—if Smiley provided substantial information to recover the maps, the government would argue for leniency.

Kelleher began by sitting down with Smiley to construct a list of what he'd stolen, detailing the maps, the libraries from which he'd taken them, and the dealers to whom he'd sold them. From years of dealing with criminals, Kelleher knew that even when they cooperated, they rarely confessed everything—at least at first. The game was to convince them that you already knew more than they realized. As Smiley sat across the table, he poured out details about how he got into the profession, how he'd built up the Leventhal and Slaughter Collections, and how he harbored resentments against other dealers and libraries that never gave him the credit he deserved.

Kelleher listened patiently but kept steering him back to the real issue—what had he stolen? Everything else to him was just noise. Early on in the investigation, Smiley turned over his computer, and the agents pored over his records and e-mails but found little solid evidence there. He worked alone, Smiley insisted, keeping no records of his sales. In most cases, he told them, the maps just fell out of the books; in others, he ripped them out or used a razor blade. After he brought the maps home, he often trimmed margins and scraped off library marks to obscure their origins.

Kelleher decided not to subject Smiley to a polygraph test; they have been shown in studies to have mixed effectiveness. (The US Supreme Court has invalidated their use in criminal investigations; now they are often used to compel subjects to confess rather than measure whether someone is telling the truth.) As he looked at the list Smiley had put together, he realized that his task would be even more difficult than he'd anticipated. Many of the maps had obscure names or could be attributed to more than one author. Some came from books or atlases, while others were single sheets. And while Smiley had total recall of some, for others he could only remember partial information—from where he stole them or to whom he'd sold them, but not both.

At least Smiley appeared to Kelleher to be genuinely remorseful for what he had done. He seemed committed to making this list his last great collection—one he'd be building for the federal government.

AT THE SAME TIME Smiley was putting together his list for Kelleher, the libraries were putting together their own lists, combing through what records they had to determine which maps Smiley had looked at and which ones were now missing. At the BPL, which had no computerized records of requests, Ron Grim and his staff had to page through thousands of call slips, organized by date, in order to find those with Smiley's name on them. Then they had to go to the card catalog to determine which maps *should* be in a given book and which ones actually *were*. For single-sheet maps, the librarians had to go through whole drawers of dozens of maps in order to determine what was missing.

"On the positive side, I always said it forced me to learn the collection a lot sooner than I would have," Grim later joked. The process took two months and one hundred hours of staff members' time. After the first month, the staff had found ten items missing from six volumes, including three maps from *Purchas His Pilgrimes* and two from Theodor de Bry's *Voyages*. The Beinecke, which had recently moved to a computerized system, found a dozen missing maps.

The Newberry Library in Chicago, which Smiley had visited twice in the last five years, identified four books he'd checked out, two of which were missing maps. One, torn from an English edition of Mercator's *Atlas*, was a bad copy of John Smith's map of Virginia by Englishman Ralph Hall, who had decorated it freely with animals and sea monsters. The other was a 1695 map of the South Carolina coast by John Thornton. The library went public with its findings to the *Chicago Tribune*. "He's the lowest of the low," the Newberry's president, Charles Cullen, said of Smiley. "He deserves to have the book thrown at him."

The Newberry's head curator, Bob Karrow, made a plea for other libraries to be similarly forthcoming about their missing items. "Full disclosure will be embarrassing, perhaps highly embarrassing for institutions and individuals, but in our hearts we all know that the world of antiquarian dealers, libraries, and collectors, like the larger world of scholarship to which it directly contributes, is a world ultimately sustained by trust," he wrote on a map community Listserv. "We must begin now to restore that trust by telling what we know when we know it and letting the chips fall where they may."

One institution that gladly took up the call was the British Library in London, which released a list of three maps that it suspected Smiley of taking, including a 1624 map of maritime Canada by Sir William Alexander and a 1578 woodcut map of the world by George Best. The last map the library reported missing was by far the most valuable. A 1520 world map by Peter Apian, it had been copied from Martin Waldseemüller's famous world map of 1507 and could be worth more than $100,000.

But the provenance of this map made it more valuable still—it originally came from a book owned by the Archbishop of Canterbury, Thomas Cranmer, who was burned at the stake by Henry VIII. The volume had the initials "T.C." lightly written inside its vellum-bound cover, and two copies of the Apian map—one folding out a few pages after the title page, and another, lighter impression about halfway through the book. Now the second copy was gone. The only person who had looked at all these books was Smiley, who had checked out the Best book on June 1, 2004; the Alexander book the following day, June 5, 2004; and the Apian book on March 5, 2005.

Boston Public also went public with its findings in early August. The other three libraries—New York, Harvard, and Yale—all maintained their silence. Except for talking privately with the feds, Smiley, too, kept quiet, refusing to respond to newspaper requests for comment. His home on the Vineyard sat half-finished behind a screen of trees, with piles of dirt still in the driveway left from the workmen. By that point, Pizzano figured he was owed more than $200,000 on the work. He left the power and water on in the house so Smiley, Lisa, and their five-year-old son, Ned, could move in.

The only time Smiley spoke publicly was on August 9, 2005, when he appeared in state court in New Haven to finally respond to the charges against him. He stood at the defendant stand, nervously stating his age as fifty before the clerk corrected him, saying he was still forty-nine. Finally, he was asked to respond to three charges of theft. When asked for his plea, he hesitated and looked over at Reeve before quietly saying, "Not guilty." After the arraignment, he and Reeve walked briskly to an elevator, trailed by a pack of reporters from publications ranging from *The New Yorker* to the *Cape Cod Times*. Smiley couldn't help grinning as Reeve kept repeating, "No comment," to their questions.

IN MID-JULY, most of the major map dealers, curators, and collectors convened in Budapest for the biannual International Conference on the History of Cartography. Smiley was the main topic, with conference-goers trading scant scraps of information and speculating on how far his crimes went. This was no petty thief like Gilbert Bland, pillaging historical societies for $100 maps; this was a known and trusted member of their own community. Rumors swirled about why he had snapped. One going around was that his son had heart trouble, and because Smiley didn't have insurance, he turned to stealing out of desperation.

Another rumor was that Smiley had gotten into a bind with one of his clients, Barry MacLean. Instead of selling him authentic antiquarian maps, he had sold him several nineteenth-century facsimiles. When MacLean found out, he told Smiley that he wouldn't press charges if he returned his money—or gave him the authentic maps. Somehow, Smiley came up with the real maps. I personally heard several versions of this story from different dealers, most of whom trace it back to Smiley's former assistant, Ashley Baynton-Williams. But he won't comment on it, and neither will MacLean, who declined to speak with me.

Some dealers were harder hit than others. Most affected of all was Harry Newman, who had looked up to Smiley professionally, considered him a friend, and even vacationed with him once in Sebec. "The professional betrayal was one thing, but the personal betrayal was worse," he told me. "It just shook my soul." As dealers started comparing notes, they realized how many rare maps Smiley had been coming up with in past years—had they shared information earlier, they might have connected the dots.

As news began to trickle out that more libraries were affected, some collectors cried out publicly for all the libraries and dealers to come clean. The loudest cries came from Tony Campbell, the former head librarian at the British Library, who had called for a central database of stolen maps after the Gilbert Bland case. Now he facilitated the web page and discussion list MapHist, the unofficial clearinghouse for the trade, and used his bully pulpit to push for change.

In a long open letter to the community called "Issues Arising out of the Smiley Affair," he chastised his colleagues for not learning the lessons from Gilbert Bland and other thieves. The very nature of books with maps in them made them vulnerable to theft, he wrote. "Steal one page from a first folio of Shakespeare, and you have nothing of value; slip into your jacket pocket a single sheet from a book with an early map of North America on it and you may have a readily saleable, broadly untraceable, artifact worth up to six figures."

The only way libraries could prevent this from happening in the future was sharing information—their reflexive silence about missing materials made them vulnerable to a thief who knew what to target. They needed to work together to identify the most valuable materials and make sure they were cataloged before a theft could occur. And after thefts did occur, they needed to circulate the missing items in a master list so dealers could know what to watch out for. Publicly, libraries protested Campbell's post, arguing they didn't have the resources for the kind of intensive cataloging that would be required. Privately, however, the librarians at all of the institutions had been frantically searching through their collections during the summer and now were ready to share with one another.

On August 28, 2005, representatives of nearly all the affected libraries filed into the third-floor trustees' room at the Boston Public Library for the first meeting of what Grim, with gallows humor, called the "Smiley Victims Support Group." Calling the meeting to order, he introduced Norman Leventhal, who now served as the honorary chair of the Leventhal Map Center. "I want to personally thank everyone for coming to this meeting," he said. "I'm delighted to see so many of the curators with whom I've had such wonderful relationships and associations in the world of maps over the past twenty years."

After that, he turned the floor over to Kit Schmeisser, the assistant US attorney who was heading up the investigation. "I am authorized to state that Mr. Smiley is cooperating fully with the investigation, and is providing information on what items he has taken," he said, adding sternly, "Mr. Smiley is providing information on items that the various institutions would not be able to establish he has taken because of record-keeping problems." It was important in the meantime, he said, that the libraries not talk to the press, warning it could hamper their ability to recover maps if they did.

After Schmeisser sat down, each of the librarians stood up in turn to share their experiences. By now, Grim had completed his own review of the materials Smiley had viewed at the BPL, and the results were worse than he could have imagined. In all, more than sixty maps were found to be missing from twenty-five books that Smiley had examined—and some of the losses were devastating. Among the worst was a 1613 edition of Samuel de Champlain's *Voyages* that was missing both of the crucial maps of Canada (Figure 15). Almost as heartbreaking were four maps pillaged from Thomas Jefferys's *American Atlas*—the volume that contained many of the foundational maps of America after the French and Indian War. There were the three maps from Sir Robert Dudley's *Dell'Arcano del Mare*, sliced through with a single cut. There were the four editions of *The American Pilot* by John and William Norman, missing seven charts among them.

Smiley had looked at all of the books—sometimes multiple times—between the late 1990s and 2005. What's more, few other people had looked at them. Only fourteen people combined had looked at all twenty-five of the books, mostly only once per book. With some books, including the Champlain and the Dudley, Smiley was the only reader during that period. Grim sent the list to the FBI and awaited a response.

IN THE FOUR MONTHS since Kelleher had started his investigation, he had received quite a cartographic education. After receiving the list of stolen maps from Smiley, he contacted the dealers he'd mentioned, including Arkway, Newman, and Burden, and asked them to provide a record of any maps Smiley had sold them. By law, it is illegal to pass on stolen goods, if it can be proven they are stolen. But with scant hard evidence in this case, he'd have to rely on the dealers' cooperation for any hope of recovering the maps Smiley had sold.

This request put the dealers in a bind. They had paid Smiley for the maps and resold them to collectors. If they were going to get them back, they would have to pay back the collectors, swallowing the loss. Kelleher promised that in return for their cooperation, he wouldn't contact any collectors directly or publicly name the dealers themselves. Implicit in that promise was a threat: If they didn't cooperate, the FBI *would* identify them, associating them with stolen goods. All three dealers—as well as a handful of smaller dealers—acquiesced, providing the agent with records of everything they had bought from Smiley for the last five years.

Comparing it against Smiley's list, Kelleher asked the dealers to recover particular maps for examination. Newman was asked to supply nineteen, including the Bonner plan of Boston from 1743, which he'd bought from Smiley back in 2002 and then advertised prominently in his catalog. He couldn't believe it. There were only five copies of that state in the world. How could Yale not have known its copy was missing?

As much as some dealers blamed the libraries, others in the map community blamed dealers for not being more diligent in determining provenance. By now, Arader was loudly asserting that he'd been alerting the map trade to Smiley's thefts ever since Smiley started in the business in 1985. "I've been telling everybody that Forbes is a crook for 20 years, and everybody says to me, 'You just think the only good maps are the ones you have,'" Graham Arader told *The New York Times*. "I'm not a bag lady walking down Madison Avenue with a grocery cart filled with bottles. I'm the oracle that was ignored."

On October 26, 2005, the US Attorney's Office faxed a list of maps to the Boston Police that Smiley had admitted taking from the BPL. When Grim saw it, his heart sank. Despite the sixty or so maps that the library's review had identified, the FBI list included only twenty-seven. Many of them were familiar—the two maps from de Jode's *Speculum Orbis Terrae*, the three Dudley charts, four of the seven Norman charts. But there were some noticeable—and devastating—omissions. The Champlain maps were absent, as were the maps from de Bry and Purchas. And some books, including the Jefferys atlas and the copies of *The American Pilot*, were missing many more maps than Smiley admitted stealing.

On the other hand, Smiley identified maps the libraries didn't even know they were missing. One from the BPL he listed only as a portolan chart of the Atlantic from 1670. Grim was confused. Most portolan charts dated from centuries earlier and covered only small areas of the Mediterranean. Seeing that Smiley said he'd sold it to Arkway, Grim scanned the dealer's catalogs, immediately seeing a map of the Atlantic on the cover of his catalog from 2003. It was crisscrossed with rhumb lines emanating from a central wind rose, just like a portolan chart. The catalog identified it as a "legendary sea chart on vellum" printed by Hendrick Doncker in 1657, with an asking price of $115,000.

Thinking this might be the "portolan chart," Grim went searching for any record that the library might have once had the map in its collection. Neither the card catalog nor the shelf list kept in the back room contained any mention of the map. Finally, he dug up a copy of the shelf list on microfiche and found a card listing "Doncker, H. West-Indische paskaert" from 1655. Returning to Smiley's call slips, he found a single slip dated September 13, 2003, for the range of maps including the chart—it must have been then that Smiley took it.

The FBI also told Grim that there was one map of the Chesapeake they were not be able to recover—since the BPL was missing several maps of that region, Grim had no idea which one they were talking about. In a private e-mail to Tony Campbell, he expressed his frustration. "Throughout this whole process, we have gotten very sketchy information from the FBI," he wrote.

WHILE MOST OF THE LIBRARIES were able to check their holdings fairly quickly, the Sterling Memorial Library had no records at all of what Smiley had examined there. Over the years, most of the map department's rarest atlases had been shifted to the Beinecke—along with the funds to support them. Up until 2001, the department had only three employees—a curator, an assistant, and a part-time cataloger. As a result, only a quarter of its eleven thousand rare maps had been put into an electronic catalog. When news broke of Smiley's arrest, all the Sterling had was the list of maps Margit Kaye had put together from Smiley's website. In the months that followed, her boss, Fred Musto, continued to stall on conducting a more thorough inventory. Finally, the university transferred him to another department and promoted one of the assistants in the map room, Abe Parrish, to acting curator.

Parrish had been hired in 2001 as a geographic information systems specialist, dealing with digital rather than paper maps. But prior to this position, he'd spent time in the army as an intelligence analyst and had experience in sifting through complex information. The university also brought in Bill Reese to help with the investigation. They started by going through Musto's office, which they found stuffed with maps stacked on shelves and file cabinets. More disturbing, they found thirty card catalog cards in his desk drawer for maps that appeared to be missing. Had Musto been covering up missing maps? Or something worse? They alerted the administration of their finds. That November, the library fired Fred Musto, citing "gross mismanagement," though he was never officially charged with any wrongdoing.

Reese started the inventory by listing one hundred maps that Smiley was likely to steal based on his specialty of the early mapping of North America. It was then up to Margit Kaye, who knew the collection better than anyone else, to determine whether the library had ever had them. Knowing how unreliable the current card catalog was, she turned to the microfiche copy of the catalog from 1978 to check for the maps. And there was another record as well—a box of cards Vietor had kept of all the maps he had acquired for the collection until his retirement in 1978, organized by year. They remained locked in a cage on the seventh floor, organized chronologically by date purchased. Going through them one by one looking for the maps Reese specified, the Sterling's staff was able to identify some fifty maps missing from the collection by August. There was only one way to truly determine everything that was missing, however—by examining all of the eleven thousand rare maps in the collection and comparing them to the record.

To do the thorough inventory, the entire map department shut down, and for three months, Parrish, Kaye, Reese, and a team of a dozen other employees went through the collection map by map. Much of the work fell on Kaye, who stayed late each night comparing the contents of folders to printed microfiche cards. Whenever someone found a map missing, it was added to a master list. By the time the inventory was complete in mid-February, the initial list had grown to eighty-nine maps in all. Some seemed unlikely targets for Smiley—including a half-dozen nineteenth-century maps of Japan—but most were by English and American mapmakers of the seventeenth and eighteenth centuries, exactly the kind of maps Smiley traded in.

When the FBI sent the Sterling its list of the maps Smiley admitted taking, however, it included only eleven. In all, the library had found eight times as many maps missing from its collection. The only problem was that it had no proof Smiley had taken them—and time was quickly running out to come up with it.

BY THE SPRING OF 2006, Kelleher was eager to wrap up his case. After a year of back-and-forth with the libraries, he was ready to put together a definitive list of maps Smiley had stolen. Federal judge Janet Bond Arterton set a judgment date for June 22, just over a year from the day after Smiley had been arrested. Smiley flew from the Vineyard to Providence, where Statt picked him up at the airport and drove him to New Haven. Smiley took the elevator up to the sixth floor and entered the courtroom at three P.M., wearing his favorite olive jacket over a blue oxford shirt and patterned navy-blue tie.

Assistant US Attorney Kit Schmeisser stood up to announce that Smiley was ready to make a plea.

"All right, Mr. Smiley, do you understand what is meant by a waiver of indictment?" Arterton asked.

"I do," said Smiley. This time, he answered correctly when asked his age—now fifty—and responded to a series of questions firmly, almost jauntily.

Schmeisser added that in addition to waiving his right to trial, Smiley had also agreed to waive the statute of limitations on his crimes—so if any additional maps were to surface, even years later, he could be charged all over again. He then announced the plea agreement. Smiley would plead guilty to "theft of major artwork," admitting to stealing ninety-seven maps—only eighteen of which the government would have otherwise been able to prove. By law, only those eighteen maps could be considered in determining his sentence, which the prosecutor recommended reducing for cooperation to a minimum of four years, nine months and a maximum of six years.

The government formally charged him with stealing only one map, however—the Gerard de Jode map of the world. By law, that was the only map for which he was required to pay restitution, and since it had been recovered the day of his arrest, that meant he didn't owe any money. Schmeisser announced, however, that Smiley had agreed to pay back the libraries and dealers for all the maps he admitted stealing, which authorities valued at more than $3 million.

Finally, the judge asked, "Then would you please tell me in your own words what it is that you did that shows you are, in fact, guilty?"

"Yes, Your Honor. On June 8, 2005, while conducting legitimate research at the Beinecke Library at Yale University, I did willingly and knowingly remove five printed maps belonging to Yale University and conceal them in my briefcase with the intention of removing them from the library," Smiley said. "I very much regret my actions, and apologize to the Court and all people and institutions who were harmed by my conduct."

Schmeisser laid out the evidence the government had to prove this crime—the X-Acto knife blade on the floor, the videotape, the policeman who found the maps on his person. "There would also be potential testimony of experts on rare books that would reflect that there were wormholes in that particular map," continued Schmeisser, "that would line up with wormholes that existed in the rare book."

The judge stopped him. "That's an interesting piece of forensic evidence, isn't it?" she asked to laughter from the gallery. She turned to Reeve. "Is there anything you disagree with?"

"Yes, Your Honor," answered Smiley's lawyer. "None of these maps were cut out of any books." He went on, "The X-Acto knife fell from his pocket, but it was not involved in these or, to my knowledge, any of these maps."

"No disagreement on the map with the wormholes?" the judge asked.

"None, Your Honor," conceded Reeve. "The worms are very distinctive wormholes, I agree."

Finally, Arterton got around to the point of the hearing. The court clerk read out the charge again, asking, "What is your plea?"

Smiley didn't hestitate. "Guilty," he said.

AS SMILEY walked out of the courthouse and into a throng of reporters, a man across the street on New Haven Green shouted at him, "Guilty! Guilty!" But his ordeal wasn't over. After his appearance in federal court, he was required to walk two blocks down the street to plead again in state court, arriving at four forty-five in the afternoon. There the judge, Richard Damiani, ordered the clerk to read the three charges for the other maps he'd stolen from the Beinecke. "Guilty," Smiley said three more times. In all, those crimes held a maximum of sixty years in prison, said the judge, before adding that the state had agreed with the federal government to limit the sentence to five or less—to run concurrently with the federal sentence. Sentencing was scheduled for late September.

As Smiley headed home with his friends, his lawyer, Dick Reeve, lingered outside the courtroom to finally comment about Smiley's crimes. "We're all a lot of mixed bags, all of us," he said. "We have a tremendous capacity to hurt the people we love the most and hurt the institutions we care about the most." He paused. "He feels terrible about that."

Not everyone was willing to let Smiley off that easily, however. "I think this is just the tip of the iceberg," an agitated Graham Arader told the *Hartford Courant.* "He turned up much more stuff than this that was *out-of-this-world!*" Certainly not all the questions about Smiley's crimes had been answered, including the question of when he began his theft. In initial interviews with the FBI, Smiley said he started stealing around 1998, which would have been around the time he was organizing the Slaughter Collection for the NYPL. But in later court filings, he amended that date to 2002, or around the time Margit Kaye first noticed the maps missing at the Sterling—a difference of four years.

The libraries commended the job done by the FBI and US Attorney's Office in recovering as many maps as they did. In private, however, they agreed with Arader that Smiley had not been as forthcoming as he could have been. All of the institutions were missing more maps than Smiley had admitted, including copies of the same maps he'd admitted stealing from other libraries. One of them was about to make those doubts public.

Chapter 12

MAP QUEST

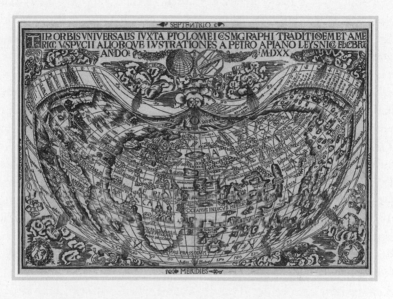

FIGURE 17 PETER APIAN. "TIPUS ORBIS UNIVERSALIS
IUXTA PTOLOMEI COSMOGRAPHI TRADITIONEM ET AMERICA
VESPUCCI." ANTWERP, 1520.

2006

KING'S CROSS STATION sits at the geographical heart of London, right
in the center of Harry Beck's iconic London Underground map. Above-
ground, Euston Road bustles with an endless clot of black cabs and red
double-decker buses that pass by the modest home of the British Library.
Set back from the road, the library is almost buried in the buildings
around it, a four-story pile of brick and glass built in 1998 when it was
spun off from the British Museum.

Inside, however, it's hard not to be impressed by the central tower of glass holding the once-private library owned by King George III. Like a grander version of the Beinecke's aquarium of books, the tower soars upward with forty feet of leather- and vellum-bound volumes. Among them are Shakespeare's plays—some in the original quarto versions that preceded the folios—a first edition of *The Canterbury Tales*, and dozens of medieval illuminated manuscripts. It's fitting that this tower of knowledge should sit at the center of the library at the center of the city that was once the economic, political, and cartographic center of the world. But the tower isn't just a monument to the past. Every so often, a case of shelves will disappear from the window as a librarian rolls it out to retrieve a volume to bring to a reader.

I was met at the base of the tower by map department head Peter Barber, a short man with a hawkish nose and wisps of white hair who is prone to Britishisms like "rather curious." He led me three flights up a stone spiral staircase to an office crammed with papers and books, including his own—*The Map Book*, one of the most popular general books about cartography. Barber remembered the day he first met Forbes Smiley: June 1, 2004. Map dealer Philip Burden brought him in for a meeting. As he wrote in his diary that night, Barber was puzzled by Smiley, who stood awkward and remote, seemingly uncomfortable to be there. His strange passivity made him stick in Barber's mind more than if he'd been friendly and open.

The next time he heard Smiley's name was a year later, on May 27, 2005—less than two weeks before Smiley was arrested at the Beinecke. That day, a patron requested a digital image of William Alexander's 1624 map of New Scotland from a small blue book titled *An Encouragement to Colonies*. When the photographer went to shoot the image, however, he discovered the map was missing. Barber went back over everyone who had requested the book, and the last one stood out: Forbes Smiley, who had looked at the book on June 5, 2004, four days after their awkward meeting.

"I said 'Aha,'" remembered Barber. "Well, this would sort of make things understandable." Going back over the rest of the books Smiley requested, he discovered two other missing maps—a 1578 world map by George Best and the 1520 world map by Peter Apian from the volume owned by the Archbishop of Canterbury (Figure 17). Barber contacted Scotland Yard, which had just begun its investigation when news of

Smiley's arrest crossed the Atlantic. A few months later, Kelleher flew to England to pay a visit to the library, asking the staff to determine if any more maps were missing from volumes Smiley had used. That fall, it discovered one more—another Alexander map of New Scotland, this one missing from a copy of *Purchas His Pilgrimes*. The book had once been a part of the library of the British East India Company—in fact, it had been given to the company by Samuel Purchas himself and was instrumental in the corporation's early voyages of colonization and trade.

The library shared all the information with Kelleher. When the plea bargain came out in June 2006, however, Barber was surprised to find that Smiley had admitted taking only one of the four maps the library had accused him of taking—the Apian map. The head of the library's collections, Clive Field, sent a stern letter to the FBI in protest, writing, "We continue to entertain serious doubts about the completeness of the investigation and the extent of Mr. Smiley's co-operation with the authorities."

On its own, the library reached out to Burden, who had purchased an Alexander map from Smiley, and to Maine collector Harold Osher, who had bought a Best world map. But the margins on both maps had been trimmed down, and the library couldn't match them up with the ripped edges in the book. The only way the library could prove which maps were theirs, it seemed, was to put more pressure on Smiley to admit more thefts.

After Smiley's plea, Barber contacted all the libraries, urging a more forceful approach. "Are your institutions minded to make common cause with the BL over this so as to maximize all of our chances of success?" he asked. The library's former head, Tony Campbell, was even more insistent. In a posting on his MapHist Listserv, he described the FBI's list of admitted maps as "cartographically semi-literate" and expressed shock that the bureau should take the word of Smiley, "a regular, and presumably accomplished liar," over that of the libraries. Barber's and Campbell's entreaties, however, met with a resounding silence from the other curators. If the British Library was going to press its case in the United States, it would need to find someone across the Atlantic to represent it.

BOB GOLDMAN THINKS a lot about Theodore Roosevelt. He's collected more than two hundred books about the former president, quotes him often, and even looks like a skinny T.R. himself. An attorney working in a small town north of Philadelphia, he sports small oval glasses and a thick droopy mustache that lends him a serious expression even when he smiles. When I met with him, he led me into an office in a brick town house dating to the 1870s. His own house was built in the 1700s. "I told the British that, and they laughed at me," he said. "To them, that's a new house."

British Library staff contacted him in the summer of 2006, telling him about the disappointing plea bargain in the Smiley case and their concerns that Smiley had been less than forthcoming. A former prosecutor himself, Goldman knew only too well the importance of applying pressure to bring cases to a swift conclusion. As he listened to Clive Field talk, it sounded to him like the government had moved too quickly to reach an agreement with Smiley without pushing him hard enough on the missing maps.

Goldman had worked in the US Attorney's Office for nineteen years, spending much of that time tracking down and prosecuting thieves looting and defacing cultural artifacts. He doggedly pursued his task, personally helping convict thirty-five smugglers and dealers, and recovering more than $150 million worth of art and heirlooms, including Geronimo's war bonnet, an original copy of the Bill of Rights, and, particularly sweet to him, a .38-caliber revolver Theodore Roosevelt carried during the charge of the Rough Riders at San Juan Hill.

In 1996, Goldman was the first prosecutor to use the newly created Theft of Major Artwork statute, leading to the prosecution of a janitor at the Historical Society of Pennsylvania who stole, among other artifacts, a ceremonial sword presented to General George Meade after the battle of Gettysburg. In that case, he succeeded in doubling the janitor's sentence to four years. Goldman's particular specialty was in writing indictments that captured the sweep of history and showed the importance of these artifacts to the larger story of civilization. For the case involving Meade's sword, he quoted prominent historians and Roosevelt himself to bring alive the sword's connection to some of our country's most heroic deeds.

He left the US Attorney's Office to start a private practice devoted to solving art crimes in 2006, the same year the British Library contacted him. If they were going to be successful, Goldman told Field and

Barber, they'd need to act fast. "Your best shot on getting a defendant to fess up and disclose and cooperate is prior to sentencing," he later told me. "Once a person is sentenced there is little incentive to come clean." Since Smiley's sentencing was scheduled for September, they had little time to come up with a strategy.

It would be a two-pronged approach, they finally agreed. They'd urge federal prosecutors to take a stronger hand with Smiley, threatening him with serious jail time if he didn't confess to taking more maps. At the same time, they'd entreat the other libraries to join them in a civil suit, in which they could take Smiley's deposition under oath, subpoena dealers and collectors who had bought from him, and dig into his client base to track down more maps. "Working together, we might get the government to take a stronger stance with Smiley and develop evidence on where the other maps might be," Goldman said.

THE BRITISH LIBRARY wasn't alone in suspecting Smiley of taking more maps than he admitted taking. Soon after the verdict, Yale's Sterling Memorial Library went public with its list of eighty-nine maps missing from its inventory, most of which Smiley had not admitted taking. Many were maps Margit Kaye had seen on Smiley's website back in 2002, including the Pelham map of Boston. There were others too. On his site, Smiley had advertised a map of the District of Columbia by Andrew Ellicott for $32,000. It was the same rare diamond-shaped map that Smiley had once found for Larry Slaughter, showing the district's original topography. Smiley mentioned the fact on his website, noting "the last copy that we are aware of was purchased by us on behalf of Mr. Lawrence Slaughter during the Howard Welsh Sale at Sotheby's New York, in 1991." Smiley sold the map to Harry Newman, who listed it on the cover of his map catalog that fall, asking $40,000. Despite such circumstantial evidence, however, Kaye had nothing to prove that the map was the same one that was missing from Yale.

In the same catalog, Newman listed an even rarer map—a 1676 map of New England by Robert Morden and William Berry drawn from the same survey John Seller had used in his map of the region. "Of great rarity, the map is known in only three other examples, one on vellum,"

Smiley wrote on his site. "This appears to be the only copy in private hands." Newman copied that language verbatim for his catalog, with one correction, writing, "Of great rarity, his map is known in only *four* other examples, one of which is printed on vellum. . . . This impression appears to be the only copy in private hands" (emphasis added). As Newman could determine from carto-bibliographies, two copies were held at Brown, one at Osher Map Library, and one at the Sterling. If Smiley left that last library out of his calculations, it may be because he knew the Sterling no longer had its copy.

In addition to the maps in Newman's catalogs, Kaye found more than a half-dozen copies of its missing maps in Arkway's catalogs, including De L'Isle's 1718 map of Lousiane; a 1780 map of the Northeast by John Thornton and his apprentices Robert Morden and Philip Lea; and a map by William Faden of the Battle of Bunker Hill. Again, there was no evidence that any of these maps had come from Yale or even from Smiley, though all of them were rare.

No matter what further suspicions the map department's curators may have had about Smiley, Yale University's official line was that the FBI had done everything it could do to identify the stolen maps. Smiley's lawyer, Dick Reeve, readily agreed. "It's really unfortunate that Yale has lost or misplaced or had stolen so many maps," he told the press. "I don't believe any of those maps are connected to Forbes Smiley." Not all of the libraries were so publicly confident, however. Shortly after Yale released its list, Harvard released its own list of thirteen missing maps—only eight of which Smiley had admitted taking. Harvard didn't go so far as to accuse Smiley of taking the maps, but they also didn't rule it out. "We have some missing maps, and we know that he looked at them, so that's very interesting to us," said a spokesperson.

The BPL was more explicit. "I think all of the affected institutions believe he took other maps," BPL's president, Bernard Margolis, bluntly told *The Boston Globe.* In all, curator Ron Grim had identified thirty-five maps he suspected Smiley of taking beyond those he had admitted. Nine of them had particularly troubling chronologies. Smiley examined de Bry's *Voyages* on January 28, 2003, and less than a month later he sold Le Moyne's map of Florida to Philip Burden. He looked at the book again in September 2004, and just ten days later, he sold a copy of John White's map of Virginia to an unidentified buyer. He examined Boston's copy of Seller's *Atlas Maritimus* in May 2004, and six days later, he sold a map by Seller of the West Indies to Arkway. And three days after he examined Herman Moll's *The World Described*, he sold a copy of Moll's influential map of the Colonies to Arkway.

As the libraries each in turn published their lists, many of them listed the same maps—despite Smiley never admitting to stealing the same map twice. Harvard and Yale were both missing Hernán Cortés's map of Tenochtitlán, for example, while Boston and Harvard were both missing Samuel de Champlain's map of New France. (New York, which hadn't yet released its list, was missing both.) In addition to suspecting that he'd stolen more maps, many of the libraries questioned whether all the recovered maps had gone back to the right places.

IN ORDER TO FIND OUT, the curators from all the affected libraries assembled at ten thirty in the morning on August 7, 2006, at the office of Yale's lawyer in New Haven. They walked the several blocks to the FBI headquarters, which occupied a block by itself near the highway. There they met Steve Kelleher—many of them for the first time in person. As he led them into a large conference room with several tables, Harvard map collection curator David Cobb tried to contain his excitement.

The maps from Harvard had been stolen from the Houghton Library, not the map collection, but Cobb had been called down to help identify—and defend, if necessary—Harvard's maps. In particular, he hoped that he might be able to identify the map by Samuel de Champlain of New France, one of the most valuable of all the maps Smiley had stolen from Harvard. The copy that had been recovered, however, had been attributed to the New York Public Library. All the curators tried to appear calm—they didn't want to seem like they were gunning for one another's maps.

Kelleher and several other agents emerged with a few large cardboard boxes wrapped in packing tape. Just as Cobb was thinking that there was no way they would be keeping the maps in there, Kelleher brandished a large folding tactical knife and sliced open the first package to the collective intake of breath of all the librarians in the room. He began to lift individual maps out of the package and put them in piles on the table as the stunned librarians looked on. Each group took a selection of maps to a table and pored over them, comparing them to photographs and trying to fit them into books they'd brought with them.

Almost immediately, Cobb saw that the Champlain map's folds were all wrong for the way the map fit into Harvard's book. He tried to hide his disappointment, even as Harvard was able to pick up another map of New France by French missionary Claude Dablon that had been attributed to Yale. He watched anxiously as other curators examined maps that had been attributed to Harvard. None of them were able to make a match with any of Harvard's maps with the evidence they'd brought. Boston, however, was able to claim from the NYPL the map of Charleston from Des Barres's *Atlantic Neptune*, when Grim identified a stain in the upper right corner that matched a similar stain on the next page of the atlas in Boston. In return, New York was able to claim from the BPL a map of New York by John Montresor from Jefferys's atlas.

Goldman was unable to identify any of the British Library's other three missing maps from the boxes. The bigger disappointment for Goldman came, however, when the curators headed back to Yale for a working buffet lunch to craft their "victim impact statements" to share with the judge. Goldman urged them to go further by pursing a civil lawsuit against Smiley that would allow them to dig into Smiley's records and put him on the stand to testify under oath. None of the other libraries were willing to go along. It seemed too risky to expose themselves in court and open themselves up to cross-examination by Smiley's lawyers about their security procedures and the extent of their losses. Such a public display could alienate donors, who relied upon institutions to safeguard their generous gifts. One by one, they told Goldman that they wouldn't be participating.

GOLDMAN FAILED IN his efforts to urge the prosecutors to take a tougher stance as well. When he contacted Schmeisser, he was even rebuffed in his requests for copies of Smiley's business records so the library could pursue its own investigations. Unable to get the government or the other libraries to go along, he decided along with Field and Barber that the British Library would have to go it alone, making its own case in criminal court for a harsher sentence.

Congress had given victims the right to argue separately from the government only in 2004, and that right had almost never been exercised. On September 21, 2006, a week before Smiley was scheduled for sentencing, the British Library filed its own sentencing memorandum with the court. With a former prosecutor's zeal, Goldman argued that Smiley had taken four maps, not one, and that the government had grossly underestimated the seriousness of Smiley's crimes.

"The maps stolen by Smiley created the dreams of the explorer, merchant and powerful," he wrote. "They charted the paths of national expansion and empire building. They marked the rise of British dominance, the origins of a new nation and the demise of a native population. The maps drew the lines between where knowledge ended and imagination began. They represented man's timeless drive to explore the unknown and bring definition to the void." Because of the incalculable loss to history, Goldman argued, Smiley's offenses warranted an upward departure from the guidelines that would add years to the sentence—both as a punishment and as an example to others.

He took the Apian world map as an example, detailing how the Archbishop of Canterbury Thomas Cranmer had married Henry VIII to Anne Boleyn in 1533, only to later be burned at the stake for heresy. "The volume and map remained intact surviving catastrophic events: the execution of its owner and the disbursement of his property; Civil War and the ascendance of Oliver Cromwell; royal intrigue; times of economic depression; and the Nazi bombing of London. The volume remained intact until visited by Smiley."

Each of the maps Smiley stole, he argued, had similarly improbable stories of survival over the centuries. "Like a drop of oil on a still pond," he wrote, "the number of his victims spreads with time. Smiley's victims include students, scholars, academics, the general public, and individuals yet to be born who will not have the opportunity to sit at a desk, open a leather-bound volume and see the world as Archbishop Cranmer and others saw it in the 16th century."

Smiley's lawyer, Dick Reeve, shot back, lambasting the British Library for spreading false rumors about how many maps Smiley had stolen. He should be sentenced on "the basis of what he has in fact done, including his cooperation, and not on the basis of what some speculate he *might* have done," he wrote. After all, what incentive did Smiley have to hold back? If it hadn't have been for his cooperation, the libraries would have gotten back only the eighteen maps the government was able to prove Smiley took, not the close to one hundred that he had admitted to stealing.

"The British Library's rhetoric neglects an important and fundamental truth," he continued. "The Apian World Map will soon be back in its collection. All 'students, scholars, academics, the general public, and individuals yet to be born' will then be able to utilize the map." He went on to argue that rather than harming the libraries, Smiley may have inadvertently helped them. "If the institutions now do what is needed to improve overall security, it is possible that the positive side effects of this tragic case will benefit future generations of scholars and explorers 'like a drop of oil on a still pond.'"

Most important, he wrote, the call for an upward departure, was completely unwarranted, since changes to the sentencing guidelines after the Spiegelman case had already taken into account the cultural harm done through thefts of historical items. "To the degree that the sentence here is a potential deterrent to others, no sane person would look at all the ramifications of this proposed sentence and conclude that stealing maps should be the next activity to try," Reeve wrote.

The next day, the government submitted its own memo, siding with Reeve in praising Smiley's decision to cooperate with authorities. In fact, prosecutors wrote in an accompanying motion, his extraordinary cooperation actually warranted a downward departure to reduce Smiley's sentence even below the four-and-a-half-year minimum they had previously urged.

FORBES SMILEY ARRIVED for sentencing at the federal courthouse in New Haven on the morning of September 27, 2006, looking sharp in a dark suit and patterned green tie (Figure P). He had undergone back surgery in Boston a few days earlier and was able to stand up straight without pain for the first time in years. Smiley took a seat at the defense table with his attorney, Dick Reeve, while agent Steve Kelleher and US attorneys Kit Schmeisser and Kevin O'Connor took seats at the prosecution table.

Behind them in the front row sat Smiley's friends Paul Statt, Scott Slater, and Bennett Fischer, veterans of so many Sebec Boys' Weekends.

The rest of the courtroom was taken up with media and representatives of all six libraries Smiley had harmed. Only Alice Hudson was absent—though she had planned to go until the last minute, in the end she found herself too upset to attend.

Calling the hearing to order, Judge Arterton explained how the sentencing would work. Under the guidelines, a charge of art theft for the dollar value of the maps the government could prove carried a level 22. Add 2 points for stealing from a museum, 2 more for stealing "cultural property," and 2 more for stealing for "pecuniary gain," and that brought the total to 28. On the other hand, the assistance Smiley had provided knocked the level down by 3 points to 25. That meant a minimum sentence of four years, nine months, and a maximum of five years, eleven months. Even though that range was agreed upon by both sides, the British Library was still arguing for an upward departure to as much as eight years, while the US attorney was arguing for a downward departure to as little as three years. It was Arterton's job to decide where within that range the sentence should fall.

One by one, the representatives from the libraries stood up to detail the impact of the thefts. First Beinecke head Frank Turner spoke for several minutes about the damage Smiley had done to Yale's libraries, the "tens of thousands of dollars" the university would have to spend on new security systems, and the "negative impact on the lives, morale, and self-esteem" to staff. David Ferriero, head of the research libraries at New York Public Library, took up a similar theme. "I'm here today to talk about the actions of a thief, a thief who assaulted history, betrayed personal trust, and caused irreparable loss of treasures whose value to future scholarship will never now be known," he said.

Boston Public Library president Bernie Margolis took a lighter tack, saying, "I could of course invoke the old library line and urge you to throw the book at him."

"It would be an atlas in this case," the judge deadpanned.

"It would be a big one," agreed Margolis, before turning serious. "It is my clear opinion, and I believe there is no lack of evidence to suggest, that Mr. Smiley may have stolen additional maps," he said. "I hope that the Court will see it appropriate to impose restrictions so that he is never in a place to profit in any manner, shape, or form from the sale of these kinds of maps." Next, the British Library's Clive Field reiterated the points that Goldman had made in his sentencing memo, stressing the open question of what additional maps Smiley may have stolen. "Mr. Smiley will doubtless not be the last thief of cultural property," he told the judge. A strong sentence "would serve as a powerful deterrent and firm evidence that the free world will not tolerate such assaults on our global cultural patrimony."

The last speaker was Bob Karrow of the Newberry Library, which had suffered the least from Smiley's crimes. It was missing only two maps. Karrow's testimony, however, was arguably the most powerful. "Now we arrive on the day of reckoning," he said, addressing Judge Arterton. "A day on which you, your Honor, must decide on the penalty Mr. Smiley owes society. And what, after all, are Mr. Smiley's crimes? He did no physical harm to anyone. He stole some elaborately printed sheets of paper from old books and sold them for profit to willing buyers. Imprisonment will protect society from Mr. Smiley, but I'm not sure that he's much of a threat anymore.

"So what is the point of this hearing today and of your decision? It seems to me the point is that Mr. Smiley, through his systemic plundering of libraries, stealing some 100 maps over the course of eight years, has managed to transcend himself. He has become—actually he has made himself—a symbol, a symbol of the vulnerability of libraries, a symbol of the fragility of the public trust that is required for the operation of our cultural institutions, a symbol of the commodification of historical artifacts, a symbol of the erosion of civility, and his status as a symbol must be weighed in his sentence.

"Research libraries are not like other businesses. At the end of our business day we cannot put a value on the day's acquisitions or transactions, nor do we even try to do so, at least in monetary terms. As nonprofits, we use a different calculus. We count readers served, books, maps, and manuscripts paged, the numbers of rare documents of all kinds added to our collections and made available to our public.

"This is the kind of business that Mr. Smiley chose to ransack for his personal gain. In doing so, he not only robbed his and our contemporaries of the ability to study these documents, he also robbed all those who will come after us. If Mr. Smiley never steals again, his fame and the monetary value of the objects he pillaged almost guarantee that he will have imitators, and some of them will learn from his mistakes and outwit us again. We have taken extraordinary precautions to guard our capital, and we will take others in the future. That is all we can do, for we must continue to make these materials available, that is our business.

"Respectfully, I request that you, Your Honor, craft a sentence that will serve to tell Mr. Smiley's successors that the stakes in this game of cultural hijacking have been raised."

OVER THE NEXT FEW MINUTES, Reeve tried to undo the damage, starting by attacking the libraries' contention that Smiley hadn't admitted everything. "It does disturb me again and again," he said, "they still come before the Court and say, do you know, Judge, you ought to take into account other thefts. It's wrong, it's inappropriate, and I know that it won't happen."

There was no question that Smiley had done indelible damage to cultural heritage, he continued, but he had also done everything he could to undo that damage. "For institutions to come into the courtroom and say 'Impose the maximum sentence on Forbes Smiley' seems to me, with all respect to the institutions and the emotions and difficulties they are having, not in their interest," Reeve continued. The British Library's Clive Field himself admitted that Smiley wouldn't be the last thief the libraries would see. What kind of message would it send if the judge didn't reward cooperation? "The message that is sent is it doesn't matter what you do, it's just so bad, we're just going to sentence you, we are not going to take into account your cooperation, the libraries won't get their materials back, the government won't be assisted in their investigation, and I don't think that anyone, any of the institutional representatives here or elsewhere would say that that's the result they want."

Next, it was Smiley's turn to speak. Standing up at the podium, he cleared his throat and took a deep breath before talking. "Your honor, I have hurt many people," he began. "I stole very valuable research materials from institutions that made it their business to provide those materials to the public for valuable research. I am deeply ashamed of having done that. It was wrong. I have also caused great financial loss both within the institutions and to the dealers. I am very anxious to meet my obligations and pay back the money that those institutions and dealers both need and deserve.

"Within that group of institutions and dealers, there are individuals with whom I've worked closely for many years and whom I once called friends. I cannot imagine the pain and anger that I have made them suffer, the betrayal of trust, not only of our professional relationships, but of our friendship. I am very, very deeply sorry and distressed that I allowed myself to get into a place of such selfishness that I was able to put their well-being at risk. I am deeply sorry."

Finally, it was time for the judge to hand down the sentence. She started with the maps themselves, which the FBI agents had delivered to her before the hearing. She and her staff had spent several hours looking through them, and they now sat behind her in three cardboard cartons. "I wanted firsthand to have that experience, and have therefore, had the privilege of handling these maps of such antiquity," she said, before coming to the point of the hearing. "The enormity of the theft and the thievery is hardly capable of being [overstated]," she said. "In contrast, the enormity of the assistance of the repatriation, if you will, of these cultural heritage resources back to where they belong stands in counterpoise." The case contained many contradictions, she continued. Here was a man who loved maps and history and yet "stole and defaced or compromised and lost historic treasures." Here was someone who had been generous to a fault with friends but "betrayed those who trusted him."

Despite the seriousness of that betrayal, however, she said it was important to honor his cooperation. "To use the product of Mr. Smiley's cooperation and assistance, to then punish him in excess of what he would have been punished were he to have remained silent, seems counterproductive, to say nothing of patently unfair," she said. The justice system had a dual message to send: "If you steal humankind's treasures, you will go to prison, but if you help recover them, that will be taken into account and weighed in the balance."

Because of all that, said the judge, she was denying the British Library's request for an upward departure and granting the prosecution's request for a downward departure. His sentence, she announced, would be forty-two months—three and a half years. She noted a certain poetic justice in the time, which was "approximately the length of time that you report having been engaged in the stealing of these artifacts." Furthermore, he would be required to pay back $1,926,160 in restitution—or whatever final amount prosecutors determined when they sorted out all the recovered maps.

At that, Schmeisser asked that Smiley be allowed to remain free for several months so they could continue to rely on his cooperation to resolve final questions about where maps belonged. The judge agreed, setting Thursday, January 4, 2007, as the date for him to report to prison at the satellite camp at Fort Devens, in Massachusetts, a minimum-security medical facility. Smiley smiled with relief as the judge announced the sentence. After court adjourned, he hugged his three friends who had accompanied him. As he left the courtroom, Reeve spoke with reporters, praising the fairness of the sentence. After everyone else had left, Steve Kelleher and several other FBI agents emerged, carrying the three cardboard boxes full of maps. They placed them in the backseat of a black Pontiac Bonneville sedan and drove away.

Chapter 13

TERRA INCOGNITA

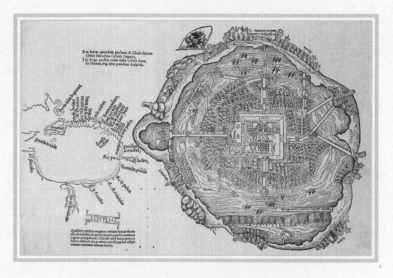

FIGURE 18 HERNÁN CORTÉS. "UNTITLED"
(MAP OF TENOCHTITLÁN AND THE GULF OF MEXICO).
NUREMBURG, 1524.

2007–2013

THE RESPONSE TO Arteron's sentence was swift and almost uniformly critical. "Obviously we are disappointed in the leniency of the sentence, which amounts to about 12 days' imprisonment for every map that he has stolen," Clive Field told the press. "It doesn't send any message of deterrence at all," said Bill Reese, speaking to the *Hartford Courant.* An editoral in the same paper went much further, criticizing the leniency shown Smiley for cooperating: "Should a judge forgive a car thief because he returned the vehicle? Should a mass murderer get a lighter sentence because he led police to more bodies?"

Librarians and newspaper editors weren't the only ones who disapproved. A few weeks after his federal sentencing hearing, Smiley appeared at a near-empty courtroom at New Haven Superior Court to face the state charges for his crimes. Unlike federal prosecutors, State's Attorney Mike Dearington wasn't impressed with Smiley's contrition. "I think he really is just a crook and a thief," he said in court.

Judge Richard Damiani seemed to agree, criticizing the length of the federal sentence. "I have young people coming in here who rob convenience stores at knife point and gun point. I'm giving them four or five years," he said from the bench. "But here I've got a man who stole two million dollars and now he gets three and a half." But he'd already agreed to a maximum state sentence of five years—with eligibility for parole after two and a half. Since that sentence would run concurrently with the federal sentence, that most likely meant no additional jail time.

In the aftermath of the sentence, the dealers fared the worst. The recovered maps went back to the libraries, and the dealers paid back their clients for selling them stolen property. Smiley was responsible for paying back the dealers. In the restitution order delivered by the court, he owed $263,520 to Philip Burden, $425,740 to Harry and Robert Newman at the Old Print Shop, and $886,400 to Paul Cohen and Henry Taliaferro, who had assumed Arkway's company. (Technically, Cohen and Taliaferro never merged with Arkway and never took on Arkway's debt, which accounted for the lion's share of what Smiley owed the two firms. For convenience, however, prosecutors lumped the two companies together in the restitution order.) A handful of collectors to whom Smiley had sold directly were also on the hook, including Bob Gordon, who was owed $115,000 for maps including the Dudley chart of the Chesapeake, and Harold Osher, who was owed $69,500 for the John Seller map of New England.

To make their payments, the Newmans were forced to sell a valuable painting they had put aside for a "rainy day." Paul Cohen struggled to keep his new business afloat. "To have that kind of loss early in our career, you are lucky to still be talking to me," he said. Smiley's assets covered a fraction of the money he owed the dealers. Most of his money had disappeared—into plane tickets, construction costs on the Vineyard, payroll up in Maine. After the sentence, Smiley sold his Sebec farmhouse and shops for a combined $125,000. He kept the Vineyard home, however. By Massachusetts law, the government is forbidden from seizing a person's home if it is a primary residence, so while the government could put a lien on Smiley's half of the property (his wife owned the other half), it could not take it outright.

This incensed Philip Burden, whom I met at the Miami map fair. "Let me get this straight: Someone steals millions of dollars and he gets to keep his house?" he asked with an agitated public school accent. "The British system would have nailed him to the wall." Even more frustrating to the dealers, the restitution order was written so creditors would receive what money Smiley did pay in equal shares, rather than shares proportional to how much they'd lost." The proper way to do it would be to divide it up as a percentage," Burden said. "This way the person owed the least gets paid off first."

EVEN AS THE DEALERS struggled to pay their debts, the libraries fought to recover as many of their maps as they could—both those Smiley had admitted stealing and those he hadn't. Last among the libraries, the NYPL finally released its list of missing maps after sentencing. Of the sixty listed, Smiley had admitted taking only thirty-four of them. Even those would not all be coming back. The FBI told Alice Hudson that despite their best efforts, they'd never be able to recover three of New York's maps, including John Seller's "Map of East and West New Jarsey," the one she'd written about in the first Mercator Society book. She'd been hurt when she discovered that Smiley had taken the map; now she was doubly hurt that it would not be returned.

She blamed the FBI for not trying hard enough. "The FBI agent said, 'I think a lot of them are in England and they are not coming back,'" she told me. "Meaning we are not going to go after them. They weren't diamonds; they weren't jewelry. So who cares?" When I told Kelleher, he said he understood Hudson's frustration, but without any physical evidence to prove the map belonged to the NYPL, he couldn't demand the collector return it. "It was one person who was not cooperative, very, very much so uncooperative," he said of the collector, whom he declined to name.

At the BPL, Grim faced his own challenges. The FBI told him that it was unable to recover one map—a chart of Carolina from *The American*

Pilot that Smiley had sold to the Old Print Shop, which had then sold it to a collector named Jim Curtis. Another collector, Bob Gordon, was still dragging his feet on returning the Dudley map of the Chesapeake, the middle map of the three Smiley had sliced out of *Dell'Arcano della Mare.* When he finally did send it back, Grim took one look before realizing it wasn't Boston's map. Not only was it the wrong size, but it also had fold marks that the BPL's atlas didn't have. Grim called Hudson at the NYPL, which was missing the same map, and it matched their description perfectly.

That begged the question, however: If Smiley hadn't sold the BPL's Chesapeake chart to Gordon, where had he sold it? Because the razor mark had sliced through all three maps together, this was the first definitive proof that Smiley had stolen at least one map that he hadn't admitted to. And it wasn't the only one Grim suspected Smiley of failing to admit to. There were still six maps with suspicious chronologies, in which he'd sold a map to a dealer soon after viewing a book at the BPL that should have contained it. After sentencing, Grim repeatedly called Kelleher and Schmeisser to ask them to view those maps, finally getting them both on the phone for a conference call on November 22, 2006— the day before Thanksgiving. They told him he'd have to deal with the dealers directly—clearing up any outstanding issues by December 21, ninety days after sentencing.

Grim scheduled a meeting with Arkway in New York for December 7 to examine the Herman Moll map of the colonies and the John Seller chart of the West Indies, taking the train from Boston along with his conservator. Even as they were examining maps worth tens of thousands of dollars, they paid $12.87 for lunch between the two of them and were back on the train before dinner. Viewing the maps immediately confirmed Grim's suspicions—the Moll map had folds that lined up perfectly with others in the atlas, and the Seller map had a telltale number stamp in the corner. A month later, Arkway's Paul Cohen and Henry Taliaferro sent another map to Boston—the John White map of Virginia from the book by de Bry. Not only did the map match the book's dimensions, but several creases in the map matched creases on the preceding page—all signs that it was Boston's map. Cohen and Taliaferro agreed to return all three maps, adding to the list of maps Smiley had taken but not admitted to.

There were more as well. Harvard spotted a copy of the world map by George Best posted on the website of a private collector that matched a digital photo made by the university. When Cobb contacted the collector, he agreed to return it. At Yale, Margit Kaye struggled to find evidence to link the maps she found in the Arkway and Old Print Shop catalogs with those missing from the Sterling. She had a digital photograph of only one of them—a map of New France by Jean Boisseau, which matched the coloring of the map in Arkway's catalog. They returned that one as well.

After the sentencing, the Beinecke posted its own digital photographs of its missing maps. Looking at them in his office one morning, Harry Newman closely examined the image of the map of Tenochtitlán by Hernán Cortés. Smiley had sold him a copy of the map, and he'd recently resold it but hadn't yet shipped it to the buyer. Newman shook his head when he looked at the image, which had a hole punched in the fold. Who would do that to a map that rare? No matter, since he was sure his map didn't have such a hole.

Something about the photo bothered him, however, and that afternoon he pulled out the map to compare it to the image. Both maps had been left untrimmed, and the pattern of feathered paper fibers seemed to match. Now as he bent his face down to the paper to the spot where the hole punch should have been, he saw a small circular indentation where someone had added wet fibers to fill in the gap. *Shit,* he thought. There was no doubt this was Yale's map. He picked up the phone to return it.

Most of the maps that had surfaced since sentencing were rare, but not incredibly so. The Cortés map, however, hadn't shown up at auction for thirty years. It wasn't the kind of map a major dealer was likely to forget. "He doesn't have a photographic memory for each theft," lawyer Dick Reeve told the *Hartford Courant* in Smiley's defense.

The last map to be recovered before the FBI closed the case was the Norman chart of Carolina, which Smiley had also sold to Harry Newman. Finally recovering it from collector Jim Curtis that spring, Newman brought it up to Boston to examine the BPL's 1816 edition of *The American Pilot.* Not only was the chart the same version that occurred in that edition, it also had evidence of abrasion in the upper-right corner where the other charts from the atlas had a purple number stamped on them. Newman agreed it was Boston's map and agreed to leave it with Grim.

In all, libraries were able to prove that Smiley had stolen at least a dozen maps he hadn't admitted to taking. Prosecutors didn't see any evidence that he was deliberately withholding information—after all, he had admitted taking almost a hundred maps, including some the libraries didn't know were missing. While Kelleher was sympathetic to the libraries' claims that Smiley had stolen more maps than he'd admitted to, he also had to be careful not to take maps away from dealers and collectors without solid evidence. "There was a constant worry in this case that I wasn't getting enough back for the libraries," Kelleher told me. "[But] we were taking maps from people that, if we had to prove it in court, we wouldn't have gotten them back. And there were more that we couldn't prove than we could. If he says, 'I don't remember,' we couldn't go to a dealer and say you know, we think [it's stolen], can you shell out this money that you gave to this person and bring the map back?' There has to be an endpoint."

That point came on May 8, 2007, when prosecutors submitted a new order for restitution to reflect the new maps that had been recovered. Almost all the dealers saw their losses increase—Burden to $357,520; The Old Print Shop to $567,639; and Cohen and Taliaferro to $938,400. The total value of the maps Smiley stole increased as well, to a final tally of $2,295,209.

NOW SITTING WITH with me at the picnic table in Martha's Vineyard five years later, Forbes Smiley seemed contrite and subdued as he talked about his past as a map dealer. "I was playing at it," he said. "I never took it seriously. I've had to look back on these things and, you know, ask myself the question why someone with all of those opportunities, and someone who really, really, really wanted to do well, why in a sense couldn't I get that to go well." The burglary of his studio in 1989 was the beginning of his problems, he told me, followed by his heart difficulties and the bypass surgery. Then came Sebec. "The hole that I dug in Sebec was much more insidious, and I was really blind to it," he said. "You don't buy the town and force your vision on everybody else— because you are going to get a backlash. And the backlash on me cost me an enormous amount of money, but more important it destroyed the safe haven and refuge of that farmhouse, not only for me, but for everybody."

Recently, he said, he was looking for old photographs and came across a box full of picture after picture of the bulldozer destroying the shore in front of his home—two hundred of them in all. "It was as fast as I could take the pictures, in a complete and absolute panic," he said. "And that's probably not a bad image of who I was at the time and how I dealt with stress." From there it was only a small leap to justify stealing given the resentments he had developed over the years toward the other dealers and libraries. "You talk yourself into a place that the reasons you are feeling so alone and so upset and have these resentments is because people aren't treating you as well as they should treat you, and they aren't as appreciative and you are not getting paid the way you should," he said. "So it festers."

Once he started stealing, he said, he couldn't see any other way out of his predicament. "Why did I steal? I stole for the money. You could write that in one sentence. The question I have to ask myself is, Why did I think I needed the money so much? I worked for many years and was very successful, but you couldn't have put enough money into my pocket to cover that level of mismanagement." Stealing became his way of trying to control an increasingly unmanageable life. "I never took pleasure in stealing," he said. "I stole because I was trying to relieve myself from this feeling of desperation, and that's a word I never understood until it happened to me."

Smiley justified the thefts by telling himself that at least the items he sold would be cared for by collectors. "That's not an observation, that's a confession, because that is really fucked up," he said. "That state of mind feels like a different movie." After his arrest in June 2005, he joined a twelve-step program on the Vineyard, in part to deal with the heavy drinking he'd begun doing in the previous few years. At the beginning of each meeting, the facilitator read a passage that mentioned the importance of "rigorous honesty."

"I used to hear those words in despair and fear that I couldn't do this," he told me. He began by telling his seven-year-old son what he'd done. "I didn't want to do it, man!" he said, finally letting go with a belly laugh. "I thought he was going to be devastated by this. I thought this little boy was going to get his life destroyed." In the end, he rose to the challenge, telling his son, "I made terrible mistakes and I hurt people and I was going to have to go away and work very, very hard to make that better." Not only did his son understand, he said, but going through that ordeal allowed him to start opening up to other family members and friends and finally be honest about what he'd kept hidden.

As for how he stole the maps, he would only say: "They fall out. I mean, three-hundred-year-old glue, they are not bound in. Some of them tear but the paper is so fragile. They fall out." Despite the evidence, he was adamant he never removed a map with a blade. "I always had a razor blade—I wouldn't expect anyone to believe that, but I'm a print dealer," he said. "I don't believe that I ever cut a map out of a book." He also continued to insist that he has admitted the full extent of his crimes. "I was honest and straightforward and worked hard, and where we left it was, if not perfect, then extraordinarily close," he said. "There were no Swiss bank accounts." The Boston Foster map stolen from Yale in the 1980s? "I did not take it." The Alexander map the British Library accused him of stealing? "I have no recollection whatsoever of taking that map." After all, he said, if he had a cache of maps hidden somewhere, would he even be talking to me? "There is not a single map," he said definitively. "I do not know of one."

SMILEY ARRIVED AT Fort Devens Federal Medical Center to report to its minimum-security "satellite camp" on January 4, 2007. There, he was given an orange jumpsuit and a new identity: prisoner 15867-014. Smiley tried to make the best of the situation, telling himself at least he'd be in with other white-collar criminals and not hardened offenders. Upon arrival, he was put into solitary confinement for what he was told would be two days. He didn't get out for several months.

According to Smiley (and corroborated by letters and interviews with people he spoke with at the time), he was locked in a cell for twenty-three hours a day. In the mornings he was woken by the loud banter of other inmates echoing off the prison walls. He was allowed to exercise in the yard for an hour a day with other inmates. Twice a week, he was given a toothbrush. Smiley was outraged at first at the injustice—but eventually, he said, he just gave up any pretense of having control over his life. All of his notions about managing his time in prison disappeared, as he dealt with the reality of his new situation. "You are in an orange suit and you are in shackles. You are on your knees to make a telephone call once a month and the phone doesn't work. You are getting screamed at, and the guy next door is losing it, I mean, getting taken away in strait-jackets. I mean, this is happening."

Finally, after three months, he said, he was let out of solitary on the condition that he agree to spend the rest of his time in a medium-security prison. In those first moments walking out into the yard, he was terrified, not knowing where to turn for support. Eventually, he found his footing, however, continuing AA meetings and taking classes in web design and watercolor painting. He began teaching English classes to fellow inmates along with life skills such as—ironically—how to balance a checkbook.

During his time in prison, he clung to letters from friends and family, opening up emotionally to them for the first time. "It is impossible to explain how I held on to those letters," he said. "I cried when I saw the return addresses." When fall came, the "boys" gathered for their annual weekend at Bob von Elgg's home in Santa Cruz rather than Sebec. Scott Slater read a long "Lament for Sebec," describing to his friends the painful effect of watching their clubhouse "stripped of all the furnishings, artwork, books, memorabilia . . . maps, photographs, moose antlers, beds, French cookware, his beloved cookbooks, his billards table, his tube amp, and the front porch table and chairs. . . . No music or laughter emanates from his once beautiful house," he concluded, before proposing a toast to "The Squire!"

Then von Elgg performed a parody of Johnny Cash's "Folsom Prison Blues" that he had composed in Smiley's honor, sending the rest of the crew into fits of laughter.

> *I hear the boys a drinkin'*
> *Drinkin' up again*
> *And I ain't seen the sunshine since I don't know when,*
> *I'm stuck in Devens prison, and time keeps draggin' on*
> *But those bastards keep a pourin'*
> *While I sit here all alone*

When I was just a baby my mama told me. Son
Always be a good boy, don't steal antiques for fun
But I stole a map at Yale-O and left the blade behind
Now every time I hear the boys a drinkin' I hang my head and cry . . .

Following the song, Smiley's friends sang a rendition of "For He's a Jolly Good Fellow" as the whiskey continued to pour.

After two and a half years of good behavior, Smiley was transferred to spend a final six months in a work-release program at a halfway house on Cape Cod. Finally, the prison released him on a furlough on December 23, 2009, allowing him to go home with an electronic bracelet to spend the holidays with his family. On January 17, 2010, he officially earned parole, being released from his sentence six months earlier than the forty-two months he'd been given. In all, he served a total of three years and six days—or about eleven days for each of the ninety-seven maps he'd admitted stealing.

OF COURSE, IF you add all the maps libraries accuse Smiley of stealing, his time spent in prison for each map is considerably less. Adding the twelve maps recovered by libraries after sentencing brings the total number of maps attributed to Smiley to 108. But the total number of maps libraries are missing is 257, more than double what's been accounted for. And there are those who believe he stole many, many more. "My guess is that five percent have been returned," said Graham Arader. "My feeling has always been that he went to the big places after he cleaned out the little places," he said, referring to historical societies up and down the East Coast where security is more lax than at the libraries. He isn't the only one who thinks so. One of the librarians victimized by Smiley claims that other institutions have admitted privately that Smiley stole from them, but they've never publicized the fact.

Despite the circumstantial evidence linking some of the missing maps to Smiley, however, some libraries have discovered evidence to prove the opposite—that he didn't take particular maps. Such was the case when two curators at the British Library were conducting a routine office move in January 2012 and came across the missing George Best map of the world that the library had accused Smiley of taking during the court trial. "We now know that our assessment of the probable cause of the loss was incorrect," a library representative wrote me in an e-mail, "but in our view it was not an unreasonable assessment, given the context."

If Smiley did steal more maps, it begs the obvious question: Where are they? Arader thinks he knows. "I le turned in the dealers, but he didn't turn in the clients," he said, speculating that they are still hanging on the walls of some collectors' houses today. Bob Goldman agrees. "There are collectors out there who think that there is no better protector of items than themselves," he says. "It is such a passion they come to believe that nobody appreciates them and nobody is in a better position to possess or protect them than they are." It's the *Dr. No* theory of art theft—only in the case of maps, it could actually be true. Unlike a one-of-a-kind work of art, a rare map could be displayed openly by its owner without anyone even knowing it was stolen.

Harvard's David Cobb will never forget a map conference he attended in Guatemala a few years after Smiley's thefts. Giving a talk about security to a few dozen map collectors, he asked, "Do any of you think you have stolen maps in your collection?" None of the collectors raised their hands. Next he asked, "Would any of you refuse to purchase a map for which a dealer had not provided you a known provenance?" Again, none of them raised their hands. "I'm like, you can't have it both ways, guys," he told me. "The four maps Harvard is still missing are in somebody's collection. And those people know they are in their collection."

In October 2008, Cobb and others at Harvard were hopeful that one of their maps had turned up when Sotheby's announced it was auctioning a copy of Samuel de Champlain's map of "Nouvelle Franse" from *Les Voyages*, billing it as "perhaps the most important single map" in Canadian history. Harvard immediately contacted the auction in hopes that this might be its lost map. After a flurry of initial excitement, however, the university confirmed that the map did not match a digital copy and cleared it for auction. (The map eventually went for a record $250,000.)

Whether or not Smiley took them, the maps missing from the libraries are out there somewhere—and despite the efforts of people like Tony Campbell, libraries and dealers have never gotten together to create a comprehensive list of stolen maps that could be used to recover these materials. After Smiley's thefts, a New York Map Society member named John Woram took it upon himself to create a master list of all the missing maps attributed to Smiley by combining all the lists released by the victimized libraries. None of the libraries, however, were willing to give him pictures that he could post, which are essential to identification of particular maps. "When a kid goes missing or something like that, you have to put a photo out," he told me. "Unfortunately none of the institutions were willing to cooperate," he told me. "After about a year or so, I gave up."

Campbell put the blame on the institutions for not being more open about their missing material. "It's not the map librarians who are the problem; it's the people up there, it's the PR people," he told me over pints at a London pub. "What they don't realize is that the policy of trying to keep a lid on it has helped the thieves." It's for that reason Smiley was able to commit his thefts a decade after Gilbert Bland had done the same thing, Campbell insisted, and it's for that reason another thief will be able to do it in the future if libraries don't change their ways. "The best time to have done something was shortly after Smiley. When the next Smiley comes, people will say, why didn't we do that?"

Other map thieves *have* already struck since Smiley's arrest. Even while Smiley was awaiting sentencing in the fall of 2006, librarians at Western Washington University found more than one hundred maps and prints ripped out of its government documents department. The trail led to James Brubaker, a seventy-three-year-old man living in Great Falls, Montana, who had stashed more than a thousand books and twenty thousand pages of documents, selling them for cash on eBay. All told, his thefts totaled $220,000, enough to earn him two years in prison.

Since Brubaker, no major map thieves have targeted US institutions—though many have struck in Europe. In August 2008, sixty-year-old César Gómez Rivero stole sixteen items from Madrid's Biblioteca Nacional, including a 1482 world map from the Ulm Ptolemy and a 1507 world map by Johann Ruysch. Around the same time, electrician and heroin addict Richard Delaney stole £89,000 worth of historic maps and books from England's Birmingham University while performing electrical work on the library. In November 2008, the British Library discovered that a wealthy Iranian-born scholar, Farhad Hakimzadeh, had sliced maps and other pages from 150 rare volumes, totaling £400,000. In 2009, a Hungarian thief stole some seventy maps from libraries in Spain; and in the Czech Republic, a thief stole two maps, including Peter Apian's 1520 world map, from the Scientific Library in Olomouc.

Even though the libraries haven't banded together systematically to track map thefts, some have individually gone to extraordinary lengths to improve their security. In addition to its new state-of-the-art control room, the Beinecke launched a project to recatalog all its rare books with detailed information on the maps they include. The British Library, too, began recataloging its rare books, requiring readers to view the rarest in a specially designated area under the close watch of a monitoring desk. The BL's map department also spearheaded an innovative project to take digital photos of its rarest sheet maps—photographing each map while backlit to show a unique pattern of paper fibers that can identify it as certainly as a fingerprint.

The Leventhal Map Center in Boston also began an ambitious digitization project with a half-million-dollar grant from the National Endowment for the Humanities to photograph its rarest atlases. In order to do that, however, each must be taken apart and put back together, at a cost of more than $10,000 apiece. It would take twice the grant to photograph all the library's one hundred pre-1800 atlases, to say nothing of its three thousand later atlases. The BPL recently spent some $200,000 in security upgrades for its rare-book room to improve sightlines and install cameras.

Thanks to a $100,000 donation from Bill Reese, the Sterling Memorial Library has been able to finally catalog its map collection; it also installed a new camera for its map department reading room. New director Abe Parrish, however, sees that as only the last line of defense. As a former military intelligence officer in Iraq and Afghanistan, Parrish knows the importance of establishing a "chain of custody" for classified documents. He applied the same logic to maps at the Sterling, installing bar codes on the sleeves of all of its rarest sheet maps, which are scanned in and out after each use.

Not all libraries seemed to have learned their lessons, however. At the New York Public Library, a sign just inside the doorway at Room 117 states that all patrons must check bags and coats downstairs. In each of the half-dozen times I visited the department, however, the tables and chairs were strewn with numerous bags and coats. During days of research, I was never asked to check my bag, despite working with some of the rarest maps in the collection.

HARRY NEWMAN AND his brother Robert still get checks in the mail to cover Smiley's restitution costs—$25 or $50 every few months, Harry Newman told me. The biggest portion came after Smiley's mother passed away in February 2009, leaving equal amounts of family money to each of her children. Smiley's share came to $165,000—of which $32,000 went to taxes and $40,000 went to his lawyers; he was allowed to keep $28,500. That left $65,000 to pay the victims of his crimes, a fraction of the more than $1 million he still owed. At least this time, the money was paid out as a percentage of what he owed each one, rather than being proportioned in even shares.

When Newman sees one of the other affected dealers now, they joke about Smiley's home on the Vineyard, saying they should be able to use it as a time-share in the summer. But the thefts seriously affected Newman, who spent months in therapy to recover from Smiley's betrayal.

Alice Hudson was hit even harder. Though her fears of being fired were unfounded, her work in Room 117 was never the same. She withdrew from the map community for a time, declining invitations to conferences and even making excuses not to research the antiquarian maps that had been Smiley's specialty. She had always hoped to work at least forty years in the Map Division. But when the opportunity came in 2008 for a buyout, she took it, one year short at thirty-nine. "It was the end of the world—not the end of the map world—but the end of it for me," she later said. "There was just this sense of loss, of sadness, you know, responsibility. It hit me so hard."

Little remains to show for all the money Smiley earned off the maps he stole. In Sebec, a new public boat launch sits along the shore in front of the Smileys' old home, which they sold in 2007. A rock garden with flowers and birch trees sits before a tall flagpole flying the American flag. Across the bridge, however, the Sebec Village Shops are again derelict. White paint blisters and peels on the side of the building, and unused Christmas lights dangle year-round from the ceiling of the wraparound porch. Inside, all the fixtures are still in place, and all the tables for the café are still set six years after it closed, as if it might open for breakfast in the morning. Across the street, the Sebec Village Marina looks dilapidated as well. Three small docks bob in the water, but the Moriartys never achieved their dream of a takeout restaurant. The paint on the storefront is peeling here too, and half the windows are boarded up, even though the marina still operates and the Moriartys still live there.

With Smiley out of the business, Graham Arader has continued to prosper—finally announcing in 2009 that he would be donating all his wealth to philanthrophic causes at the rate of $2 million a year. In 2013, he announced a gift of fifteen thousand antique maps and prints to the University of South Carolina to establish the W. Graham Arader III Collection—a total value of $30 million. He's made smaller gifts over the past few years to the University of Florida, the University of California–Irvine, and Northeastern University to establish programs to teach college students using real antique maps. "Rich kids grow up in houses with things like these in them," he told me. "Well, why can't poor kids have this? So there are all these empty walls in American universities and they're begging for a chance to put something there."

More walls were filled with maps at the Boston Public Library after the official opening of the Norman B. Leventhal Map Center in a new space on October 22, 2011. Visitors to the long-awaited center find exhibits on geography, a room for kids to learn about maps, and, in the back, a glassed-in reading room where patrons can view the two hundred thousand maps in the library's collection.

The maps Smiley helped Norman Leventhal acquire, however, are not among them. While technically on loan to the BPL, most of Leventhal's maps still hang in the Boston Harbor Hotel along Boston's waterfront. There, tourists circulate among them in a lobby filled with plush couches and the smell of the harbor and the restaurant next door. If they stop and look, they can trace the chronological history of the city laid out on three walls—starting with John Smith's map of New England.

WHEN SMILEY FIRST got out of prison, he had no idea what he was going to do. He'd spent his entire career in the map business—and now was expressly forbidden from handling these objects again. Not that he'd want to anyway. Even reading about maps now was painful for him. He returned to the Vineyard worried that he would no longer be accepted by the island community. Through his AA meetings and parents of his son's friends, however, he began meeting other high-powered business-people who had crashed and burned in their careers. "There are a lot of broken toys on this island," he told me.

A friend helped get him a job that first summer working at a catering company for $9 an hour. Eventually, he was able to use his skill in work-ing with his hands to find employment as a landscaper and laborer on building sites for $12 an hour. With the computer skills he picked up in prison, he began building websites on the side for extra cash. His life is simpler now than it was around the wealthy world of map collectors, when he was flying off to London and Paris and dining at top restau-rants. He now eats out with his family at the neighborhood clam shack and attends Ned's Little League games, watching the teams rather than pacing the sidelines with a cell phone to his ear.

As if to signal the change, he stopped calling himself Forbes and began calling himself Ed—or even Eddie among close friends. "I am on the road to being well," he told me cautiously. "I've taken the time to learn how the world actually works, instead of having a childish idea in my head of how it works and trying to force it." One day, he said, he hopes to pay back the money he owes and make it up to those he hurt. "At the end of the day, I stole people's money as much as anything, even though I never looked at it that way. But the final effect is these were people I was genuinely fond of, and who entrusted me with their expec-tation that I would never hurt them or their institutions. They put their good faith and trust in me and I let them down."

It wasn't just librarians and dealers who Smiley let down; some of his best friends also felt betrayed by his actions—if only because he wasn't the person he'd always presented himself to be. "It was quite a revelation to realize there was something wrong with the guy who was paying for all the drinks all those years," said Paul Statt. "And there were a lot of free drinks over the years." It felt good to be the one helping Forbes for a change, but he also felt like his life was diminished some-how from the deception. "It's a little hard for some of us for whom he represented boundlessness over the years to accept the boundedness."

Scott Slater had the opposite feeling—like he could finally talk to Forbes the way he always wanted him to be, absent the pretentions of "the Squire." In long letters from prison, Smiley opened up about his childhood and the mistakes he made; about how much he missed his son and what it meant to be a man. As much as Slater was grateful for this new honesty and openness, however, he, too, sometimes missed some of the larger parts of Smiley's personality that had disappeared since his arrest—telling stories over beers and his big belly laugh. "I miss the parts of Forbes where there was never a problem about anything," he told me, sighing.

Above the couch in Slater's living room is the only map Smiley had left before he went to prison, the map of Sebec Lake that hung in the house up in Maine. Slater has all of Smiley's jazz and blues records, too, neatly stacked on cinder blocks in his dining room. Smiley has yet to pick them up, perhaps because they remind him of a time in his life when he was too out of control. "My wife keeps telling me we should sell them," Slater said. "We need money for our roof. But if I did that, it would be stealing."

Slater also has several watercolor paintings Smiley sent him from prison. When he began taking painting classes, he and his fellow prisoners were forbidden from looking at art books because of the frequent paintings of nudes they contained. So he began copying pictures from magazines and catalogs, painting farmhouses and snowy landscapes he sent to his friends for Christmas. Once he sent a painting to Slater's disabled son, Gordon, depicting *The Dying Gaul,* a famous Roman marble statue of a fallen warrior, lying slumped and defeated on his shield.

Months after I spoke with Smiley, I again took the ferry to Martha's Vineyard, this time in the middle of December. A stiff wind was blowing off the ocean and shaking the leafless trees as I took a cab out to a farmhouse a few miles from Vineyard Haven. The building is home to the Featherstone Center for the Arts, a small gallery that was putting on a Christmas craft fair and art show. A local nonprofit had given grants of $200 to $5,000 to various island artists to present their work, which ranged from paintings of Revolutionary War generals to circus costumes for kids.

Tucked in one corner were three small watercolors, accompanied by a short artist statement from Edward Smiley. It read: "During a difficult period of my life (including prison) I turned to painting as a way of regaining my balance, and beginning a period of renewal of mind and spirit. Self-taught, I found an ability to see the world with fresh eyes and express myself and my feelings in watercolors."

One of the paintings showed a village scene, with a small figure emerging from a cottage to walk across a peaceful snowy square. Another depicted a moody snow-colored field with a single, bare tree rising into a cloudy sky. The last, and most accomplished, painting showed a seascape with a gauzy light descending from a break in the clouds. In the foreground, a thicket of black and green brambles choked the shoreline.

The painting calls to mind a letter Smiley sent his friends Statt and Slater from prison, in which he wrote:

> When painters paint, it is often the case that light is their primary interest. . . . What painters like Rembrandt discovered, is that you "paint" light by painting very dark areas in contrast. Painting "darks" proves to be much easier with pigment, and the only way to express light.
>
> I love to paint the light. For me and others learning to paint, the challenge has been to risk getting comfortable with adding very dark areas to the painting, not just in the shadows but in the unexpected places. But it works—very dark areas do not wreck the painting as one might expect, but rather tend to [recede] in the brilliant expression of sunlight or the subtle silver light of the moon. What the brain notices and is the primary effect, is that of lightness.
>
> As often as I examine good paintings and notice all the "darks," it still feels very uncomfortable to drop black or dark blue into a perfectly clean watercolor. Maybe it will always feel uncomfortable. But I am told that my paintings are now more realistic and I am beginning to like them myself.

Reading that, I couldn't help but think of the terra incognita found on antique maps, those blank spaces that represented endless possibility to early explorers—an ancient city of gold or a blue-water passage to the Orient waiting to be discovered. But those spaces could also be dangerous, as early mapmakers reminded us when they filled in the blanks with savage beasts and sea monsters. Other times, in the absence of real knowledge, those mapmakers filled in those dark spaces with their own desires, the way John Smith inserted his fictitious English cities in the middle of hostile wilderness. Perhaps what Smiley was groping toward in his letter was a comfort in finally leaving the imperfections in place, resisting the impulse to fill in the dark spots with a desired geography, and allowing them to simply exist. His life now may not be as grandiose or imaginative as the one he created while he was selling and stealing maps, but in that sense at least it is truer.

EPILOGUE

ON JULY 13, 2013—more than eight years after Smiley had been arrested, and three and a half years after he'd been released from prison—the FBI made an unexpected announcement. "After a well-known dealer of rare maps was caught stealing from a Yale University library in [2005], a subsequent FBI investigation revealed that the man had stolen antique maps and other valuable items from institutions around the world," read the agency's press release. "Most of the pilfered material was eventually returned to its rightful owners—but not all of it."

The bureau went on to reveal that it was still in possession of twenty-eight rare maps and books that had been recovered from Smiley at the time of his arrest but had never been identified or returned. Some of them were quite familiar, matching maps that Smiley had stolen from libraries, including Thomas Holme's map of Philadelphia (which he'd stolen from the BPL but was still missing from Yale); Hernán Cortés' map of Tenochtitlán (which he'd stolen from Harvard and the Beinecke but was still missing from New York); George Best's map of the Northwest Passage (which he'd stolen from the NYPL); and several sea charts from John Thornton, Mount and Page, and J.F.W. Des Barres. Others seem strange—like a mix of nineteenth-century state maps and US Coast Guard surveys.

What's more strange is that the FBI should choose to release the list so long after Smiley had been arrested and sentenced. The case has since passed from Steve Kelleher to another agent in the New Haven office, Special Agent Lisa MacNamara. When I called to ask her where the items came from, she said they were "acquired in August 2005 as a result of a search warrant." Smiley said he didn't recall where he'd gotten them, and so the FBI had no idea whether they had been stolen or had been legitimately acquired. So far, MacNamara told me, no one had come forward to claim any of them. In fact, in the weeks after the release, she received only one call—from a dealer who said he legitimately sold Smiley one of the maps.

The rest of them sit at the New Haven field office, each item individually packaged in a box or tube. If no one comes to claim them, they may eventually be donated to the Library of Congress. Until then, they sit in evidence, one more mystery in a case full of mysteries.

Appendix A

MAPS SMILEY ADMITTED STEALING

KEY:

Boston/M = Norman B. Leventhal Map Center, Boston Public Library

Boston/B = Boston Public Library, Rare Books Department

British Library — British Library, Map Library

Harvard = Harvard University, Houghton Library

Newberry = Newberry Library

New York/M = New York Public Library, Map Division

New York/B = New York Public Library, Rare Book Division

Yale/B = Yale University, Beinecke Rare Book and Manuscript Library

Yale/M = Yale University, Sterling Memorial Library Map Collection

Date	Creator	Title	Owner	Status
1520	Peter Apian	Tipus Orbis Universalis (world)	British Library	Recovered
1524	Hernán Cortés	Untitled (Tenochtitlán/Gulf of Mexico)	Harvard	Recovered
1532	Oronce Fine	Nova et Integra Vniversi Orbis Descriptio (double-cordiform world)	Yale/B	Unrecovered

Date	Creator	Title	Owner	Status
1535	Gregorius Reisch	Typus Universalis Terrae (world)	New York/M	Recovered
1572	Antonio Lafreri	Untitled (Salamanca world map)	New York/B	Recovered
1577	Pietro Martire d'Anghiera	Untitled (West Indies)	New York/B	Recovered
1578	George Best	Untitled (Northwest Passage)	New York/B	Recovered
1578	Gerard de Jode	Vniversi Orbis Sev Terreni Globi (world)	Yale/B	Recovered
1581	Nicola van Sype	La Herdike Enterprinse Faict (world/Drake circumnavigation)	New York/B	Recovered
1582	Richard Hakluyt and Robert Thorne	Untitled (world)	New York/B	Recovered
1587	Richard Hakluyt and Pietro Martire d'Anghiera	De Orbe Novo (America)	Yale/B	Recovered
1589	Richard Hakluyt	Typus Orbis Terrarum (world)	Yale/B	Recovered
1593	Cornelius de Jode	Hemisphaerium Ab Aequinoctiali Linea (double-hemisphere world)	Boston/M	Recovered
1593	Cornelius de Jode	Americae Pars Borealis	Boston/M	Recovered
1596	Theodor de Bry	America sive Novus	Boston/B	Recovered
1599	Edward Wright	A Particular Sea Chart for the Islands Azores	Yale/B	Recovered

Date	Creator	Title	Owner	Status
1599	Edward Wright	A Plat of All the World	Yale/B	Recovered
1609	Marc Lescarbot	Figvre de la Terre Nevve, Grand Riviere de Canada	Harvard	Recovered
1613	Samuel de Champlain	Carte Géographique de la Nouvelle France	New York/B	Recovered
1616	Gabriel Tatton	Californiae Nouae Hispaniae Mexicanae et Peruviae	Yale/M	Recovered
1618	Jodocus Hondius and Dirk Grijp	Nova Virginiae Tabula	New York/M	Recovered
1625	Henry Briggs	The North Part of America	Boston/B	Recovered
1630	Jodocus Hondius	America Noviter Delineata	Boston/B	Recovered
1631	John Smith	New England	Yale/B	Recovered
1632	Samuel de Champlain	Carte Géographique de la Nouvelle France	New York/B	Recovered
1634	William Wood	The South Part of New England	Boston/M	Recovered
1635	John Ogilby	Nova Terrae-Mariae Tabula ("Lord Baltimore" map of Maryland)	New York/B	Unrecovered
1635	Luke Foxe	Part of China, Part of America	Yale/B	Recovered
1636	Ralph Hall	Virginia	Newberry	Recovered

Date	Creator	Title	Owner	Status
1646	Robert Dudley	Carta Particolare della Nuoua Belgia è Parte della Nuoua Anglia (New England)	Boston/M	Recovered
1646	Robert Dudley	Carta Particolare della Costa di Florida e di Virginia (Carolina)	Boston/M	Recovered
1646	Robert Dudley	Carta Particolare della Virginia Vecchia e Nuoua (Chesapeake)	Boston/M	Unrecovered
1655	John Smith	Virginia	Boston/B	Recovered
1655	Hendrick Doncker	West-Indische Paskaert Waer in de Graden der Breedde	Boston/M	Recovered
1656	Evert Nieuwenhof	Nova Belgica sive Nieuw Nederlandt	Harvard	Recovered
1671	Claude Dablon and Claude Allouez	Lac Tracy ov Svperievr	Harvard	Recovered
1672	John Lederer	Map of the Whole Territory Traversed by John Lederer in His Three Marches	Harvard	Recovered
1675	John Seller	A New Map of New Jersey in America	Boston/M	Recovered
1675	Arent Roggeveen	Nieu Nederland—Streckende vande Zuydt Revier tot de Noordt Revier en't Lange Eyland (New York and New Jersey)	New York/M	Recovered

Date	Creator	Title	Owner	Status
1675	Arent Roggeveen	Pascaert van Nieu Nederland, Van Hendrick Christiaens Eyland tot Staten Hoeck of Cabo Cod (New England)	New York/M	Recovered
1676	Samuel de Champlain	Canada Faict par le Sr. de Champlain (Collet copy)	New York/B	Recovered
1676	John Seller	New England	Yale/M	Recovered
1677	John Foster	A Map of New England	Harvard	Recovered
1680	Robert Morden and John Overton	Ireland	New York/M	Recovered
1680	Arent Roggeveen	Pascaerte vande Virginies, Van Baya de la Madelena tot de Zuydt Revier	New York/M	Recovered
1683	Louis Hennepin	Carte de la Nouvelle France et de la Louisiane	New York/B	Recovered
1685	Philip Lea	Mexico and America	Boston/M	Recovered
1685	Philip Lea	A New Mapp of the World	Boston/M	Recovered
1686	Philip Lea	A New Map of New England, New York, New Jarsey, Pensilvania, Maryland, and Virginia	Yale/M	Recovered
1690	Philip Lea	Map of England without Place Names (Lea 2 and State)	Boston/M	Recovered

Date	Creator	Title	Owner	Status
1690	Philip Lea	Natural Shape of England	Boston/M	Recovered
1690	Philip Lea	New Map of England and Wales	Boston/M	Recovered
1690	John Thornton	Virginia, Maryland, Pennsilvania, East & West New Jarsey	Boston/M	Recovered
1691	Ignace Rouillard	Carte Generalle de la Nouvelle France	Harvard	Recovered
1694	John Thornton	New Map of the Cheif [sic] Rivers, Bayes, Creeks, Harbours, and Settlements in South Carolina, . . .	Newberry	Unrecovered
1702	John Thornton	A New Mapp of East and West New Jarsey	New York/M	Unrecovered
1710	Thomas Holme and George Willdey	A Mapp of Ye Improved Part of Pennsilvania in America	Boston/M	Recovered
1724	Cadwallader Colden	A Map of the (New York) Country of the Five Nations	Yale/B	Recovered
1737	Cyprian Southack	A Correct Map of the Coast of New England	Boston/M	Recovered
1741	Daniel Coxe	Map of Carolana and of the River Meschacebe	Boston/B	Recovered
1743	John Bonner and William Price	A New Plan of Ye Great Town of Boston in New England in America	Yale/M	Recovered

Date	Creator	Title	Owner	Status
1758	Lewis Evans	A General Map of the Middle British Colonies	New York/M	Recovered
1759	Nicholas Scull	Map of the Improved Part of the Province of Pennsylvania	Yale/M	Recovered
1761	Joseph Blanchard and Samuel Langdon	An Accurate Map of His Majesty's Province of New-Hampshire in New England	Yale/M	Recovered
1764	Henry Dawkins	A General Chart of Louisiana	New York/M	Recovered
1765	Thomas Hutchins	A Map of the Country on the Ohio and Muskingum Rivers	New York/B	Recovered
1768	Joshua Fry and Peter Jefferson	A Map of the Most Inhabited Part of Virginia	Boston/M	Recovered
1768	Thomas Jefferys	A Map of the Country between Wills Creek & Monongahela River	Boston/M	Recovered
1768	John Montresor and Thomas Jefferys	A Plan of the City of New York & Its Environs	New York/M	Recovered
1770	John Abraham Collet	A Compleat Map of North Carolina	New York/M	Recovered
1770	William Scull	Map of the Province of Pennsylvania	New York/M	Unrecovered
1772	William Gerard de Brahm	The Ancient Tegesta East Florida	Boston/M	Recovered

Date	Creator	Title	Owner	Status
1772	William Gerard de Brahm	Chart of the South End of East Florida	Boston/M	Recovered
1772	William Gerard de Brahm	Hydrographical Map of Atlantic Ocean	Boston/M	Recovered
1775	Lewis Evans	A General Map of the Middle British Colonies	Yale/M	Recovered
1777	William Faden	A Plan of the City and Environs of Philadelphia	New York/M	Recovered
1777	William Faden	Plan of the Seige of Savannah	New York/M	Recovered
1777	William Faden	Sketch of the Position of the British Forces at Elizabeth Town Point	New York/M	Recovered
1777	William Faden	Sketch of the Surprise of German Town	New York/M	Recovered
1778	Michel Capitaine du Chesnoy	Amérique Septentrionale	Yale/M	Recovered
178?	Anonymous	Caroline Meridionale et Partie de la Georgie (manuscript)	Boston/M	Unrecovered
178?	Anonymous	Manuscript Map of the Operations at the Siege of Savannah in 1779	Boston/M	Recovered
1780	Joseph F.W. Des Barres	A Sketch of the Environs of Charlestown in South Carolina	New York/M	Unrecovered

Date	Creator	Title	Owner	Status
1780	Joseph F.W. Des Barres	A Sketch of the Operations before Charlestown the Capital of South Carolina	New York/M	Recovered
1784	Jean Lattre	Carte des États-Unis de l'Amerique	Yale/M	Recovered
1792	William Blodgett	A New and Correct Map of Connecticut	New York/M	Recovered
1792	Andrew Ellicott	Plan of the City of Washington	Harvard	Recovered
1794	Carleton Osgood (Norman Chart)	A New General Chart of the West Indies	Boston/M	Recovered
1794	A.P. Folie	Plan of the City and Suburbs of Philadelphia	New York/M	Recovered
1796	Aaron Arrowsmith	United States of North America	New York/M	Recovered
ca. 1798	Anthony Smith (Norman Chart)	A New and Accurate Chart of the Bay of Chesapeak	Boston/M	Recovered
1801	Osgood Carleton	Map of Massachusetts Proper Compiled from Actual Surveys	New York/M	Recovered
1815	William Darby and John Melish	A Map of the State of Louisiana	Yale/M	Recovered
1816	D.L. Dunbibin (Norman Chart)	Chart of the Coast of America from Cape Hatteras to Cape Roman	Boston/M	Recovered

Date	Creator	Title	Owner	Status
1816	T. Rogers (Norman Chart)	New Chart of the Gulf of Florida and Bahama Banks	Boston/M	Recovered
1816	John Melish	Map of the United States with the Contiguous British & Spanish Possessions	New York/M	Recovered
1822	John Wilson	A Map of South Carolina	Yale/M	Recovered

Appendix B

ADDITIONAL MAPS LIBRARIES REPORTED MISSING

KEY:

Boston/M = Norman B. Leventhal Map Center, Boston Public Library

Boston/B = Boston Public Library, Rare Books Department

British Library — British Library, Map Library

Harvard = Harvard University, Houghton Library

New York/M = New York Public Library, Map Division

New York/B = New York Public Library, Rare Book Division

Yale/B = Yale University, Beinecke Rare Book and Manuscript Library

Yale/M = Yale University, Sterling Memorial Library Map Collection

Date	Creator	Title	Owner	Status
1524	Hernán Cortés	Facsimile of Untitled (Tenochtitlán/Gulf of Mexico)	New York/B	Missing
1524	Hernán Cortés	Untitled (Tenochtitlán/Gulf of Mexico)	Yale/B	Recovered

Date	Creator	Title	Owner	Status
1525	Martin Waldseemüller	Terra Nova Ocaenus Occidentalis (world)	New York/M	Missing
1530	Oronce Fine	Nova et Integra Vniversi Orbis Descriptio (double-cordiform world)	New York/B	Missing
1540	Oronce Fine	Nova et Integra Vniversi Orbis Descriptio (double-cordiform world)	Harvard	Missing
1562	Abraham Ortelius	Russiae, Moscoviae et Tartariae Descriptio	Yale/M	Missing
1578	George Best	Untitled (world)	British Library	Found
1578	George Best	Untitled (world)	Harvard	Recovered
1589	Humphrey Gilbert and Richard Hakluyt	A General Map Made Onelye for the Particuler Declaration of this Discovery (world)	New York/B	Missing
1590	Abraham Ortelius	Islandia circa 1590	Yale/M	Missing
1591	Theodor de Bry	Occidentalis Americae Partis (West Indies)	Boston/B	Missing
1591	Jacques Le Moyne	Floridae Americae Provinciae Recens & Exactissima Descriptio	Boston/B	Recovered
1591	John White	Americae Pars, Nunc Virginia Dicta (Virginia)	Boston/B	Recovered

Date	Creator	Title	Owner	Status
1595	Gerard Mercator	Septentrionalium Terrarum Descriptio (polar regions)	Yale/M	Missing
1600	Jodocus Hondius	Tartaria (black and white)	Yale/M	Missing
1600	Jodocus Hondius	Tartaria (color)	Yale/M	Missing
1612	Samuel de Champlain	Carte Géographique de la Nouvelle France Faictte . . .	Harvard	Missing
1613	Samuel de Champlain	Carte Géographique de la Nouvelle France Faictte . . .	Boston/B	Missing
1613	Samuel de Champlain	Carte Géographique de la Nouvelle France en Son Vray Mondia	Boston/B	Missing
1613	Samuel de Champlain	Carte Géographique de la Nouvelle France en Son Vray Mondia	New York/B	Missing
1624	William Alexander	Untitled (New England and New France)	British Library	Missing
1624	William Alexander	Untitled (New England and New France)	New York/B	Missing
1625	William Alexander	Untitled (New England and New France)	Boston/B	Missing
1625	John Smith	Virginia	Boston/B	Recovered
1625	William Alexander	Untitled (New England and New France)	British Library	Missing
1625	William Alexander	Untitled (New England and New France)	Harvard	Missing

Date	Creator	Title	Owner	Status
1631	Guijelmo Blaeuw [Blaeu]	Nova Totius Terrarum Orbis Geografica ac Hy'Drografica Tablua (world)	Yale/M	Missing
1632	Samuel de Champlain	Carte de la Nouvelle France	New York/B	Missing
1635	John Smith	New England	New York/B	Missing
1635	Luke Foxe	Untitled (Northwest Passage)	Yale/B	Missing
1639	Hendrik Hondius	Nova Totius Terrarum Orbis Geografica ac Hy'drografica Tablua (world)	Yale/M	Missing
1643	Jean Boisseau	Description de la Nouvelle France	Yale/M	Recovered
1646	Robert Dudley	Carte Seconda Generale del America (Florida to St. Lawrence Gulf)	Boston/M	Missing
1647	Robert Dudley	Carta Particolare della Nuova Belgia è Parte della Nuoua Angelica (New England)	Yale/M	Missing
1647	Robert Dudley	Carta Particolare della Virginia Vecchia e Nuoua (Chesapeake)	New York/M	Recovered
1653	Jan Jansson	Nova Belgica et Anglia Nova (New England)	Yale/M	Missing
1660	Nicolaes Visscher	Plate 86	New York/M	Missing

Date	Creator	Title	Owner	Status
1660	Nicolaes Visscher	Plate 89	New York/M	Missing
1660	Nicolaes Visscher	Plate 90	New York/M	Missing
1666	Robert Horne	Carolina Described	New York/B	Missing
1671	Claude Dablon and Claude Allouez	Lac Tracy ov Svperievr	Harvard	Missing
1671	Jacobsz (Lootsman) and Jacob & Casparus	Pascaerte van Nieu Nederlant, Virginies, Nieu Englant en Nova Francia (Plate 28)	New York/M	Missing
1671	James Moxon	A New Description of Carolina by Order of the Lords Proprietors	New York/M	Missing
1672	Claude Dablon and Claude Allouez	Lac Tracy ov Svperievr	New York/B	Missing
1672	John Lederer	Map of the Whole Territory Traversed by John Lederer in His Three Marches	Boston/B	Missing
1672	John Lederer	Map of the Whole Territory Traversed by John Lederer in His Three Marches	New York/B	Missing
1672	John Seller	Chart of West Indies from Cape Cod to the River Oronoque	Boston/M	Missing
1672	John Speed	A Map of New England and New York	Yale/M	Missing
1673	Claude Dablon and Claude Allouez	Lac Svperieur et Autres Lieux	Boston/B	Missing

Date	Creator	Title	Owner	Status
1675	John Morden and William Berry	A Map of New England New Yorke New Jersey Maryland & Virginia	Yale/M	Missing
1675	John Seller	A Chart of the South Sea	Yale/M	Missing
1676	John Speed	America with Those Known Parts in That Unknowne Worlde	Boston/M	Missing
1676	Matthei Seutteri [Seutter]	Recens Edita Totius Novi Belgii in America Septentrionali circa 1676	Yale/M	Missing
1676	John Speed/ Francis Lamb	A Map of New England and New York	Yale/M	Missing
1678	Theunis Jacobsz Lootsman and Jacob & Casparus	De Noord Oost Zyde van Yerlandt van Caap de Hoorn tot aen Hedehde (Ireland, northeast side)	Boston/M	Missing
1680	F. De Witt [Van Keulen?]	Imperii Russici sive Moscoviae	Yale/M	Missing
1680	Frederik de Wit/John Thornton	A New Map Containing All the Citties. Market Townes. Rivers. Bridges. & Other Co[n]siderable places in England and Wales (Plate 5)	New York/M	Missing
1680	Frederik de Wit/John Thornton	A New Map of Ireland (Plate 3)	New York/M	Missing

Date	Creator	Title	Owner	Status
1680	Frederik de Wit/John Thornton	A New Map of the Kingdome of England and Principality of Wales (Plate 7)	New York/M	Missing
1680	Frederik de Wit/John Thornton	A New Mapp of England, Scotland, and Ireland (Plate 2)	New York/M	Missing
1680	John Thornton, Robert Morden, and Philip Lea	A New Map of New England, New York, New Iarsey, Pensilvania, Maryland, and Virginia	Yale/M	Missing
1682	Joel Gascoyne	A New Map of the Country of Carolina	Yale/M	Missing
1683	Thomas Holme	A Portraiture of the City of Philadelphia	Yale/M	Missing
1684	William Penn	A Portraiture of the City of Philadelphia	New York/B	Missing
1685	Van Keulen	Pas-Kaart vande Zee Kusten van Niew Nederland	Yale/M	Missing
1687	Thomas Holme	A Map of the Province of Pennsilvania Containing the Three Countyes	Yale/M	Missing
1690	John Thornton, William Morden, and Philip Lea (?)	New England, New York, etc.	Boston/M	Missing

Date	Creator	Title	Owner	Status
1695	Robert Morden	A New Map of the English Empire in America. Viz. Virginia, Maryland, Carolina, New York, New Iarsey, New England &c.	Yale/M	Missing
1698	John Seller	Chart of the Sea Coast of Newfoundland, New Scotland, New England	Yale/B	Missing
1702	Cotton Mather	An Exact Mapp of New England and New York	Yale/M	Missing
1708	Herman Moll	New and Exact Map of the Dominions of the King of Great Britain on Ye Continent of North America	Boston/M	Recovered
1713	Richard Daniel and W. Binneman	A New Mapp of New England and Annapolis with the Country's Adjacent . . .	Yale/M	Missing
1714	John Senex and John Maxwell	North America Corrected from the Observations . . .	Yale/M	Missing
1715	John Senex	A Map of Louisiana and of the River Mississippi	Yale/M	Missing
1718	Guillaume De L'Isle	Carte de la Louisiane et du Cours du Mississipi	Yale/M	Missing
1720	Johann Baptista Homann	Geographica Nova ex Oriente gratiosissima . . .	Yale/M	Missing

Date	Creator	Title	Owner	Status
1720	Johann Baptista Homann and Ludovico Hennepin	Amplissimae Regionis Mississippi seu Provinciae Ludovicianae	Yale/M	Missing
1720	Tobias Conrad Lotter	Pensylvania, Nova Jersey, et Nova York cum Regionibus ed Fluvium Delaware	Yale/M	Missing
1730	Guillaume De L'Isle	Antilles Françoises et des Isles Voisines (French Antilles)	Yale/M	Missing
1735	Guillaume De L'Isle	Carte de la Louisiane et du Cours du Mississipi	Yale/M	Missing
1737	John Seller	New and Accurate Chart Shewing the Variations of the Compass in the Western & Southern Oceans	Boston/M	Missing
1737	John Seller	New and Correct Chart of North Part of America from New Found Land to Hudsons Bay	Boston/M	Missing
1737	John Warner	A Survey of the Northern Neck of Virginia	Yale/M	Missing
1739	B. Roberts & W.H. Toms	The Ichnography of Charles-Town at High Water	Yale/M	Missing
1740	Carington Bowles	A Map of the Most Inhabited Part of New England	Yale/M	Missing

Date	Creator	Title	Owner	Status
1745	Louis Renard (Joshua Ottens)	Nova et Accruatissima Totius Terrarum Orbis Tabula (World) (Plate 1)	New York/M	Missing
1745	Louis Renard (Joshua Ottens)	Nova & Accuratissima Totius Terrarum Orbis Tabula Nautica Variationum Magneticarum	New York/M	Missing
1745	Louis Renard (Joshua Ottens)	Terra Neuf (New World) (Plate 30)	New York/M	Missing
1748	Matthaeus Seutter	Pensylvania Nova Jersey et Nova York cum Regionibus ad Fluvium Delaware	Yale/M	Missing
1748	Samuel Thornton	A Generall Chart of the South Sea from the River of Plate to Dampiers Streights on Ye Coast of New Guinea	Yale/M	Missing
1750	Jacques Nicolas Bellin	Carte de la Louisiane et des Pays Voisins	Yale/M	Missing
1750	Cyprian Southack	A Map of the Coast of New England, from Staten Island to the Island of Breton	Yale/M	Missing
1750	Gerard Van Keulen	Carte de la Nouvelle France Ou se Voit le Cours des Grandes Rivieres	Yale/M	Missing
1754	Emanuel Bowen	A Map of the British American Plantations	Yale/M	Missing

Date	Creator	Title	Owner	Status
1755	Lewis Evans	A General Map of the Middle British Colonies, in America	Boston/B	Missing
1759	Johann Baptiste Homann	Amplissimae Regionis Mississipi Seu Provinciae Ludovicianae	Yale/M	Missing
1761	Thomas Jefferys	An Accurate Map of His Majesty's Province of New-Hampshire in New England	New York/M	Missing
1768	George Heap and Nicholas Scull	East Prospect of the City of Philadelphia	Boston/M	Missing
1770	Tomás Lopez de Vargas Machuca	Mapa de Africa	Boston/M	Missing
1773	James Cook	A Map of the Province of South Carolina	Yale/M	Missing
1774	Thomas Jefferys and Braddock Mead	A Map of the Most Inhabited Part of New England	Yale/M	Missing
1775	Thomas Jefferys and William Faden	Sketch of the Action between the British Forces and American Provincials, on the Heights of the Peninsula of Charlestown	Yale/M	Missing
1775	Henry Mouzon	North and South Carolina with Their Indian Frontiers	Yale/M	Missing
1775	Bernard Ratzer	Plan of the City of New York	Yale/M	Missing

Date	Creator	Title	Owner	Status
1775	Bernard Ratzer	Plan of the City of New York in North America	New York/M	Missing
1775	Bernard Romans	Map of the Seat of Civil War in America (Massachusetts)	Yale/M	Missing
1775	William Scull	Map of the Province of Pennsylvania	Yale/M	Missing
1776	William Faden	A Plan of the Action at Bunkers Hill (Plate II)	New York/M	Missing
1777	Jean de Beaurain	Amerique Septle. Pour Servir a l'Intelligence de la Guerre entre les Anglois et les Insurgents	Yale/M	Missing
1777	Joseph F.W. Des Barres	Bay and Harbour of Pensacola	Boston/M	Missing
1777	Joseph F.W. Des Barres	Gulph of Mexico	Boston/M	Missing
1777	Joseph F.W. Des Barres	Nantucket Island	Boston/M	Missing
1777	Joseph F.W. Des Barres	Northeast Shore of Gulph of Mexico	Boston/M	Missing
1777	Joseph F.W. Des Barres	A Plan of the Harbour of St. Augustin in the Province of Georgia	Boston/M	Missing
1777	Joseph F.W. Des Barres	A Sketch of the Operations before Charlestown the Capital of South Carolina	Boston/M	Missing

Date	Creator	Title	Owner	Status
1777	Joseph F.W. Des Barres	View of Plaister Cliffs on the West Shore of George's Bay	Boston/M	Missing
1777	Henry Pelham	A Plan of Boston in New England with Its Environs	Yale/M	Missing
1778	Thomas Kitchin	Map of New York I.: with the Adjacent Rocks and Other Remarkable Parts of Hell-Gate	New York/M	Missing
1780	Joseph F.W. Des Barres	The Coast of New York, New Jersey and Pennsylvania	New York/M	Missing
1780	Joseph F.W. Des Barres	Plan of the Posts of York and Gloucester in the Province of Virginia	New York/M	Missing
1780	Joseph F.W. Des Barres	Port Royal in South Carolina	New York/M	Missing
1780	Joseph F.W. Des Barres	View of Boston	New York/M	Recovered
1780	William Mount and Thomas Page	A Draught of South Carolina and Georgia from Sewee to St. Estaca	Yale/M	Missing
1784	Joseph Blanchard and Langdon	An Accurate Map of the State and Province of New-Hampshire in New England	Yale/M	Missing
1784	Brion de la Tour	Carte des Etats-Unis d'Amérique, et du Cours du Mississipi	Yale/M	Missing

Date	Creator	Title	Owner	Status
1784	William Faden and Samuel Holland	A Topographical Map of the Province of New Hampshire	Yale/M	Missing
1785	William Faden	United States of North America with the British Territories and Those of Spain	Yale/M	Missing
1787	Thomas Jefferson	Map of the Country between Albemarle Sound and Lake Erie, Comprehending the Whole of Virginia, Maryland, Delaware and Pensylvania	Boston/B	Missing
1792	Andrew Ellicott	Plan of the City of Washington	Boston/B	Missing
1792	Andrew Ellicott	Plan of Washington in the Territory of Columbia	Yale/M	Missing
1792	Reading Howell	A Map of the State of Pennsylvania	Yale/M	Recovered
1793	Andrew Ellicott	Territory of Columbia	Yale/M	Missing
1795	Dennis Griffith	Map of the State of Maryland	Yale/M	Missing
1798	Osgood Carleton and John Norman	An Accurate Map of the Commonwealth of Massachusetts	Yale/M	Missing
1798	Nathaniel Holland (Norman Charts)	Chart of the Coast of New England from South Shoal to Cape Sable	Boston/M	Missing

Date	Creator	Title	Owner	Status
1798	William Norman	Chart of the Coast of Maine	Boston/M	Missing
1798 ca.	Carleton Osgood (Norman Chart)	A New General Chart of the West Indies	Boston/M	Recovered
1798	Paul Pinkham (Norman Chart)	Chart of Nantucket Shoals	Boston/M	Missing
1798	Anthony Smith (Norman Chart)	A New and Accurate Chart of the Bay of Chesapeak	Boston/M	Missing
1801	(unknown)	Map of Yedo	Yale/M	Missing
1802	Osgood Carleton and J. Loring	Map of Massachusetts Proper	Yale/M	Missing
1807	James Madison	A Map of Virginia, Formed from Actual Surveys	New York/M	Recovered
1814	Aaron Arrowsmith	A Map Exhibiting All the New Discoveries in the Interior Parts of North America	Yale/M	Missing
1820	Moses Greenleaf	A Map of the State of Maine, from the Latest and Best Authorities	New York/M	Missing
1825	(unknown)	Martinique [West Indies] [306]	Yale/M	Missing
1825	(unknown)	West Indies Martinque St Pierre Roadstead [305]	Yale/M	Missing
1840	Maruya Zenbei	Map of Kyoto	Yale/M	Missing
1841	(unknown)	Dai Nihon Dochu Hayabiki Saiken no Dzu	Yale/M	Missing

Date	Creator	Title	Owner	Status
1847	Albert Alden	Alden's Pictorial Map of the United States	Yale/M	Missing
1851	(unknown)	Map of Sakai	Yale/M	Missing
1853	(unknown)	Map of the World in the Ortelius Manner	Yale/M	Missing
1854	Juan de Cordova	J. de Cordova's Map of the State of Texas, Compiled from the Record of the General Land Office	New York/M	Missing
1854	J.H. Colton	United States of America, the British Provinces, Mexico, the West Indies, and Central America	Yale/M	Missing
1854	Suido Nakajima	Nihon Yochi Zenzu	Yale/M	Missing
1858	H.F. Walling	Map of the Counties of Barnstable, Dukes and Nantucket, Mass.	Yale/M	Missing
1860	Yagi Isaburo	Nagasaki Ko	Yale/M	Missing
1889	Saito Torakichi	Picture of Nikko	Yale/M	Missing
1891	(unknown)	Map of Niigate in 1891	Yale/M	Missing

Acknowledgments

I'VE ALWAYS HAD a tremendous respect and admiration for librarians—who helped introduce me to the joys of reading at an early age and later helped me track down countless sources and facts as a reporter. But working on this project has convinced me they are some of the nicest and most generous people on the planet. I deeply appreciate the unstinting knowledge and honesty they shared with me in the interest of the historical record. In particular, I have to thank Ron Grim, E.C. Schroeder, Margit Kaye, Abe Parrish, Alice Hudson, Nancy Kandoian, David Cobb, Tony Campbell, and Peter Barber.

I also owe a debt to the journalists who plowed this field before me, in particular Kim Martineau and Bill Finnegan, whose stories I relied upon to track down sources and information. I am also thankful for the assistance of the law enforcement officials who spent their time untangling Smiley's web of deceit, especially Steve Kelleher and Marty Buonfiglio. I also have to acknowledge the map collectors and dealers who helped me understand their world, including Harry Newman, Bill Reese, Graham Arader, Barry Ruderman, Paul Cohen, and Douglas Marshall; as well as crime experts Anthony Amore, Travis McDade, and Bob Goldman, who explained the ins and outs of art, book, and map theft to me.

Thanks as well to Smiley's friends, who helped me write a more human story than I would otherwise have been able to do, including Paul Statt, Hilary Chaplain, Bob von Elgg, Fred Melamed, Scott Haas, David Mallett, Jayne Lello, and especially Scott Slater, who spent hours with me sharing stories, letters, paintings, and videos to make sure that I got the portrait of his best friend right.

I can't say enough about the support provided to me by the Schuster Institute for Investigative Journalism at Brandeis University, as well as the support it provides to great journalism in general. Specifically I have to thank Florence Graves, Claire Pavlik Purgus, Melissa Ludtke, Sophie Elsner, Neena Pathak, Molly Taft, and Elizabeth Eckley; as well as their team of indefatigable research assistants, including Gilda Di Carli, Megan Kerrigan, Adelina Simpson, Aliya Bean, Simon Diamond Cramer, and especially Tate Herbert, who helped corral many of the wonderful maps that illustrate this volume. Thanks as well to Sophie Luke-Hall and Maura Fields for their own crucial research assistance and to Jelmer Noordeman and Koen Harmsma, who provided such excellent original maps to accompany the narrative. I am thankful to those who helped me first conceive of this story, including Janice O'Leary, who first suggested I try to interview Smiley, and Alexandra Hall, who encouraged me from the outset to pursue this book.

I am also grateful for the support of Grub Street Writer's Launch Lab, including Katrin Schulman, Lynne Griffin, and all my wonderful fellow authors, including Peggy Shriner, Tasneem Zehra, and Elizabeth Earley, who all read a draft of the manuscript and provided much helpful advice. Thanks to my mother, Ann Blanding, who lent her own eagle eye to catching typos in the penultimate draft, and to my father, Bob Blanding, who inspired my love of maps to begin with. A special shout-out to Rebecca Uchill, who also read the manuscript and offered generous amounts of advice and support in a plethora of multimedia styles.

Finally, this book would not have been possible without the unflagging support of my agent, the incomparable Elisabeth Weed, who immediately saw the potential in this strange tale and helped me shape it into a compelling narrative. And last but not least, I have to thank the wonderful team at Gotham who helped to make this a reality, including my talented editor, Megan Newman, who rightly encouraged me to let the story tell itself; her always-positive assistant, Gigi Campo; and all of the people behind the scenes who helped make this book a reality. It is because of them that you now hold this book in your hands, and for that I am endlessly grateful.

Bibliography

American Book Prices Current. Washington, CT: Bancroft-Parkman, 1983–2006.

Amore, Anthony M., and Tom Mashberg. *Stealing Rembrandts: The Untold Stories of Notorious Art Heists.* New York: Palgrave Macmillan, 2011.

Antique Map Price Record. Cambridge, MA: MapRecord Publications, 1983–2011.

Bagrow, Leo. *History of Cartography.* Cambridge, MA: Harvard University Press, 1964.

Baker, Emerson W. *American Beginnings: Exploration, Culture, and Cartography in the Land of Norumbega.* Lincoln, NE: University of Nebraska Press, 1994.

Barber, Peter. *The Map Book.* London: Walker and Company, 2005.

Barber, Peter, and Tom Harper. *Magnificent Maps: Power, Propaganda and Art.* London: British Library, 2010.

Baynton-Williams, Ashley, and Miles Baynton-Williams. *New Worlds: Maps from the Age of Discovery.* London: Quercus, 2006.

Bedford, New Hampshire: A Glimpse of the Past. Bedford, NH: Bedford Bulletin, 2000.

Binding, Paul. *Imagined Corners: Exploring the World's First Atlas.* London: Review, 2003.

Black, Jeremy. *Maps and Politics.* London: Reaktion Books, 1997.

Borges, J.L. *Collected Fictions.* Trans. Andrew Hurley. New York: Penguin Books, 1999.

Boyle, David. *Voyages of Discovery.* New York: Thames and Hudson, 2011.

Brandt, Anthony. *The Man Who Ate His Boots: The Tragic History of the Search for the Northwest Passage.* New York: Alfred A. Knopf, 2010.

Bricker, Charles, and R.V. Tooley. *Landmarks of Mapmaking: An Illustrated Survey of Maps and Mapmakers.* Amsterdam: Elsevier, 1968.

Brown, Lloyd A. *The Story of Maps.* New York: Little, Brown, and Company, 1949.

Burden, Philip D. *The Mapping of North America: A List of Printed Maps, 1511–1670.* Rickmansworth, Hertfordshire, England: Raleigh Publications, 1996.

Campell, Tony. *Early Maps.* New York: Abbeville Press, 1981.

Clark, John Owen Edward. *100 Maps: The Science, Art and Politics of Cartography throughout History.* New York: Sterling, 2005.

Crane, Nicholas. *Mercator: The Man Who Mapped the Planet.* New York: Henry Holt, 2003.

Crone, G.R. *Maps and Their Makers: An Introduction to the History of Cartography.* Folkestone, England: Wm. Dawson and Sons, 1978.

Cumming, William Patterson. *British Maps of Colonial America.* Chicago: University of Chicago Press, 1974.

Davidson, Marshall B., and Bernard McTigue. *Treasures of the New York Public Library,* New York: H. N. Abrams, 1988.

Deetz, Charles Henry. *Cartography: A Review and Guide for the Construction and Use of Maps and Charts.* Washington, DC: US Government Printing Office, 1943.

Dexter, Lincoln A. *Maps of Early Massachusetts; Pre-history through the Seventeenth Century.* L.A. Dexter: Brookfield, MA, 1984.

Ehrenberg, Ralph E. *Mapping the World: An Illustrated History of Cartography.* Washington, DC: National Geographic, 2005.

English Mapping of America, 1675–1715: An Informal Selection of Printed and Manuscript Maps Produced during the Formative Years of the English Map Trade. New York: Mercator Society, 1986.

Fairstein, Linda A. *Lethal Legacy: A Novel.* New York: Doubleday, 2009.

Fite, Emerson David, and Archibald Freeman. *A Book of Old Maps Delineating American History from the Earliest Days down to the Close of the Revolutionary War.* New York: Dover, 1969.

Garfield, Simon. *On the Map: A Mind-Expanding Exploration of the Way the World Looks.* New York: Gotham, 2013.

Gohm, Douglas Charles. *Maps and Prints for Pleasure and Investment.* New York: Arco, 1969.

Goss, John. *The Mapmaker's Art: An Illustrated History of Cartography.* Skokie, IL: Rand McNally, 1993.

———. *The Mapping of North America: Three Centuries of Map-Making, 1500–1860.* Secaucus, NJ: Wellfleet, 1990.

Greenhood, David. *Mapping.* Chicago, IL: University of Chicago Press, 1964.

Grim, Ronald. *Journeys of the Imagination: An Exhibition of World Maps and Atlases from the Collections of the Norman B. Leventhal Map Center.* Boston: Boston Public Library, 2006.

Harley, J.B. *Maps and the Columbian Encounter: An Interpretive Guide to the Travelling Exhibition.* Milwaukee, WI: Golda Meir Library, 1990.

Harvey, Miles. *The Island of Lost Maps: A True Story of Cartographic Crime.* New York: Random House, 2000.

History of Bedford, New Hampshire, 1737–1971. Bedford, NH: Bedford Historical Society, 1972.

Hoobler, Dorothy, and Thomas Hoobler. *Captain John Smith: Jamestown and the Birth of the American Dream.* Hoboken, NJ: John Wiley and Sons, 2006.

Hornsby, Stephen, and Hope Stege. *Surveyors of Empire: Samuel Holland, J.F.W. Des Barres, and the Making of the Atlantic Neptune.* Montreal: McGill-Queen's University Press, 2011.

Howse, Derek, and Michael W.B. Sanderson. *The Sea Chart: An Historical Survey Based on the Collections in the National Maritime Museum.* New York: McGraw-Hill, 1973.

Jennings, Ken, and Stuart McArthur. *Maphead: Charting the Wide, Weird World of Geography Wonks.* New York: Scribner, 2011.

Karrow, Robert W. *Mapmakers of the Sixteenth Century and Their Maps: Bio-Bibliographies of the*

Cartographers of Abraham Ortelius, 1570. Chicago: Published for the Newberry Library by Speculum Orbis, 1993.

Kebabian, John S. *The Henry C. Taylor Collection.* New Haven, CT: Yale University Library, 1971.

Kennedy, Hugh. *Original Color.* New York: Nan A. Talese, 1996.

Know Your Town: Bedford, N.H. Bedford, NH: League of Women Voters Education Fund, 1967.

Krieger, Alex, David A. Cobb, Amy Turner, and David C. Bosse. *Mapping Boston.* Cambridge, MA: MIT Press, 1999.

Lester, Toby. *The Fourth Part of the World: An Astonishing Epic of Global Discovery, Imperial Ambition and the Birth of America.* New York: Free Press, 2010.

Lister, Raymond. *How to Identify Old Maps and Globes.* Hamden, CT: Archon Books, 1965.

Marshall, Douglas W., and Howard H. Peckham. *Campaigns of the American Revolution: An Atlas of Manuscript Maps.* Ann Arbor: University of Michigan Press, 1976.

McCorkle, Barbara B. *New England in Early Printed Maps, 1513 to 1800: An Illustrated Carto-bibliography.* Providence, RI: John Carter Brown Library, 2001.

McCoy, Roger M. *On the Edge: Mapping North America's Coasts.* New York: Oxford University Press, 2012.

McDade, Travis. *The Book Thief: The True Crimes of Daniel Spiegelman.* Westport, CT: Praeger, 2006.

Mercator Society. *English Mapping of America, 1675–1715: An Informal Selection of Printed and Manuscript Maps Produced During the Formative Years of the English Map Trade.* New York: The New York Public Library, 1986.

Monmonier, Mark S. *Drawing the Line: Tales of Maps and Cartocontroversy.* New York: Henry Holt, 1995.

———. *How to Lie with Maps.* Chicago, IL: University of Chicago Press, 1991.

Moreland, Carl, and David Bannister. *Antique Maps.* London: Phaidon, 1989.

Nordenskiold, A.E. *Facsmilie-Atlas to the Early History of Cartography with Reproduction of the Most Important Maps Printed in the XV and XVI Centuries.* New York: Dover, 1973.

Portinaro, Pierluigi, and Franco Knirsch. *The Cartography of North America, 1500–1800.* New York: Facts on File, 1987.

Potter, Jonathan. *Country Life Book of Antique Maps: An Introduction to the History of Maps and How to Appreciate Them.* Secaucus, NJ: Chartwell, 1989.

Price, David A. *Love and Hate in Jamestown: John Smith, Pocahontas, and the Heart of a New Nation.* New York: Knopf, 2003.

Pritchard, Margaret Beck., and Henry G. Taliaferro. *Degrees of Latitude: Mapping Colonial America.* Williamsburg, VA: Colonial Williamsburg Foundation, in Association with Harry N. Abrams, 2002.

Reed, Henry Hope. *The New York Public Library: Its Architecture and Decoration.* New York: Norton, 1986.

Reinhartz, Dennis. *The Art of the Map: An Illustrated History of Map Elements and Embellishments.* New York: Sterling, 2012.

Schwartz, Seymour I. *The French and Indian War, 1754–1763: The Imperial Struggle for North America.* New York: Simon & Schuster, 1994.

———. *This Land Is Your Land: The Geographic Evolution of the United States.* New York: Harry N. Abrams, 2000.

———. *Putting "America" on the Map: The Story of the Most Important Graphic Document in the History of the United States.* Amherst, NY: Prometheus Books, 2007.

Schwartz, Seymour I., and Ralph E. Ehrenberg. *The Mapping of America.* New York: Harry N. Abrams, 1980.

Shirley, Rodney W. *The Mapping of the World: Early Printed World Maps, 1472–1700.* London: Holland, 1983.

Short, John R. *The World through Maps: A History of Cartography.* Toronto: Firefly, 2003.

Skelton, R. A. *Maps: A Historical Survey of Their Study and Collecting.* Chicago, IL: University of Chicago Press, 1972.

Skidmore, Chris. *Death and the Virgin Queen: Elizabeth I and the Dark Scandal That Rocked the Throne.* New York: St. Martin's, 2011.

Smiley, E. Forbes III. *The Early Cartography of North America: A Selection of Maps, Atlases, and Books, 1507–1807.* Catalog Number One. New York: E. Forbes Smiley III, 1988.

Smith, John, Edward Arber, and A.G. Bradley. *Travels and Works of Captain John Smith.* Edinburgh: John Grant, 1910.

Spurway, Doris Peck. *The Book of Remembrance: 250 Years of Commitment to Christ and Community.* Bedford, NH: Bedford Presbyterian Church, 2000.

Stefoff, Rebecca. *Vasco da Gama and the Portuguese Explorers.* New York: Chelsea House, 1993.

Swift, Michael. *Historical Maps of North America.* London: PRC, 2001.

Taylor, Andrew. *The World of Gerard Mercator: The Mapmaker Who Revolutionized Geography.* London: Harper Perennial, 2005.

Terrell, Heather. *The Map Thief: A Novel.* New York: Ballantine, 2008.

Thiry, Christopher J.J. *Guide to U.S. Map Resources.* 3rd ed. Map and Geography Round Table of the American Library Association. Lanham, MD: Scarecrow Press, 2006.

Thrower, Norman Joseph William. *Maps and Civilization: Cartography in Culture and Society.* Chicago, IL: University of Chicago Press, 2008.

Tooley, Ronald Vere. *Collecting Antique Maps.* London: Stanley Gibbons Publications, 1978.

———. *An Introduction to the History of Maps and Mapmaking: A Celebration Catalogue of Fifty Selected Items Issued to Mark the Opening of Tooley's Museum Street Premises.* London: R. V. Tooley Limited, 1980.

———. *The Mapping of America.* London: Holland, 1980.

———. *Maps and Map-Makers.* New York: Bonanza, 1952.

———. *Maps and Mapmakers.* London: Batsford, 1952.

———. *Tooley's Dictionary of Mapmakers.* New York: A.R. Liss, 1979.

———. *Tooley's Handbook for Map Collectors: A Subject Index Record.* Chicago: Speculum Orbis, 1985.

Tyacke, Sarah. *London Map-Sellers, 1660–1720.* Tring, Hertfordshire, England: Map Collector Publications, 1978.

Virga, Vincent. *Cartographia: Mapping Civilizations.* New York: Little, Brown, 2007.

Wallis, Helen, and Sarah Tyacke. *My Head Is a Map: Essays and Memoirs in Honour of R. V. Tooley.* London: Francis Edwards and Carta, 1973.

Wilford, John Noble. *The Mapmakers.* New York: Vintage, 2001.

Williams, Glyndwr. *Voyages of Delusion: The Quest for the Northwest Passage.* New Haven, CT: Yale University Press, 2003.

Williams, Sam P., and William L. Coakley. *Guide to the Research Collections of the New York Public Library.* Chicago, IL: American Library Association, 1975.

Wilson, Derek. *The Uncrowned Kings of England: The Black Legend of the Dudleys.* London: Constable and Robinson, 2005.

———. *Her Majesty's Captain: Being the Manuscript of Robert Dudley, Duke of Northumberland, Earl of Warwick, and Earl of Leicester in the Holy Roman Empire, from His Own Hand: A Novel.* Boston, MA: Little, Brown, 1978.

Wood, Denis. *The Power of Maps.* London: Routledge, 1992.

Worms, Laurence, and Ashley Baynton-Williams. *British Map Engravers: A Dictionary of Engravers, Lithographers and Their Principal Employers to 1850.* London: Rare Book Society, 2011.

Wright, Shirley Nason. *The History of Sebec 1812–1987.* Presque Isle, ME: Print Works, 1987.

———. *Recollections of Sebec, Maine: Stories Across Two Generations.* Lulu.com, 2012.

Zinsser, William K. *Search and Research: The Collections and Uses of the New York Public Library.* New York: New York Public Library, 1961.

Notes

AUTHOR NOTE: For cartobibliographies, including Burden, McCorkle, and Shirley, the number of the map is included (in parenthesis) along with the page numbers on which it appears.

1 **"[As] Geography without History":** John Smith, *The Generall Historie of the Bermvdas, now called the Summer Iles, 1624,* in Smith, *Travels and Works of Captain John Smith,* 625.

INTRODUCTION

4 **"closest confidant & adviser":** E. Forbes Smiley III, e-mail to the author, October 24, 2012.
5 **"On Exactitude in Science":** Borges, *Collected Fictions,* 325.

CHAPTER 1

10 **Smiley in the Beinecke and his arrest:** Marty Buonfiglio, Ellen Cordes, Ralph Mannarino, E.C. Schroeder, E. Forbes Smiley III, interviews with the author; Marty Buonfiglio, walking tour with the author, July 1, 2013; "Z702 is for book thief: the role of technical services in collection security," panel discussion with Ellen Cordes, American Library Association Rare Books and Manuscripts Section preconference, June 22, 2011; Yale University Police Department, incident report, complaint #0205001914, June 8, 2005; Martin Buonfiglio, affidavit, arrest warrant, July 10, 2005; Beinecke Library security video, June 8, 2005.
11 **Beinecke Library:** "About the building," Beinecke Rare Book and Manuscript Library, http://beinecke.library.yale.edu/about/about-building.
12 **world map by Henricus Martellus:** "Henricus Martellus Germanus," Beinecke Rare Book and Manuscript Library, http://brbl-dl.library.yale.edu/vufind/Author?author=Martellus%2C+Henricus; Lester, *Fourth Part of the World,* 229–232.
14 **Captain John Smith:** Hoobler and Hoobler, *Captain John Smith*; Price, *Love and Hate in Jamestown*; Smith, Arber, and Bradley, *Travels and Works of Captain John Smith.*

17 **"Could I have but the means"**: Smith, Arber, and Bradley, *Travels and Works of Captain John Smith*, 193–194.

17 **"If he have nothing but his hands"**: Ibid., 213.

17 **fifteen-year-old crown prince**: According to Smith, Arber, and Bradley (*Travels and Works of Captain John Smith*, 232), *A Description of New England* was printed on June 3, 1616. England's King Charles I was born on November 19, 1600.

17 **previously known as Cape Cod**: Schwartz and Ehrenberg, *Mapping of America*, 85.

18 **unprecedented act of virtual colonization**: Harley, *Maps and the Columbian Encounter*, 134–136.

18 **His map of New England**: Smith, Arber, and Bradley, *Travels and Works of Captain John Smith*, 699; Burden, *Mapping of North America*, (187) 226–228; Krieger and Cobb, *Mapping Boston*, 82–83; Dexter, *Maps of Early Massachusetts*, 58–59; Baker, *American Beginnings*, 290–293, 297–298; Fite and Freeman, *Book of Old Maps*, (34) 124–127; Schwartz and Ehrenberg, *Mapping of America*, 96–99.

25 **Gerard de Jode world map**: Shirley, *Mapping of the World*, (124, Pl. 105) 146–147; Richard B. Arkway, Inc., *Catalog 54: World Maps, c. 1200–1700*, 18; Buonfiglio, affidavit, arrest warrant; *Antique Map Price Record*, 2001, 2008.

26 **other maps**: Buonfiglio, affidavit, arrest warrant.

CHAPTER 2

28 **B. Altman and Co.:** E. Forbes Smiley III, interview with the author; Angela Taylor, "For delegates and others, a guide to New York's emporiums," *The New York Times*, August 11, 1980; Jennifer Merin, "After 124 years in business, the grand dame of fifth avenue, B. Altman & Co., is closing its doors," *Los Angeles Times*, November 26, 1989; David D'Arcy, "Going, going, gone: the liquidation and closing of B. Altman in New York comes as a warning to other retail giants: no one is safe," *Los Angeles Times*, January 31, 1990.

28 **"Most maps are bad"**: Smiley interview.

29 **Technical lessons**: Smiley interview; Gohm, *Maps and Prints*, 2–62; Potter, *Country Life Book of Antique Maps*, 9–27; Lister, *How to Identify Old Maps and Globes*, 51–70; Moreland and Bannister, *Antique Maps*, 11–18; Reinhartz, *Art of the Map*, 1–40; Ashley Baynton-Williams, lecture, London Map Fair, June 9, 2013.

29 **Edward Forbes Smiley III (grandfather)** : "Rev. Smiley, 78, of Bedford dies," *New Hampshire Union Leader* (Manchester), October 23, 1973; "87 degrees confirmed," *The Harvard Crimson*, March 1, 1917; United Church of Christ, *Year Book*, (New York: The Church, 1975; *General Catalogue of Andover Theological Seminary* (Boston: The Fort Hill Press, 1927); Spurway, *Book of Remembrance*; Edward Forbes Smiley, "English historians' and theologians' opinions of Luther in the eighteenth and nineteenth centuries" (master's thesis, Columbia University, 1917).

29 **Edward Forbes Smiley II (father)**: Edward Forbes Smiley II gravestone, Bedford Cemetery; "Sixty-third annual commencement," University of Connecticut, Storrs, CT, June 6, 1946; E. Forbes Smiley II, "A two crystal feedback aioustical interferometer for the measurement of ultrasonic velocities and attenuation in rarefied gases" (master's thesis, Brown University, June 1949).

30 **Adele (Moreau) Smiley (mother)**: "Adele M. Smiley obituary," *New Hampshire Union Leader* (Manchester), February 18, 2009.

30 **Marilyn and Marion Smiley**: Peoplesmart.com.

30 **Edward Forbes Smiley III and Susan Smiley:** Peoplesmart.com; Yale University Police Department, incident report, complaint #0205001914, June 8, 2005.

30 **Bedford, New Hampshire, history:** Bedford Historical Society, *History of Bedford, New Hampshire, 1737–1971;* Bedford, New Hampshire, League of Women Voters, *Know Your Town;* Bedford Presbyterian Church, *The Book of Remembrance: 250 Years of Commitment to Christ and Community;* Bedford Bulletin, *Bedford, New Hampshire: A Glimpse of the Past;* Betty Lessard, "A history of Bedford, New Hampshire 1735–1979," Merchants Savings Bank, 1979; Bedford Historical Society, "Self-guided walking tour Bedford Center"; exhibits at Bedford Historical Society; loose materials in the New Hampshire Room of the Bedford Public Library.

31 **Smiley family in Bedford:** Paul Statt and Hilary Chaplain, interviews with the author; deed, James G. Driscoll and Marguerite D. Driscoll to Edward F. Smiley and Adele M. Smiley, vol. 1557, 314, December 6, 1958, NHDeeds.com; Bedford Historical Society, photos from garden club tour, undated.

32 **Derryfield School:** "About Derryfield," Derryfield School, http://www.derryfield.org/about-DS/our-school/history; Initium, Derryfield School yearbooks, 1971, 1972, accessed through Classmates.com.

32 **Smiley at Derryfield:** Statt and Chaplain interviews.

33 **Smiley at Hampshire:** Scott Slater, Scott Haas, Dick Cantwell, and Fred Melamed, interviews with the author; Statt and Chaplain interviews; *Hampshire College Frogbook,* 1976, 1977–1978, 1978.

34 **"the dollhouse":** Slater, Statt, Chaplain, Haas, and Melamed interviews; Stephen Oravecz, "House of houses," *Hampshire Gazette,* October 15, 1977; Stephen Mease, "The little pleasures of Victorian living," *Hampshire Gazette,* September 30, 1983.

35 **Small Hope:** Slater and Statt interviews.

37 **New York Public Library Map Division:** New York Public Library, *Annual Report,* 1984, 1986; Henry Hope Reed, *The New York Public Library: Its Architecture and Decoration;* Alice Hudson, "A brief history of the New York Public Library Map Division," *Meridian,* Map and Geography Round Table of the American Library Association, no. 13 (1988); Alice C. Hudson, "The cartographic treasures in the New York Public Library, Astor, Lenox and Tilden foundations: part one: the map division," *The Map Collector,* no. 43 (Summer 1988): 2–7; Alice Hudson, "Report of what's happening at the Map Division, N.Y.P.L., 1989–1990," *SLA* Geography and Map Division, *Bulletin,* no. 161 (September 1990); Glenn Collins, "Restoring vivid palette of library's map chamber," *The New York Times,* December 12, 2005.

37 **Alice Hudson:** Alice Hudson, interview with the author; "Alice C. Hudson resume," *SLA Geography and Map Division Bulletin,* no. 167 (March 1992); Dawn Youngblood, "Alice Hudson: New York Public Library's treasure among maps," *Journal of Map and Geography Libraries* 6, no. 2 (2010): 151–173; Andrew Friedman, "City lore; the kingdom of the map," *The New York Times,* March 11, 2001.

38 **"water map":** D.D. Guttenplan, "Invisible metropolis bustles beneath city," *Newsday* (New York), October 1, 1989; Natalie Keith, "Maps to the heart of the city; at the New York Public Library," *Real Estate Weekly,* September 13, 2000.

38 **Rare Book Division:** Maud C. Cole, "The cartographic treasures in the New York Public Library, Astor, Lenox and Tilden foundations: part two: the rare books division and manuscripts division," *The Map Collector,* no. 43 (Summer 1988): 8–10; Davidson and McTeague, *Treasures of the New York Public Library,*

168–189; Williams and Coakley, *Guide to the Research Collections of the New York Public Library*.

39 **Norman Leventhal:** Krieger and Cobb, *Mapping Boston*, viii; Jerry Ackerman, "The Leventhal touch," *The Boston Globe Sunday Magazine*, October 27, 2006; Michael Blanding, "The old and the restless: for some, life begins at 80," *Boston Magazine*, April 2002.

40 **B. Altman and Co. struggled:** Daniel F. Cuff, "Altman's head resigns," *The New York Times*, December 17, 1982; "FAO Schwarz to open shops at B. Altman," *Daily News Record* (Harrisonburg, Va.), August 25, 1986; Rita Reif, "Auctions," *The New York Times*, September 5, 1986; Christine Dugas, "B. Altman's new luster fades," *Newsday* (New York), July 9, 1989; Isadore Barmash, "No bidder to rescue B. Altman," *The New York Times*, November 18, 1989; Jennifer Merin, "A Christmas bonus: B. Altman's going-out-of-business bargains in New York," *Chicago Tribune*, December 10, 1989.

40 **North American Maps & Autographs:** Forbes Smiley, *A Celebrated Collection of Aeronautica*, New York: North American Maps & Autographs, 1984; advertisement, *Map Collector* (March 1985).

40 **Leventhal's call finally came:** Smiley interview.

CHAPTER 3

44 **maps from all of ancient civilization:** Barber, *Map Book*, 6–27; Brown, *Story of Maps*, 6–8, 12–57; Bagrow, *History of Cartography*, 19–34; Bricker and Tooley, *Landmarks of Mapmaking*, 9–23; Clark, *100 Maps*, 18–34; Crone, *Maps and Their Makers*, 1–3; Goss, *Mapmaker's Art*, 18–26; Thrower, *Maps and Civilization*, 1–26; Tooley, *Maps and Map-Makers*, 1–5; Virga, *Cartographia*, 9–26; Wilford, *Mapmakers*, 6–13.

44 **Alexandria . . . Eratosthenes:** Bricker and Tooley, *Landmarks of Mapmaking*, 13; Brown, *Story of Maps*, 46–50; Wilford, *Mapmakers*, 18–28.

45 **Ptolemy:** Bagrow, *History of Cartography*, 34–37; Bricker and Tooley, *Landmarks of Mapmaking*, 15–22; Brown, *Story of Maps*, 58–80; Clark, *100 Maps*, 38–40; Goss, *Mapmaker's Art*, 24; Lester, *Fourth Part of the World*, 131–144; Thrower, *Maps and Civilization*, 23–35; Virga, *Cartographia*, 21–24; Wilford, *Mapmakers*, 29–39.

46 **Ptolemy's influence on the Renaissance:** Bagrow, *History of Cartography*, 77–86; Lester, *Fourth Part of the World*, 153–165.

46 **"raises us above the limits":** Lester, *Fourth Part of the World*, 162.

46 **scholars meeting at church conferences:** Ibid., 166–171.

46 **Mapmaking in the Middle Ages:** Bagrow, *History of Cartography*, 41–50, 61–73; Bricker and Tooley, *Landmarks of Mapmaking*, 23–31; Brown, *Story of Maps*, 81–107; Goss, *Mapmaker's Art*, 11, 35, 42; Lester, *Fourth Part of the World*, 65–128; Wilford, *Mapmakers*, 40–65.

47 **Prester John:** Lester, *Fourth Part of the World*, 45–53; Wilford, *Mapmakers*, 48–53.

47 **Portuguese discoveries:** Stefoff, *Vasco da Gama*, 13–79; Brown, *Story of Maps*, 108–112; Goss, *Mapmaker's Art*, 60; Wilford, *Mapmakers*, 67–70; Lester, *Fourth Part of the World*, 223–229.

48 **Printing press:** Brown, *Story of Maps*, 150–152; Gohm, *Maps and Prints*, 12–16.

48 **early editions of Ptolemy:** Brown, *Story of Maps*, 153–156; Shirley, *Mapping of the World*, 630; Tooley, *Maps and Map-Makers*, 6–7.

48 **altering Ptolemy's maps:** Fite and Freeman, *Book of Old Maps*, I; Lester, *Fourth Part of the World*, 203–205.

48 **Henricus Martellus:** Lester, *Fourth Part of the World*, 229–232.

49 **discovery of Waldseemüller map:** Ibid., 12–17; Schwartz, *Putting "America" on the Map*, 143–167.

49 **purchase of Waldseemüller map:** Lester, *Fourth Part of the World*, 17–19; Schwartz, *Putting "America" on the Map*, 243–255; John R. Herbert, "The map that named America: library acquires 1507 Waldseemüller map of the world," Library of Congress, Information Bulletin, September 2003, http://www.loc.gov/loc/lcib/0309/maps.html; "Library of Congress and NIST build a case for Waldseemüller map display," Library of Congress, Information Bulletin, January–February 2008, http://www.loc.gov/loc/lcib/08012/map.html.

49 **Christopher Columbus:** Lester, *Fourth Part of the World*, 236–270; Wilford, *Mapmakers*, 73–85.

51 **Amerigo Vespucci:** Lester, *Fourth Part of the World*, 302–323; Schwartz, *Putting "America" on the Map*, 109–123; Wilford, *Mapmakers*, 83–84.

51 **"Everyone of both sexes goes about naked":** Schwartz, *Putting "America" on the Map*, 296.

51 **"The women . . . not as revolting as one might think":** Ibid., 297.

51 **"I have deemed it best . . . insatiable lust":** Ibid., 310.

52 **Martin Waldseemüller map of the world:** Lester, *Fourth Part of the World*, 327–370; Schwartz, *Putting "America" on the Map*, 27–49, 123–126.

52 **"Within the memory of man":** Crane, *Mercator*, 36–37.

52 **Low Countries:** Ibid., 19–21; Taylor, *World of Gerard Mercator*, 39–47; Binding, *Imagined Corners*, 7–18; Ashley Baynton-Williams, interview with the author.

54 **Gerard Mercator:** Crane, *Mercator*; Taylor, *World of Gerard Mercator*; Binding, *Imagined Corners*, 94–102; Brown, *Story of Maps*, 158–160; Wilford, *Mapmakers*, 87–92.

55 **Abraham Ortelius:** Binding, *Imagined Corners*; Brown, *Story of Maps*, 160–165; Tooley, *Maps and Map-Makers*, 29–30; Virga, *Cartographia*, 1–3; Wilford, *Mapmakers*, 103.

56 **Gerard de Jode:** Binding, *Imagined Corners*, 131; Brown, *Story of Maps*, 166; Burden, *Mapping of North America*, 104; Crane, *Mercator*, 246, 268; Tooley, *Maps and Map-Makers*, 30–31.

56 **published at least thirty:** Tooley, *Maps and Map-Makers*, 30.

56 **Cornelius de Jode:** Burden, *Mapping of North America*, (81–82, Pl. 81), 104–106.

56 **dozen or so copies of de Jode:** Burden, *Mapping of North America*, 104.

57 **Mercator's *Atlas*, Hondius, and Jansson:** Brown, *Story of Maps*, 164–168; Tooley, *Maps and Map-Makers*, 31–35.

57 **maps in Vermeer:** Krieger and Cobb, *Mapping Boston*, 88; Jonathan Janson, "Vermeer's Maps," Essential Vermeer, http://www.essentialvermeer.com/maps/delft/maps_of_delft.html.

57 **rival family of Willem Blaeu:** Brown, *Story of Maps*, 168–173; Tooley, *Maps and Map-Makers*, 33–34.

Chapter 4

59 **R.V. Tooley:** Tooley, *Introduction to the History of Maps and Mapmaking*, 7–8; Wallis and Tyacke, *My Head Is a Map*; Valerie G. Scott, "R. V. Tooley: the 'Grand Old

Man of Maps,'" *Mercator's World* 4, no. 6 (November 1999): 12; Tony Campbell and Valerie Scott, interviews with the author.

60 **"To hold an ancient atlas"**: Scott, *Mercator's World.*

61 **"A collection of maps"**: Smiley interview, Martha's Vineyard, Massachusetts, August 2011; Campbell interview.

61 **"No dealer is really successful"**: Tooley, *Introduction to the History of Maps and Mapmaking,* 8.

62 **John Smith map of New England (1635)**: John Smith, "New England . . . 1614," London, 1635, Norman B. Leventhal Collection, Boston Harbor Hotel; Alex Krieger, interview with the author; Alex Krieger, e-mail to the author, December 2, 2013; Burden, *Mapping of North America,* (187), 226–228. (Through Krieger, Leventhal and his family declined requests for an interview.)

62 **John Smith map of New England (1624)**: John Smith, "New England . . . 1614," London, 1624, Norman B. Leventhal Collection, Boston Harbor Hotel; Krieger interview; Krieger e-mail; Krieger and Cobb, Mapping Boston, 82–83; Map 4, "New England—The Most Remarquable Parts Thus Named by the High and Mighty Prince Charles, Prince of Great Britaine," *Mapping Boston* website, http://www.mappingboston.com/html/map4-0.htm.

62 **Wood map of New England (1634)** : The copy in Leventhal's collection is a reissue from 1639. Krieger and Cobb, *Mapping Boston,* 87; Map 7, "The South Part of New-England, as It Is Planted This Yeare, 1639," Mapping Boston, http://www.mappingboston.org/html/map7-0.htm#full.

62 **Blaeu map of New England (1635)**: Willem Janz Blaeu, "Nova Belgica et Anglia Nova," Amsterdam, 1635, Norman B. Leventhal Collection, Boston Harbor Hotel.

62 **Jansson map of New England (1651)**: Jan Jansson, "Belgii Novi, Anglia Novae . . . ," Amsterdam, 1651, Norman B. Leventhal Collection, Boston Harbor Hotel; Krieger and Cobb, *Mapping Boston,* 89; Map 8, "Belgii Novi, Angliae Novae, et Partis Virginiae Novissima Delineatio," Mapping Boston, http://www.mappingboston.org/html/map8-0.htm.

62 **Speed map of New England (1676)**: John Speed, "A Map of New England and New York," London, 1676, Norman B. Leventhal Collection, Boston Harbor Hotel; Schwartz and Ehrenberg, *Mapping of America,* 113; "John Speed: A Map of New England and New York," Barry Lawrence Ruderman Antique Maps Inc., https://www.raremaps.com/gallery/detail/33489?view=print.

63 **mapmaking began in France**: Brown, *Story of Maps,* 241–255; Crone, *Maps and Their Makers,* 85–91; Tooley, *Maps and Map-Makers,* 38–45; Wilford, *Mapmakers,* 111–151.

64 **"waggoners"**: Brown, *Story of Maps,* 145–146.

64 **"So completely did the Dutch"**: E. Forbes Smiley III, "The Origins of the English Map Trade, 1670–1710," *AB Bookman's Weekly,* June 9, 1986, 2685–2694.

64–66 **John Seller . . . John Thornton . . . Mount and Page**: Smiley, "Origins"; Rodney Shirley, "The maritime atlases of Seller, Thornton, Mount & Page," *The Map Collector,* no. 73 (December 1995); Ashley Baynton-Williams, "The Charting of New England," Map Forum, http://www.mapforum.com/02/neweng.htm; Ashley Baynton-Williams, "John Seller, Sr.: the 'Atlas Maritimus,'" *Map Forum* 6 (Summer 2005); New York Public Library, "*In Thy*

Map Securely Saile": Maps, Charts, Atlases, and Globes from the Lawrence H. Slaughter Collection, 1998; Baynton-Williams and Worms, *British Map Engravers,* 469–470, 595–598, 662–663; Baynton-Williams interview; Bricker and Tooley, *Landmarks of Mapmaking,* 134; Cumming, *British Maps of Colonial America,* 39–40; Krieger and Cobb, *Mapping Boston,* 94–95.

66 **"must have been a godsend":** Cumming, *British Maps of Colonial America,* 39.

67 **Seller map of New England (c. 1675):** "John Seller. A Mapp / of New England" and "Morden & Berry. A Map of / New ENGLAND . . . [1676]," E. Forbes Smiley III, www.efsmaps.com (site discontinued; accessed through Internet Archive, www.archive.org); Smiley, "Origins"; Burden, *Mapping of North America,* (473, Pl. 473), 102–103; Goss, *Mapping of North America,* 96–97; Krieger and Cobb, *Mapping Boston,* 22, 24, 92; "John Seller," wall text, Norman B. Leventhal Collection, Boston Harbor Hotel.

67 **"first true map of New England":** Krieger and Cobb, *Mapping Boston,* 24.

68 **Smiley got a bead . . . most historians didn't:** Smiley interview.

68 **Mount and Page chart of Boston Harbor (1708):** Smiley interview; "Anonymous, 1708," Mercator Society, *English Mapping of America, 1675–1715.*

68 **Lawrence Slaughter:** Bill Dentzer, "Lawrence Havron Slaughter, computer system expert, dies," June 4, 1998, unknown publication found in Lawrence H. Slaughter Collection (LHS) archives, New York Public Library; Nancy Kandoian, "The Lawrence H. Slaughter Map Collection: the cataloguer's viewpoint," *Meridian,* no. 13 (1998); Hudson interview; "LHS List," New York Public Library Map Division, October 27, 2006, LHS archives.

69 **October 12, 1985:** Alice Hudson, memorandum to Mercator Society Committee, October 21, 1985, NYPL Map Division Archives; Scott Slater, interview with the author.

69 **Smiley's wedding:** Slater interview; photographs shown by Scott Slater.

69 **Mercator Society:** "New York Public Library forms Mercator Society," *SLA Geography and Map Division Bulletin,* no. 144 (June 1986); New York Public Library, *Annual Report,* 1986; *Mercator Society Newsletter,* June 1986, New York Public Library, Map Division Archives; "Mercator Society Income Report," February 22, 1995, NYPL Map Division Archives; Hudson memo to Mercator Society Committee, October 21, 1985, NYPL Map Division Archives.

70 ***English Mapping of America:*** Mercator Society, *English Mapping of America;* "Libraries Celebrate Edmond Halley," *Mapline,* no. 44, December 1986; "Letter from Alice Hudson," *Mercator Society News,* January 1987, NYPL Map Division Archives; Alice Hudson, memorandum to Dick Newman et al., September 24, 1986, NYPL Map Division Archives.

70 **Smiley donated $4,000:** NYPL president Vartan Gregorian, letter to E. Forbes Smiley III, November 17, 1986, NYPL Map Division Archives; Alice Hudson, memorandum to Faye Simkin, October 26, 1986, NYPL Map Division Archives.

70 **"apparently moved mountains":** "Woolridge/Thornton, c. 1702–1707," Mercator Society, *English Mapping of America.*

70 **"earliest navigable chart of Boston Harbor":** "Anonymous, 1708," Mercator Society, *English Mapping of America.*

70 **"considers the maintenance and enrichment":** Mercator Society, *English Mapping of America.*

71 **new "gallery":** "E. Forbes Smiley III," advertisement, *The Map Collector* (Spring 1987); author site visit, April 4, 2013.

71 **Matthew Clark:** Krieger and Cobb, *Mapping Boston*, 53–54.

71 **Bill Reese:** Barbara Mundy, "Object Lesson: Descendants of the Aztecs," *Yale Alumni Magazine*, July–August 2013.

71 **Franklin Institute auction:** Bill Reese, interview with the author; Lita Solis-Cohen, "Franklin Institute's rare books," *The Philadelphia Inquirer*, September 12, 1986; Stephan Salisbury, "The sale of the stacks: the Franklin Institute is selling or giving away most of its library," *The Philadelphia Inquirer*, August 16, 1986.

72–73 **"Hello, this is Forbes Smiley" . . . nothing to do with him again:** Reese interview; Smiley interview.

CHAPTER 5

77 **W. Graham Arader III:** Deborah Randolph, "A rare map dealer stirs some turmoil in a very small world," *The Wall Street Journal*, January 3, 1980; "Vallijeanne Hartrampf weds W.G. Arader 3rd," *The New York Times*, June 6, 1983; Mark Singer, "Profiles: wall power," *The New Yorker*, November 30, 1987; Phil Patton, "'Arader is up again!' and his galleries are in full bloom," *Smithsonian*, December 1, 1989; Sarah Vowell, "Futures market," *This American Life*, National Public Radio, December 12, 1997, transcript, http://www.thisamericanlife.org/radio-archives/episode/86/transcript.

77 **"then there was Graham Arader":** Singer, "Profiles."

77 **"best in the world at what I do":** "Dealer in rare maps covers a lot of ground," Associated Press, March 9, 1979.

77 **"Muhammad Ali of the map world":** Randolph, "A rare map dealer."

78 **"His most overriding concern":** Singer, "Profiles."

78 **"sees competitors as adversaries":** Ibid.

78 **boomlet in the bird and animal prints:** Peter Carlsen, "Affordable bits of botany can warm up rooms," *Chicago Tribune*, February 5, 1989; Marilyn Hoffman, "A boom year ahead for antiques," *Christian Science Monitor*, January 22, 1998; Anne Gilbert, "It takes eagle eye to spot valuable bird, plant prints," *Miami Herald*, June 4, 1989.

79 **selling their clients on maps:** Jane Margolies, "Maps that aren't for getting somewhere," *The New York Times*, March 29, 1990; Frank D. Roylance, "Big money is said to spur mutilations of rare books," *The Baltimore Sun*, December 15, 1995; Doris Athineos, "Windows of the world," *Forbes*, January 1, 1996.

79 **Place des Antiquaries:** Joseph Giovanni, "International antiques center opens its doors with a gala," *The New York Times*, November 19, 1987; Rita Reif, "Antiques center still expanding as new dealers move into shops," *The New York Times*, October 14, 1988.

79 **one of few American vendors:** "E. Forbes Smiley III," advertisement, *The Map Collector* (Winter 1987).

79 **Smiley published a list:** "Collector's Barometer," *The Map Collector* (Autumn 1987).

79 **took out a full-page ad:** "E. Forbes Smiley III," advertisement, *House & Garden*, March 1988.

79 **"Maps have a history"**: Laurie Schechter, "Maps—graphic alternatives with a worldview," *House & Garden,* June 1988.

80 **"He'd talk about the beauty of the design"**: Anonymous, interview with the author.

80 **"He was a wonderful salesman"**: Paul Cohen, interview with the author.

80 **watched him steal away one client**: Graham Arader, interview with the author. (MacLean declined requests for an interview.)

81 **Harry Newman**: Harry Newman, interview with the author.

81 **"let me sell you a few things"**: Ibid.

81 **acquired a rare "proof state"**: "E. Forbes Smiley III," advertisement, *The Map Collector* (Autumn 1987); Krieger and Cobb, *Mapping Boston,* 22, 24, 92; Burden, *Mapping of North America,* (473, pl. 473), 102–103; John Seller, "A Mapp of New England," Norman B. Leventhal Collection, Boston Harbor Hotel; Alex Krieger, e-mail to the author, December 2, 2013.

81–82 **wouldn't have anything left . . . new plan**: Krieger and Cobb, *Mapping Boston,* viii.

82 **Ruysch map of world (1507)**: Fite and Freeman, *Book of Old Maps,* 29; Smiley, *Early Cartography* (1); Virga, *Cartographia,* 173–176.

82 **Larry Slaughter**: Smiley interview; Judith Doolin Spikes, "Larchmont man leaves legacy of maps, atlases to NYC library," *Daily Times* (New Rochelle), September 20, 1997.

82 **Andrew Ellicott**: Tooley, *Mapping of America,* 216; Schwartz and Ehrenberg, *Mapping of America,* 212; Schwartz, *This Land Is Your Land,* 163; Ian McKay, "Bids and pieces," *Mercator's World* (September 1999); "Samuel Hill / Massachusetts Magazine: *Plan of the City of Washington [Second Printed Plan of Washington],*" Barry Ruderman Antique Maps Inc., http://www.raremaps.com/gallery/detail/23342?view=print; Ashley Baynton-Williams, "Plans of Washington, DC," Map Forum, http://www.mapforum.com/12/12washb.htm; Donald Heald, "Ellicott, Andrew (1754–1820) and Pierre Charles L'Enfant (1754–1825), Plan of the City of Washington," Donald A. Heald Rare Books, Prints, and Maps, http://www.donaldheald.com/maps/North%20America/maps_list_01. php?cat=North%20America&pg=13; Jed Graham, "Architect of a capital idea," July 21, 2006, Arlington National Cemetery, http://www. arlingtoncemetery.net/l-enfant.htm.

82 **Smiley originally acquired versions**: "LHS List," New York Public Library Map Division, October 27, 2006, LHS Archives; Krieger interview.

82 **appearances began to matter more**: Newman and Cohen interviews; Scott Slater, Paul Statt, Fred Melamed, Scott Haas, Paul Cohen, and Harry Newman, interviews with the author.

83 **flipping through real estate circular . . . $89,000**: Slater interview.

83 **Smiley flew up . . . elements in check**: Statt interview.

83 **$50,000 . . . "Forbes dollars"**: Slater interview.

84 **warrants for two years of back taxes**: New York state tax warrant, $4,578.93, issued May 18, 1988, satisfied April 7, 1989; New York state tax warrant, $3,844.88, issued May 18, 1988, satisfied April 7, 1989.

84 **in one instance . . . Newman forgave him**: Newman interview.

84 **other dealers, like Reese, stopped**: Reese interview.

84 **not the natural scholar:** Singer, "Profiles."

84 **unravel a complicated web:** E. Forbes Smiley III, "The Origins of the English Map Trade, 1670–1710," *AB Bookman's Weekly,* June 9, 1986, 2685–2694.

85 **Ogilby map of Carolina (1673):** Smiley, "Origins"; Cumming, *British Maps of Colonial America,* 3; Goss, *Mapping of North America,* 90–91.

85 **Holme map of Pennsylvania (1671):** Smiley, "Origins"; Burden, *Mapping of North America,* (557, Pl. 557) 214–215, 218; Smiley, *Early Cartography* (28); "The Quaker Province," Pennsylvania Historical and Museum Commission, http://www .portal.state.pa.us/portal/server.pt/community/overview_of_pennsylvania_ history/4281/1681-1776__the_quaker_province/478727.

85 **"These, then, were the men":** Smiley, "Origins."

85 **action in North America had shifted inland . . . England and France:** Schwartz and Ehrenberg, *Mapping of America,* 133–162; Pritchard and Taliaferro, *Degrees of Latitude,* 13–24, 114–125, 134–141, 152–175.

85 **Moll "Beaver Map" (1715):** Pritchard and Taliaferro, *Degrees of Latitude,* 114–117; Baynton-Williams and Baynton-Williams, *New Worlds,* 132; Reinhartz, *Art of the Map,* xiv–xxi, 14–15.

86 **De L'Isle map of Louisiane (1718):** Pritchard and Taliafarro, *Degrees of Latitude,* 118–121; Goss, *Mapping of North America,* 114–115; Fite and Freeman, *Book of Old Maps,* 176–177.

86 **Moll map of North America (1720):** Pritchard and Taliaferro, *Degrees of Latitude,* 123–125; Goss, *Mapping of North America,* 118–119; Smiley, *Early Cartography* (43, 44).

86 **Popple map of North America (1733):** Goss, *Mapping of North America,* 122–123; Smiley, *Early Cartography* (45).

86 **John Mitchell map of North America (1755):** Goss, *Mapping of North America,* 130–131; Smiley, *Early Cartography* (50); Fite and Freeman, *Book of Old Maps,* 180–184.

86 **Lewis Evans map of North America (1755):** Goss, *Mapping of North America,* 128–129; Smiley, "Survey of American Cartography," *AB Bookman's Weekly,* March 18, 1985; Schwartz, *French and Indian War,* 72.

86 **"greatest effort of American cartography":** Smiley, "Survey."

86 **French and Indian War:** Schwartz, *French and Indian War;* Schwartz and Ehrenberg, *Mapping of America,* 162–166; Pritchard and Taliaferro, *Degrees of Latitude,* 24–27.

87 **Thomas Jefferys:** Pritchard and Taliaferro, *Degrees of Latitude,* 28, Baynton-Williams and Worms, *Dictionary of English Map Engravers,* 347–351, Cumming, *British Maps of Colonial America,* 45–47.

88 **William Faden:** Pritchard and Taliaferro, *Degrees of Latitude,* 28–38; Baynton-Williams and Worms, *Dictionary of English Map Engravers,* 221–225; Cumming, *British Maps of Colonial America,* 68, 71–72.

88 **Joseph F.W. Des Barres:** Hornsby and Stege, *Surveyors of Empire,* 1–9; Krieger and Cobb, *Mapping Boston,* 106–107; Cumming, *British Maps of Colonial America,* 52–56.

88 **"one of the most remarkable products":** Cumming, *British Maps of Colonial America,* 56; Schwartz and Ehrenberg, *Mapping of America,* 202.

88 **"handsomest collection of hydrographic maps":** Ibid., 202.

89 **"one of the great rare Americana Catalogues":** William Finnegan, "A theft in the library," *The New Yorker*, October 17, 2005.

89 **"our small contribution to the history" . . . on the market for a century:** Smiley, *Early Cartography*.

CHAPTER 6

91 **one April morning in 1989:** Smiley interview. Author could uncover no independent sources to verify the date. In a letter written on March 12, 1990, Smiley set the date of the burglary as April 8, 1989 (Jose Porrja v. E. Forbes Smiley III, Supreme Court of the State of New York, Index No. 25040/90). In a sentencing memorandum submitted on September 19, 2006, Smiley's lawyer set the date as April 13, 1989 (US v. Smiley, US District Court of the District of Connecticut, 3:06-cr-00189).

91 **rare 1713 edition of *The English Pilot*:** Smiley interview.

92 **Paul Cohen remembers Smiley calling:** Cohen interview.

92 **Alex Krieger . . . remembers being questioned:** Krieger interview.

92 **Ashley Baynton-Williams . . . remembers seeing pictures:** Baynton-Williams interview.

92 **referred to the incident in court papers several times:** In response to a lawsuit by Cosmos Communications on November 8, 1989, Smiley claimed "uninsured loss of $220,000" (New York County District Court, Index No. 54546/1989); in response to a lawsuit by American Express Travel Services, on March 1, 1990, he claimed "uninsured loss of $220,000" (New York County District Court, Index No. 5678/90); in response to a lawsuit by Jose Porrja, on March 12, 1990, he claimed "an uninsured loss of $330,000; in response to the same lawsuit on November 13, 1990, he claimed "uninsured loss of $225,000" (Supreme Court of the State of New York, Index No. 25040/90). In an interview with the author in 2012, he put his losses at "a half a million dollars."

92 **"Though I may be an 'expert' in cartography":** E. Forbes Smiley III, Affidavit in Support of Order to Show Cause to Vacate Default Judgment, Jose Porrja v. E. Forbes Smiley III, Supreme Court of the State of New York, Index No. 25040/90.

93 **"I can't say it never happened":** Building superintendent (name withheld by request), 16 East Seventy-Ninth Street, New York, New York, interview with the author.

93 **friends said Smiley grew despondent:** Slater and Statt interviews.

93 *You do this alone*: Smiley interview.

93 **friends and family urged him to cut his losses:** Ibid.

93 **Baynton-Williams:** Cedrid Pulford, "Roger Baynton-Williams obituary: key figure in the growing popularity of antiquarian maps," *The Guardian* (UK), August 18, 2011; Kim Martineau, "From life among the elite to charges of theft," *Hartford Courant*, September 25, 2005. (Baynton-Williams declined to comment directly on his relationship with Smiley.)

93 **sold Smiley several maps . . . Nicholas Scull:** Arader interview.

93 **Smiley signed a note . . . attorney fees:** W. Graham Arader III v. E. Forbes

Smiley III, New York County Supreme Court, filed April 16, 1990, index no. 18994/89.

94 **took out a mortgage:** Mortgage, E. Forbes Smiley III and Fleet Bank, Piscataquis County Registry of Deeds, filed May 26, 1989, Doc. #2962 Book 725, 95.

94 **Creditors began suing him:** Cosmos Communications *v.* E. Forbes Smiley III, New York County District Court, filed February 7, 1991, index no. 54546/89. Judgment: $3,535.

94 **IRS hit him with liens:** Federal tax lien, $3,233, case no. 00000004430, July 17, 1990; federal tax lien, $1,689, case no. 00000901490, filed December 11, 1990.

94 **failed to pay the bill . . . to a burglar alarm company:** Holmes Protection of NY Inc. *v.* E. Forbes Smiley III, New York County District Court, filed April 25, 1990, index no. 12807/90. Judgment: $9,982.

94 **dispute with a Spanish map collector:** José Porrúa *v.* E. Forbes Smiley III, New York County Supreme Court, filed March 28, 1991, index no. 25040/90. Judgment: $34,682.

94 **Alex Krieger:** Krieger interview; Krieger and Cobb, *Mapping Boston*, viii; William Finnegan, "A theft in the library," *The New Yorker*, October 17, 2005.

95 **"I thought he was slimy":** Krieger interview.

95 **calling around to other dealers:** Krieger interview; Finnegan, "theft in the library."

95 **Leventhal hadn't been too concerned . . . parted ways:** Krieger interview; Kenneth Nebenzahl, interview with the author; Krieger, e-mail to the author, December 2, 2013; Smiley, *Early Cartography*, "60. Norman & Coles"; John Norman, "An accurate map of the four New England states," 1785, Boston Public Library, Mapping Boston Collection.

96 **remembered his falling-out . . . "nothing to do with me":** Smiley interview.

96 **gradually they parted ways:** Smiley and Krieger interviews.

96–97 **Slaughter . . . assemble a collection:** Judith Doolin Spikes, "Larchmont man leaves legacy of maps, atlases to NYC library," *Daily Times* (New Rochelle), September 20, 1997.

97 **"finding the really nice things":** Jane Margolies, "Maps that aren't for getting somewhere," *The New York Times*, March 29, 1990.

97 **Howard Welsh:** Helen Dalrymple, "Collector enriches LC's map holdings," *LC Information Bulletin*, 1994; Alice C. Hudson, "Obituary: Howard Welsh," *SLA Geography and Map Division Bulletin*, no. 163 (March 1991); Smiley interview; Hudson interview.

97 **Smiley showed up at the auction:** Catalog, Sotheby's New York, June 13, 1991.

97 **among other maps:** Lawrence H. Slaughter Collection (LHS) archives, New York Public Library, #1, 4, 5, 10.

97 **acquiring . . . John Seller map of New Jersey:** LHS archives, #234.

97 **another buyer picked up a group of four books:** *American Book Prices Current:* "English Pilot, 1713–68, 4 vol. Sotheby's New York, June 13, 1991, lot 288, $15,000."

97 **buy a pair of maps:** LHS archives, #1, 4.

97 **Thomas Jefferson map of Virginia (1787):** Jane Hallisey, "Thomas Jefferson,

cartographer: a father's legacy to his Renaissance son," *Mercator's World* I, no. 3 (1996).

97 **Smiley purchased a copy in 1991:** LHS archives, #100.

97 **adding it to three others:** LHS archives, #99, 101, 102.

97 *The English Pilot, Fourth Book* **from 1689:** "The Pierre S. DuPont III collection of navigation, voyages, cartography and literature of the sea," Christie's New York, October 8, 1991, Lot #101; LHS archives, #312.

98 *Atlas Maritimus* **from 1682:** LHS archives, #334.

98 **1713 edition of:** *The English Pilot* LHS archives, #324.

98 **carto-bibliography of New England:** Mercator Society Steering Committee, minutes of the meetings of May 18, 1991; January 14, 1992; and February 11, 1993; Barbara McCorkle, draft introduction to "The Printed Charts of New England 1614–1800"; all from NYPL Map Division archives.

98 **Smiley and Baynton-Williams got into a dispute:** Hudson interview. (Baynton-Williams declined to comment.)

98 **IRS filing a lien:** Federal tax lien, $21,388, March 31, 1992; federal tax lien, $25,374, September 7, 1994.

99 **largest town in Piscataquis County:** Helen Kelly, "Sebec Village reading room," *The Piscataquis Observer,* October 21, 1998.

99 **population of more than a thousand:** "Sebec, Piscataquis County, Maine," compiled from History of Piscataquis County, by Amasa Loring, c. 1880, Three Rivers Community, http://www.trcmaine.org/community/sebec.

99 **dropped to only six hundred:** US Census Bureau, 2007–2011 American Community Survey, https://www.census.gov/acs/www/.

99 **second-poorest county in Maine:** Anne W. Acheson, *Poverty in Maine,* Margaret Chase Smith Policy Center, University of Maine, Orono, 2010. (Washington County is the poorest.)

99 **most sparsely populated areas east of the Mississippi:** Sarah Goodyear, "Can one of Maine's emptiest counties become an urbanist paradise?" *The Atlantic Cities,* February 2012, http://www.theatlanticcities.com/design/2012/02/can-one-maines-emptiest-counties-become-urbanist-paradise/1154/.

99 **"Big house, little house":** Thomas C. Hubka, *Big House, Little House, Back House Barn: The Connected Farm Buildings of New England,* Lebanon, NH: University Press of New England, 2004.

99 **five-over-five Colonial . . . rebuilt the chimney:** "Sebec Lake Colonial" (real estate brochure), George Applegate, Trimble Private Brokerage, Bangor, Maine; house tour, July 4, 2013, by Andrew and April Taylor, 11 Cove Road, Sebec, Maine.

99 **rustic, country aesthetic:** VHS video by Scott Slater, August 18, 1993.

99 **map of Sebec Lake:** "Sebec Lake, Maine," for Dover-Foxcroft Chamber of Commerce, by Prentiss and Carlisle Co, Inc., Bangor, Maine, May 24, 1962.

100 **video from August 18, 1993:** Slater video.

100–101 **Smiley doted on the children . . . stories into the night:** Scott Slater interview; Felicity Slater interview.

101–103 **Boys' Weekend . . . none of his friends knew:** Scott Slater interview; Statt interview; Bob von Elgg, interview with the author; Scott Slater, journal, October 1997; "Boys' Weekend, October 8–12, 1998, Reading Dinner Itinerary"; Bob von Elgg, "Sebec Journal," 1998.

103 "diamonds from piles of coal": Newman interview.

103 "At an auction, it's fifty-fifty": Barry Ruderman, interview with the author.

103 "a lot of money out there": Ruderman interview.

104 "take out some of the competition": Newman interview.

105 bidding more on behalf of Barry MacLean: Arader interview; Reese interview; Newman interview.

105 "Forbes didn't like going to auctions": Arader interview.

CHAPTER 7

107 Gilbert Bland . . . got into the map trade: Harvey, *Island of Lost Maps*, 25–26, 220–221.

107 Selling to other dealers: Ibid., 225.

107 Single-edged razor blade: Ibid., 101.

108 Ortelius, Hondius, and Mercator: Ibid., 279.

108 day in December 1995 . . . worth around $2,000: Ibid., 10–15; Miles Harvey, "Mr. Bland's evil plot to control the world," *Outside*, June 1997.

108 library let him off: Harvey, *Island of Lost Maps*, 81–84, 88–89.

108 contained page after page: Ibid., 89–93.

108 seventeen university libraries: Ibid., 112.

108 campus cop . . . tracked him to his home: Ibid., 175–177.

108 turned himself in: Frank Roylance, "Map theft suspect in custody; hearing of warrants, Fla. man turns self in," *The Baltimore Sun*, January 5, 1996.

108 storage locker in Boca Raton: "Feds recover 150 maps, documents taken from university libraries; some items may have been stolen from UNC, Duke," *The Chapel Hill Herald* (Durham, NC), March 2, 1996; Chris O'Brien and Todd Nelson, "Man charged in thefts of rare maps from UNC-CH," *The News and Observer* (Raleigh, NC), March 5, 1996.

108 a hundred more . . . a half-million dollars: Harvey, "Mr. Bland's evil plot to control the world."

108 "I was a real victim": Ibid., 132.

108 "I'll run over him—but in a nice way": Ibid., 133.

109 four of the affected institutions . . . $100,000 in restitution: Ibid., 313–314.

109 Some seventy of the maps were never claimed: Ibid., 338.

109 "less of a con man than an un man": Ibid., 225.

109 "Mr. Bland was bland": Ibid., 225.

109 maps were closely guarded secrets: Brown, *Story of Maps*, 7–9; Harvey, *Island of Lost Maps*, 142–145.

109 Cantino chart: Lester, *Fourth Part of the World*, 338–355; Harvey, *Island of Lost Maps*, 145–149.

110 Dutch East India Company's "Secret Atlas": Brown, *Story of Maps*, 148–149.

110 handsomely rewarded privateers: Ibid., 9.

110 map dealers stole from one another as well: Ibid., 169–170.

110 Michael Huback and Stephen Chapo: *The New York Times*, March 17, 1973; Harvey, *Island of Lost Maps*, 157–158.

111 Charles Lynn Glaser: Barnaby Conrad III, "Map quest," *Forbes*, November 7, 2011; Harvey, *Island of Lost Maps*, 159–161.

111 **Andy Antippas:** "Professor sentenced in map thefts," *The Hour* (Norwalk, CT), November 21, 1978; Emily Rose, "Tulane professor steals Yale maps," *Yale Daily News,* November 29, 1978; Emily Rose, "Thief gets year in jail," *Yale Daily News,* January 15, 1979; Petula Dvorak, "N.O. doctor, art dealer held in cemetery thefts," *The Times-Picayune* (New Orleans), November 5, 1998; Patricia Leigh Brown, "New Orleans grave theft: nothing's sacred," *The New York Times,* February 16, 1999.

112 **"The stolen items can be moved very quickly":** Emily Rose, "Map thefts plague library; lost documents worth $10,000," *Yale Daily News,* December 19, 1978.

112 **tightening its security procedures:** "The region: Yale is reassessing its library security," *The New York Times,* December 3, 1978.

112 **"relentless, unyielding due diligence":** Arader interview.

112 **common myth about theft . . . days of their crimes:** Amore and Mashberg, *Stealing Rembrandts,* 7–26.

112 **Harry Newman told . . . "millions today":** Newman interview.

113 **wet string, balled up in their mouths:** William Finnegan, "A theft in the library," *The New Yorker,* October 17, 2005.

113 **Robert "Skeet" Willingham:** Harvey, *Island of Lost Maps,* 161–162, 169–171.

113 **"insider" theft accounts for 75 percent:** Margarite Annette Nathe, "'A learned congress': a closer look at book and manuscript thieves" (master's thesis, University of North Carolina Chapel Hill, April 2005); S. Van Nort, "Archival and library theft: the problem that will not go away," *Library and Archival Security* 12 (1994): 25–49.

113 **"It's the same old story":** McDade interview.

114 **Fitzhugh Lee Opie:** David Streitfeld, "Dealer held in Library of Congress theft," *The Washington Post,* March 13, 1992; David Streitfeld, "Book thief sentenced to 6 months," *The Washington Post,* October 1, 1992; Harvey, *Island of Lost Maps,* 162–163.

114 **Daniel Spiegelman . . . rare books were kept:** McDade, *Book Thief,* 9–20.

114 **hundreds of . . . manuscripts and dozens of letters:** Ibid., 151.

114 **edition of Blaeu's *Atlas Maior* from 1667:** Ibid., 144–146.

114 **library didn't discover . . . list of stolen items:** Ibid., 1–6, 41–44.

114–15 **caught the attention . . . tried to make the sale:** Ibid., 48–52.

115 **raided a storage locker:** Ibid., 54–55.

115 **Spiegleman successfully fought extradition:** Ibid., 55–60.

115 **plea bargain in April 1997:** Ibid., 82–85.

115 **Bland left prison:** Harvey, *Island of Lost Maps,* 316.

115 **table to calculate sentences:** McDade, *Book Thief,* 73–74; McDade interview.

115 **Downward departures . . . 1 percent of cases:** McDade, *Book Thief,* 81.

115 **between thirty and thirty-seven months:** Ibid., 93.

115 **"very existence of rare books":** Ibid., 91.

116 **considering an upward departure:** Ibid., 94–99.

116 **final hearing in March 1998 . . . sixty months in prison:** Ibid., 144–146.

116 **Spiegelman escaped:** Ibid., 161.

116 **caught him in a sting:** Ibid., 161–166.

116 **left prison on July 19, 2001:** Ibid., 176.

116 **Sentencing Commission revised its guidelines:** Ibid., 171–173; U.S. Sentencing Commission press release, "Sentencing commission increases penalties for crimes against cultural heritage," March 25, 2002; U.S. Sentencing Commission, *2013 USSC Guidelines Manual*, §2B1.5 "Theft of, Damage to, or Destruction of Cultural Heritage Resources," 104–108.

117 **"essential that . . . international networks are established":** Tony Campbell, "How should we respond to early map thefts?" Map History, May 25, 2002, http://www.maphistory.info/response.html.

117 **one dealer suspected him of worse:** Reese interview; Finnegan, "A Theft in the Library."

117 **John Foster map of New England (1677):** Krieger and Cobb, *Mapping Boston*, 93; Smiley, *The Early Cartography of North America*, (20); Massachusetts Historical Society, "A Map of New England," http://www.masshist.org/database/68/project15; Finnegan, "A Theft in the Library."

117–18 **He wasn't the only one . . . "maps from him":** Norman Fiering and Susan Danforth, interviews with the author.

CHAPTER 8

119 **Slaughter . . . passed away:** Bill Dentzer, "Lawrence Havron Slaughter, computer system expert, dies," June 4, 1998, unknown publication found in Lawrence H. Slaughter Collection (LHS) archives, New York Public Library Map Division.

119–20 **assembled some six hundred maps . . . in the world:** E. Forbes Smiley III, "Analysis of need," done in preparation for Slaughter Collection donation, LHS archives.

120 **collection was built as a study collection:** Judith Doolin Spikes, "Larchmont man leaves legacy of maps, atlases to NYC library," *Daily Times* (New Rochelle), September 20, 1997.

120–21 **agreed to donate the collection . . . "non-public stack area":** Alice Hudson, letter to E. Forbes Smiley III, December 10, 1996, LHS archives.

121 **that would take money . . . "collection to the New York Public Library":** Paul LeClerc, letter to E. Forbes Smiley III, December 13, 1996, LHS archives.

121 **Smiley met again with Hudson and LeClerc:** Alice Hudson, letter to E. Forbes Smiley III, February 20, 1997 LHS archives.

121–22 **Bill Walker, who promised . . . "100K" to make it happen:** Bill Walker, letter to E. Forbes Smiley III, February 20, 1997, LHS archives.

122 **"analysis of need" . . . benefit most from the collection:** Smiley, "Analysis of need."

122 **Slaughter's heirs had decided:** E. Forbes Smiley III, letter to Alice Hudson, March 14, 1997, LHS archives.

122 **agreement was signed . . . duplicates from the collection:** Excerpt from Deed of Gift and Acceptance and Deposit Agreement between Susan D. Slaughter and New York Public Library, May 30, 1997; New York Public Library Office of Counsel, Birdie Race, memorandum to Barbara A. Roehrig, June 9, 1997, referring to deposit of Deed of Gift and Acceptance, and Deposit Agreement; E. Forbes Smiley III, letter to Paul LeClerc, March 26, 1997; all from LHS archives.

122 **invited Smiley and Susan Slaughter to tea:** Catherine Carver Dunn, letter to Susan Slaughter, June 23, 1997, LHS archives.

122 **library publicized the gift . . . "will be told here":** "The Lawrence H. Slaughter Collection: hundreds of rare English maps and atlases donated to the library," *New York Public Library News*, Friends of the New York Public Library, February–March 1998.

122 **gargantuan task . . . needed to be catalogued:** "Lawrence H. Slaughter Collection cataloging and conservation project," New York Public Library Map Division, LHS archives.

123 **organizing the notes . . . "all to be in order":** Hudson interview; Alice Hudson, handwritten notes regarding call from Susan D. Slaughter, 2001, LHS archives; Alice Hudson, e-mail to Forbes Smiley, June 26, 2001.

123 **paid off a federal tax lien:** Federal tax lien, January 28, 1997, $25,374.

123 **state tax warrant:** New York State tax warrant, $6,714.70, satisfied February 19, 1997.

123 **scoping out real estate outside the city . . . settled on Martha's Vineyard:** Slater interview.

124 **perfect combination . . . New England reserve:** Barbara Gamarekian, "An inside view of the Vineyard; it's not as exclusive as you might think," *The Washington Post*, July 7, 1996.

124 **rented the summer home . . . nicknamed the "spaceship":** Slater interview.

124 **signed the purchase agreement:** Quitclaim Deed, Dukes County Registry of Deeds, December 8, 1997, book 716, 401.

124 **putting 20 percent down:** Mortgage, Dukes County Registry of Deeds, December 19, 1997, Book 716, 403.

124 **presented . . . his list of duplicates . . . "to scholars and researchers":** Forbes Smiley, letter to Alice Hudson, November 17, 1997, LHS archives; Alice Hudson, e-mail to Bill Walker, March 6, 1998, LHS archives.

125 **among the first to view the maps:** "For donors of $250 or more, curator's choice, treasure trove of English maps," LHS archives.

125 **several dozen donors . . . putting the collection together:** Susan Slaughter Kinzie, telephone message, March 17, 1998, LHS archives.

126 **health problems . . . quadruple bypass surgery:** Smiley and Slater interviews.

126 **exhibit:** *In Thy Map Securely Saile*, New York Public Library, *Annual Report*, 1999; Roberta Smith, "Art review: envy, conquest, revenge: it's all in the maps," *The New York Times*, January 15, 1999; "In thy map securely saile: maps, atlases, charts, and globes from the Lawrence H. Slaughter collection," October 24, 1998–March 20, 1999, New York Public Library, Map Division, 98-1052.

126 **line written by English poet Robert Herrick:** Robert Herrick, "A country life, to his brother M. Tho. Herrick," *The Poetical Works of Robert Herrick*, vol. I (London: William Pickering, 1825).

126 **"advice and counsel were instrumental":** "In thy map securely saile," New York Public Library.

127 **Paul Statt and Scott Slater drove down . . . Smiley's success:** Scott Slater interview; Slater, journal, March 1999.

127 **David Cobb . . . the Harvard collection:** David Cobb, interview with author.

128 **Cobb knew as much about . . . coffee table audience:** Cobb interview; Krieger interview.

128 **within a few months . . . popular cartography books ever written:** Cobb interview; Thomas C. Palmer Jr., "Starts & Stops," *The Boston Globe*, December 27, 1999; Margy Avery, acquisitions editor, MIT Press, interview with the author.

128 **exhibition based on the book:** *Mapping Boston, The Story of Boston and the New World Told through Maps*, Boston Public Library; "A vast collection tracks the progress of an ever-changing city," *The Boston Globe Magazine*, October 10, 1999; Valerie A. Russo, "Charting Boston's past: exhibits of old and new maps trace the development of the city and the region," *The Patriot Ledger* (Quincy, Mass.), October 23, 1999.

128 **most popular . . . two hundred thousand visitors:** Beth Carney and Jim Sullivan, "Names & faces," *The Boston Globe*, April 20, 2000.

128 **Smiley brought his friends:** Slater, Bob von Elgg, and Scott Haas, interviews with the author.

129 **Apart from a thank-you by Leventhal:** Krieger and Cobb, *Mapping Boston*, viii.

129 **their son, Edward Forbes Smiley IV:** Slater, journal, November 1999.

129 **"He came in here and divided the town":** Louisa Finnemore, interview with the author.

129 **"Yeah, rules 'from away'":** Ruth Nason, interview with the author.

130 **"thought he was better than everyone else":** Anonymous, interview with the author.

130 **"He had a lot of ideas":** Carol Cress, interview with the author.

130 **Glen Fariel:** Glen Fariel, letter to Judge Janet Bond Arteron, 2005; Slater, journal, October 1997.

130 **Smiley purchased it . . . coincide with the annual parade:** Sarah MacIlroy, "Historical society launches landscaping plan in Sebec Village," *The Piscataquis Observer*, May 22, 2002; "Sebec holds 5K, canoe race to call in Fourth of July," *The Piscataquis Observer*, July 10, 2002.

130–31 **Smiley also purchased . . . market selling local produce:** E. Forbes Smiley III, application for a permit for Shoreland Zoning, Town of Sebec, March 2002; Town of Sebec, Permit No. 2014, issued to E. Forbes Smiley III, March 26, 2002; Sarah MacIlroy, "Sebec Village farmer's market opens," *The Piscataquis Observer*, August 21, 2002; Kim Martineau, "From life among the elite to charges of theft," *Hartford Courant*, September 25, 2005.

131 **"Hey, neighbor!" . . . "beaded wine skirt":** Sebec Village Shops, www .sebecvillageshops.com (site discontinued; accessed through the Internet Archive, www.archive.org).

131 **Smiley opened a restaurant:** Jessica Lee, "Café, post office, and farmers market coexist in a quaint country general store," *The Piscataquis Observer*, August 20, 2003; Slater interview; Sebec Village Shops website.

132 **"He was Robin Hood":** David Mallett, interview with the author.

132 **$600,000 on the renovations:** Lee, "Café, post office, and farmers market."

132 **"sometimes he went by my house":** Anonymous, interview with the author.

132 **Smiley tried to convince them:** Finnemore interview.

132 **Bill and Charlene Moriarty . . . free of charge:** Martineau, "From life among the elite."

132 **Moriartys purchased a home . . . rowdy boaters it would attract:** Sarah MacIlroy, "Land use continues to spur debate in Sebec," *The Piscataquis Observer,* August 7, 2002; Smiley, Slater, Mallett, and Jayne Lello, interviews with the author.

133 **word "marina" in their application:** William Moriarty, Application for Building Permit, Town of Sebec, April 24, 2001.

133 **specified "that it stays as it is":** Town of Sebec, Permit No. 2009, issued to William Moriarty, April 24, 2001.

133 **permit "pertains only to use of the buildings":** Missy Small, letter to Bill and Charlene Moriarty, May 21, 2001.

133 **"stop work" order:** William Murphy, letter to William Moriarty, June 5, 2002.

133 **"stick it up your ass":** Jayne Lello, interview with the author.

133 **"allowed to remain 'unclear'":** Susan Dow, "A problem in Sebec," *The Eastern Gazette,* July 20, 2002.

133 **"resorted to a more tribal approach":** David Mallett, "Sebec needs to be mindful of its community responsibilities," *The Piscataquis Observer,* July 31, 2002.

134 **residents approved every one:** "Sebec holds town meeting," *The Piscataquis Observer,* August 14, 2002.

134 **alleged violations at Smiley's shops:** Charlene Moriarty, Request for Code Enforcement Officer Investigation Due to Citizen Complaint, Town of Sebec, October 7, 2002; Jessica Lee, "Town aims for closure on village permit confusion," *The Piscataquis Observer,* October 23, 2002.

CHAPTER 9

136 **number is more like forty-five:** "Congratulations to these staff members celebrating 45-years of service to Yale," Working @ Yale, http://working.yale.edu/congratulations-these-staff-members-celebrating-45-years-service-yale.

136 **worked with the first curator . . . "calls me his mentor":** Margit Kaye, interview with the author.

136 **John Seller's 1675 "Mapp of New England":** John Seller, "Mapp of New England," London, 1675, Sterling Memorial Library Map Collection, 76 1675.

136–37 **dark smudge . . . shouldn't have been missing:** Kaye interview; "John Seller. A Mapp / of New England," E. Forbes Smiley III website, www.efsmaps.com/map01.html (site discontinued; accessed through Internet Archive, www.archive.org).

137 **Kaye printed out the page:** "John Seller. A Mapp / of New England," E. Forbes Smiley III website, printout, July 11, 2002.

137 **took it to the head curator . . . keep a closer eye on Smiley:** Kaye interview. (Fred Musto did not respond to interview requests.)

137 **Smiley was in the Sterling often:** Kaye interview; Abe Parrish, interview with the author.

138 **Smiley sat in the reading room . . . no one gave him a second look:** Smiley interview.

139 **thefts started in the spring of 2002:** Defendant's memorandum in aid of sentencing (20), US *v.* Edward Forbes Smiley III, September 18, 2006, 28.

139 **brought the map to his friend Harry Newman:** Newman interview.

139 **Osher . . . bought it from him:** Harold Osher and Bill Reese, interviews with the author; Smiley website; Restitution Order (29), US *v.* Smiley.

139 **stealing became easier:** Smiley interview.

139–40 **Kaye began to carefully watch . . . turning over pages:** Kaye interview.

140 **discovered four maps:** "Reading Howell, A / Map / of the / State / of / Pennsylvania," Smiley website, printout, October 22, 2002; "John Wilson, A Map / of / South Carolina," Smiley website, printout, October 23, 2002; "Samuel Thornton, A Generall chart of the / South Sea," Smiley website, printout, October 23, 2002; "William Darby, A / Map / of the State of Louisiana," Smiley website, printout October 23, 2002.

140 **Henry Pelham map of Boston:** "Henry Pelham, A Plan of Boston in New England," Smiley website, printout February 21, 2003.

140 **found the image of the card:** "Henry Pelham, A Plan of Boston in New England," catalog card in microfilm.

141 **John Bonner map of Boston (1743):** "John Bonner / William Price, A New Plan of Ye Great Town of Boston," Smiley website; Krieger and Cobb, *Mapping Boston*, 45–46.

141 **brought the map to Harry Newman:** Newman interview; Harry S. Newman, ed., *The Old Print Shop Portfolio*, Volume LXII, Number I, September 2002.

141 **International Conference on the History of Cartography:** "International Conferences on the History of Cartography," Maphistory, http://www .maphistory.info/ichcintro.html.

141 **special label of beer:** "The Shipyard Brewing Co debuts summer ale as promotion for international cartographic conference," *Modern Brewery Age*, June 23, 2003; photo on Kris Butler's photostream, Flickr.com, http://www.flickr .com/photos/kris_butler/1409516238/.

141 **"2-row British Pale Ale" . . . "seafood":** "Summer Ale," Shipyard Brewery, www.shipyard.com/taste.

142 **list of complaints . . . dismissed:** Code Enforcement Officer Bill Murphy, memorandum to Town of Sebec Board of Selectman, October 21, 2002.

142 **planning board . . . also filed a complaint:** Request for Code Enforcement Officer Investigation due to Citizen Complaint by Mary Downs/Walter Emmons, Town of Sebec, November 18, 2002.

142 **"obligation to uphold the laws":** "Planning board members seek review of Sebec Village Shops plan," *The Piscataquis Observer*, November 27, 2002.

142 **"a shot across Mr. Smiley's bow":** Edmond J. Bearor, letter to Gregory Cunningham, October 25, 2002.

142 **Glen Fariel resigned:** Jessica Lee, "Sebec selectman resigns from post," *The Piscataquis Observer*, November 20, 2002.

142 **denied by the remaining two selectmen . . . investigation into alleged violations:** Jessica Lee, "Sebec signs pact to end marina dispute," *The Piscataquis Observer*, December 4, 2002.

142–43 **"overwhelmed with all of our plans" . . . "handling local land-use issues":** Jessica Lee, "Sebec saga continues," *The Piscataquis Observer*, December 18, 2002.

143 **filed a new appeal . . . "evidence in the record":** Complaint, E. Forbes Smiley III *v.* The Inhabitants of the Town of Sebec, Piscataquis County, Maine and William and Charlene Moriarty, d/b/a Sebec Village Marina Piscataquis

County Superior Court, Docket No. AP-02-02, December 18, 2002; Jessica Lee, "Appeal of Sebec marina goes to superior court," *The Piscataquis Observer*, January 1, 2003.

143 **Buzz Small and Susan Dow . . . "don't like to lose":** Kim Martineau, "From life among the elite to charges of theft," *Hartford Courant*, October 25, 2005.

143 **violation of exceeding the permitted amount:** Jessica Lee, "Code officer finds violations at Sebec Village Shops," *The Piscataquis Observer*, February 5, 2003.

143 **grandfathered parking on 41 percent:** Gregory Cunningham, Draft Consent Agreement between E. Forbes Smiley III and the Town of Sebec, April 3, 2003; Jessica Lee, *The Piscataquis Observer*, April 2, 2003.

143 **stood over a desk . . . selectmen said:** Jessica Lee, *The Piscataquis Observer*, April 9, 2003.

143 **solidly split into two camps:** Kim Martineau, "Casting words: on the library crimes beat," GSLIScast, Graduate School of Library and Information Science, Simmons College, February 26, 2007, http://gslis.simmons.edu/podcasts.

143 **Big Bear Snowmobile Club . . . discrimination:** Jessica Lee, "Private status of snowmobile club irks selectman," *The Piscataquis Observer*, February 5, 2003; Town of Sebec, Selectmen's Meeting Notes, July 28, 2003.

144 **sign prohibiting any boater from docking:** Martineau, "From life among the elite."

144 **speedboats began buzzing . . . windows had been shattered:** Smiley interview; Mallett and Lello interviews.

144 **left on his blazer:** Ron Grim, "For the record," notes from phone conversation with Steve Kelleher, July 8, 2005; handwritten notes from phone conversation with Steve Kelleher, July 8, 2005; both from Norman B. Leventhal Map Center (LMC) archives at the Boston Public Library.

144 **greeted the librarians warmly:** Susan Glover, interview with the author.

144 **writing only "SMILEY MA":** LMC archives.

145 **checked out a copy of:** *Speculum Orbis Terrarum* Cornelius de Jode, *Speculum Orbis Terrarum*, 1593, Boston Public Library, Atlas 10.4.1593; "De Jode, Cornelius," Smiley Inventory #107, LMC archives.

145 **de Jode double-hemisphere map:** Shirley, Mapping of the World, (184, Pl. 149); Baynton-Williams and Baynton-Williams, *New Worlds*, 49; Barry Lawrence Ruderman Antique Maps Inc., "Cornelis De Jode: [World]," http://www.raremaps.com/gallery/detail/36263ct; Richard B. Arkway, *Catalog 54: World Maps* (24).

145 **de Jode map of North America:** Burden, *Mapping of North America* (81, Pl. 81), 103–105; Barry Lawrence Ruderman Antique Maps Inc. "Cornelius De Jode:Americae Pars Borealis," http://www.raremaps.com/gallery/detail/26258/; Richard B. Arkway, Inc., *Catalog 59: Antique Maps, Manuscripts, Atlases & Illustrated Works* (10).

145 **made at least a half-dozen trips:** LMC archives.

146 **Samuel de Champlain:** Burden, *Mapping of North America* (160, 161), 196–200; Schwartz and Ehrenberg, *Mapping of America*, 85–89; Fite and Freeman, *Book of Old Maps*, 120–123.

146 **Smiley looked at Boston's copy:** "Champlain, Samuel de," Smiley inventory #65, LMC archives.

146 **had only rarely come up for auction:** *Antique Maps Price Record* database search.

146 **When one finally did appear:** Randy Boswell, "Rare early maps of Canada hit the auction block," Canwest News Service, April 5, 2010.

146 **copy sold at a Bloomsbury auction:** "Rare travel book & map of the day," Graham Arader blog, June 30, 2011, http://grahamarader.blogspot.com/2011/06/map-of-day-carte-geographique-de-la.html.

146 **Smiley requested a ten-volume set:** Theodor de Bry, *Collections*, 1591, Boston Public Library, G.281.51; "Bry, Theodor de," Smiley inventory #35, LMC archives.

146 **Theodor de Bry:** Burden, *Mapping of North America* (76), 96–98.

146 **Jacques Le Moyne:** Jacques Le Moyne, "Floridae Americae Provinciae Recens," in Theodor de Bry, *Collections, Segunda Editio*, vols. 6–7, part 2, 1591, Boston Public Library, G.281.51 vol. 6; Burden, *Mapping of North America*, (79), 101–102; Fite and Freeman, *Old Maps*, 67–70; Cohen & Taliaferro Inc. and Richard B. Arkway Inc., *Catalog 62: Fine Antique Maps* (25).

147 **John White:** John White, "Americae Pars, Nunc Virginia dicta," in Theodor de Bry, *Collections, Segunda Editio*, vols. 6–7, part 1, 1591, Boston Public Library, G.281. 51 vol. 6; Burden, *Mapping of North America*, (76), 96–98; Barry Lawrence Ruderman Antique Maps Inc., "John White / Theodore De Bry: Americae pars, nunc Virginia dicta . . . ," https://www.raremaps.com/gallery/detail/36230ct/; Cohen & Taliaferro Inc. and Richard B. Arkway Inc., *Catalog 62: Fine Antique Maps* (26).

147 **Richard Hakluyt:** Gerald Roe Crone, "Richard Hakluyt," *Encyclopaedia Brittanica*, http://www.britannica.com/EBchecked/topic/252157/Richard-Hakluyt; Hoobler and Hoobler, *Captain John Smith*, 67–73.

147 **Samuel Purchas:** "Samuel Purchas," *Encylopaedia Brittanica*, http://www.britannica .com/EBchecked/topic/483810/Samuel-Purchas.

147 **Smiley requested the BPL's copy:** Samuel Purchas, *Hakluyus Postumus, or Purchas His Pilgrimes*, 1625, Boston Public Library, G.300.22; Ron Grim, Memorandum, "Subject: Inventory of missing items from publications used by Smiley at the Boston Public Library," January 3, 2006, LMC archives.

148 **the island of California:** Burden, *Mapping of North America*, (214) 265–66, 507–08; Tooley, *Mapping of America*, 110–134; Fite and Freeman, *Book of Old Maps*, 128–131; "The island of California: a persistent fallacy," *Mercator's World*, 1996; W. Michael Mathes, "Traditional, desirable, possible: origins of the island of California," *Mercator's World*, 1996.

149 **prices of up to $25,000:** *Antique Map Price Record* database search.

149 **"Let me make it up to you":** Philip Burden, interview with the author.

149 **Smiley sold Burden . . . Le Moyne map:** "Boston Public Library," list from FBI to BPL, undated (August 2006).

149 **sold Arkway . . . John White . . . John Smith:** "Boston Public Library," list from FBI to BPL, undated (August 2006).

149 **Robert Dudley . . . sold to . . . Bob Gordon:** Ron Grim, memorandum, "Unresolved issues," November 6, 2006, LMC archives; e-mail from Ron Grim to Bernard Margolis, September 6, 2006, LMC archives; Bob Gordon, interview with the author.

149 **Sir Robert Dudley:** Burden, *Mapping of North America*, (266, 278, 279, 280), 340–341, 349–364; Derek Wilson, *The Uncrowned Kings of England*, 357–370; Wilson, *Her Majesty's Captain*; O.A.W. Dilke and Margaret S. Dilke, "Sir Robert Dudley's

Contribution to Cartography," *The Map Collector* 19 (June 1982), 10–14; Chris Skidmore, *Death and the Virgin Queen*, 26–29, 76–81, 308–312.

151 **Smiley checked out the BPL's copy:** Robert Dudley, *Dell' Arcano Del Mare*, 1647, Boston Public Library, G1059 .D84 1647; "Dudley, Robert," Smiley inventory #53, LMC archives.

CHAPTER 10

154 **Norman Leventhal announced:** Catherine Foster, "Center to show off library's map collection," *The Boston Globe*, September 26, 2003.

154 **celebration that November:** Dana Bisbee, "Social scene; Joslin Center benefactors sparkle in diamond setting," *Boston Herald*, November 17, 2003.

154 **"the old kind of arrogance":** Krieger interview.

154 **friends noticed the changes too:** Slater, Statt, and Von Elgg interviews.

154 **Smiley refused to respond to requests:** Town of Sebec, Selectmen's Meeting Notes, June 16, 2003; October 20, 2003; December 1, 2003; January 14, 2004.

155 **"Do we put them in jail for noncompliance?":** Jessica Lee, "Sebec selectmen may pursue consent agreement with Sebec Village Shops' owner," *The Piscataquis Observer*, March 3, 2004.

155 **handed down her decision . . . "goal in the village":** Decision and Order, E. Forbes Smiley III v. The Inhabitants of the Town of Sebec, et al., Piscataquis County Superior Court, Docket No. AP-02-02, March 25, 2004; Jessica Lee, "Court decision sides with town," *The Piscataquis Observer*, April 7, 2004.

155 **"little oasis has been created":** Letter to the Editor, *The Piscataquis Observer*, April 7, 2004.

155 **new garage on their property:** Kim Martineau, "From life among the elite to charges of theft," *Hartford Courant*, October 25, 2005.

156 **Smiley woke to the sounds of a bulldozer . . . tearing up his land:** Smiley interview, Martha's Vineyard, Massachusetts, August 2011; Andrew Taylor, interview with the author; Jessica Lee, "Invasive weed at root of Sebec controversy," *The Piscataquis Observer*, July 23, 2003; Jessica Lee, "Sebec holds annual town meeting," *The Piscataquis Observer*, August 13, 2003.

156 **Access couldn't have been easier . . . farthest from the circulation desk:** Hudson interview.

156 **Melish map of the United States:** John Melish, "Map of the United States with the Contiguous British & Spanish Possessions," 1816, New York Public Library, Map Div. 01-11488.

157 **Collet map of North Carolina:** John Collet, "A Compleat Map of North Carolina from an Actual Survey by Captn. Collet, Governor of Fort Thurston," 1770, New York Public Library, Map Division.

157 **resold it to San Diego map dealer . . . "in our collection":** Barry Ruderman and Alice Hudson, interviews with the author.

157 **Thornton map:** John Thornton, "A New Map of East and West New Jarsey: Being an Exact Survey Taken by Mr. Wolridge," 1702–1707, New York Public Library, Map Div. 02-295 [No. 98].

157 **Des Barres's maritime atlas:** Joseph F.W. Des Barres, *Atlantic Neptune* (Lenox

Copy), 1780, New York Public Library, Atlas cases (Des Barres, J.F.W. Atlantic Neptune).

157 **William Faden's Revolutionary War atlas:** William Faden, *North American Atlas,* 1777, New York Public Library, Atlas cases (Faden, W. North American atlas).

157 **two editions of Samuel de Champlain's *Voyages*:** Samuel de Champlain, Les Voyages . . . , 1613, *KB 1613 (Champlain, S. de. Voyages dv sievr de Champlain Xaintongeois); Samuel de Champlain, Les Voyages . . . , 1632, *KB 1632 (Champlain, S. de. Voyages de la Novvelle France occidentale (P. Le-Mvr).

157 **auction at Swann Galleries:** Arader interview; Receipt from Swann Galleries, December 9, 2004; "Maps & Atlases, Natural History, Historical Prints & Ephemera," Public Auction Sale 2027, Swann Galleries, December 9, 2004.

158 **"He is a crook":** Graham Arader and anonymous collector, e-mail exchange, January 24, 2005.

158 **demolished the home in the summer:** Kim Martineau, "Map of a crime: the arrest of antique map dealer E. Forbes Smiley III has thrown the staid world of libraries and collectors into turmoil," *Hartford Courant,* July 17, 2005; William Finnegan, "A Theft in the Library," *The New Yorker,* October 17, 2005.

158 **contract . . . to build a house:** Statement of Account, David Pizzano, Dukes County Registry of Deeds, Book 1050, 105.

158 **seemed foolish, even for Smiley:** Slater and Statt interviews.

159 **proposed building a private preschool:** Chris Burrell, "Task force team presents Chilmark preschool plan to bolster enrollments," *Vineyard Gazette,* July 12, 2004; Articles of Organization, Friends of the Chilmark Pre-School, July 20, 2004, Massachusetts Secretary of State filing no. 200477433080.

159 **began looking for an exit strategy . . . unable to go back to bed:** Smiley interview.

159 **new modular home:** Nelson Sigelman, "Chilmark man pleads guilty to stealing valuable, antique maps from Yale University," *Martha's Vineyard Times,* June 29, 2006; Martineau, "From life among the elite."

159 **"left naked to the scrutiny":** Forbes Smiley, "Our house will disappear soon," letter to the editor, *Martha's Vineyard Times,* February 17, 2005.

159 **"Money was no object":** David Pizzano, interview with the author.

160 **tax lien:** Federal tax lien, $57,063, January 20, 2005, Case no. 209805705.

160 **had officially launched:** Editorial, "Planning a map room," *The Boston Globe,* October 6, 2004.

160 ***"Smiley knows this collection":*** Ron Grim, interview with the author.

160 ***The American Pilot:*** Cobb and Krieger, *Mapping Boston,* 49–52. Donald A. Heald, Rare Books, Maps, and Prints, "[NORMAN, John]—William NORMAN (1748–1817): A Chart of South Carolina and Georgia," http://www.donald heald.com/maps/North%20America/maps_list_01.php?cat=North% 20America&aut=South&sortfield=&pg=4.

160 **Boston had four of them:** John Norman, *The American Pilot,* Boston, 1794, Boston Public Library, G1106.P5 N6 1794x; William Norman, *The American Pilot,* Boston, 1798, Boston Public Library, G1106.P5 N6 1798; William Norman, *The American Pilot,* Boston, ca. 1798, Boston Public Library, G1106.P5 N6 1798.

2x; Andrew Allen, *The American Pilot,* Boston, 1816, Boston Public Library, G1106.P5 A4 1816x.

160 **examined the last copy:** Ron Grim, "Subject: inventory of missing items from publications used by Smiley at the Boston Public Library," January 3, 2006, Norman B. Leventhal Map Center (LMC) archives.

160 **took it down . . . happy to purchase it:** Newman interview.

160–61 **went to Boston to view . . . check bounced:** Grim interview; Ronald E. Grim, letter to Christopher Schmeisser, August 29, 2006, LMC archives.

161 **avoided the Harvard Map Collection:** David Cobb, interview with the author.

161 **copy of Champlain's *Voyages*:** Samuel de Champlain, *Les Voyages . . . ,* Paris, 1612, Harvard College Library, Can 205.4*.

161 **travelogues from several other:** Claude Dablon, *Relation . . . de la Compagnie de Jesus en la Nouvelle France . . . ,* Paris, 1672, Harvard College Library, Can 236. 70*; Claude Dablon, *Relation . . . de la Compagnie de Jesus en la Nouvelle France . . . ,* Paris, 1673, Harvard College Library, Can 236.71; Chrétien Le Clercq, *Establissement de la foy dans la Nouvelle France . . . ,* 1691, Harvard College Library, *FC6.L4964.691pb; Marc Lescarbot, *Histoire de la Nouvelle France . . . ,* 1609, Harvard College Library, *FC6.L5635.609hab.

161 **copy of Hubbard's book:** William Hubbard, *A Narrative of the Troubles with Indians in New-England . . . ,* 1677, *AC6.H8613.677na (A).

161 **avoided going to the Beinecke:** E.C. Schroeder, interview with the author.

161 **book by German geographer:** Johann Huttich, *Novus Orbis Regionum . . . ,* Paris, 1532, Yale University Library, CE141 +N68.

162 **unusual "double-cordiform" map:** Shirley, *Mapping of the World,* (66, Pl. 60); Richard B. Arkway, Inc., Catalog 54: World Maps, (11); Oronce Fine, "Nova et Integra Vniversi Orbis Descriptio," Paris, 1532, Yale University Library, CE141 +N68.

162 **brought it to Paul Cohen . . . never did:** Schroeder interview; Harry Newman and Paul Cohen, interviews with the author; Smiley interview.

162 **valued at more than $40,000:** *Antique Map Price Record* database search.

162 **even older book:** Hernán Cortés, *Praeclara Ferdinãdi. Cortesii de noua maris Oceani Hyspania narratio . . . ,* Nuremberg, 1524, Yale University Library; Taylor, *World of Gerard Mercator,* 58.

162 **map of the Aztec capital of Tenochtitlán:** Hernán Cortés, Untitled (Mexico City/Gulf of Mexico), 1524, Yale University Library, Taylor, *World of Gerard Mercator,* 58; Barbara E. Mundy, "Mapping the Aztec Capital: The 1524 Nuremberg Map of Tenochtitlan, Its Sources and Meanings," *Imago Mundi,* Vol. 50, 1998.

162 **already paid . . . $200,000 more:** Pizzano interview.

163 **worth only $50,000 to 60,000 at most:** *Antique Map Price Record* database search; Martin Buonfiglio, affidavit, arrest warrant, New Haven Police Department, July 10, 2005.

163 **Arkway had sold a copy . . . $125,000:** *Antique Map Price Record* database search; Buonfiglio affidavit, arrest warrant.

163–65 **guard opened a door . . . leave the library:** Beinecke Library security video, June 8, 2005; notes by Lynn Ieronimo, head of security, Beinecke Library;

Cordes interview; audio recording of Ellen Cordes in Z702 *Is for Book Thief: The Role of Technical Services in Collection Security*, 2011 RBMS Preconference, Rare Books and Manuscript Section, Association of College and Research Libraries, a division of the American Library Association, http://www.rbms.info/ conferences/preconfdocs/2011/Talks/SeminarA.mp3.

164 **"wind face"**: Dennis Reinhartz, *Art of the Map*, 10.

Chapter 11

167–68 **"dropped a file on my desk"**: Stephen Kelleher, interview with the author.

168 **share of war stories**: Damon Katz, e-mail to the author, November 27, 2013; Justin Pritchard, "148 students graduate at Bishop Feehan in Attleboro," *Providence Journal-Bulletin*, June 5, 1994; Doug Allan, "Pizza parlor fined for serving minors," *Providence Journal-Bulletin*, March 18, 1999; Doane Hulick, "Driver fired on by police held at ACI," *Providence Journal-Bulletin*, January 30, 2001; "Weddings," *Providence Journal-Bulletin*, September 9, 2001; Richard C. Dujardin, "Police promoted, honored for valor," *Providence Journal-Bulletin*, March 1, 2002; Gregory Smith, "Two injured when car rams cruiser," *Providence Journal-Bulletin*, July 2, 2003.

168–69 **drove from the New Haven . . . theft a federal offense**: Kelleher interview.

168 **the de Jode map**: Gerard de Jode, "Vniversi Orbis Sev Terreni Globi . . . ," from *Speculum Orbis Terrarum*, Antwerp, 1578, Yale University Library, 1976 Folio 2.

168 **wormholes**: LiveScience, "Medieval books hold suprising fossil record," MSNBC.com, November 21, 2012.

168 **Beinecke's copy of the *Speculum***: Gerard de Jode, *Speculum Orbis Terrarum*, Antwerp, 1578, Yale University Library, 1976 Folio 2.

169 **Theft of Major Artwork Act**: 18 US Code, sec. 668, "Theft of major artwork"; Lynne Chaffinch, "The Federal Bureau of Investigation's Art Theft Program," *The Silver Lining: Coping with Theft, Vandalism, Deterioration, and Bad Press*, Library of Congress publications, http://www.nps.gov/history/history/ online_books/presidents/chap10.html.

169 **only one of eight maps**: Buonfiglio affidavit.

169 **introduced him to Bill Reese**: Kelleher interview; Schroeder and Reese interviews.

170 **post to ExLibris**: Everett Wilkie, "Recent Map Thefts," MapHist Listserv, July 6, 2005.

170 **first appearance**: Kim Martineau, "Antique map theft charged: dealer's bail set in incidents at Yale Library," *Hartford Courant*, July 9, 2005; "Casting words: on the library crimes beat," GSLIScast, Graduate School of Library and Information Science, Simmons College, February 26, 2007, http://gslis .simmons.edu/podcasts; Eric Gershon, "Map dealer charged in theft," *Cape Cod Times*, July 10, 2005; Jeff Muskus, "Art dealer charged in Beinecke thefts," *Yale Daily News*, July 12, 2005; Nelson Sigelman, "Chilmark man charged in Yale library map thefts," *Martha's Vineyard Times*, July 14, 2005.

170 **"Da Vinci with a carving knife"**: Kim Martineau, "Map of a crime: the arrest of antique map dealer E. Forbes Smiley III, left, has thrown the staid world of libraries and collectors into turmoil," *Hartford Courant*, July 17, 2005.

170 **"made me crazy"**: Ibid.

170 **Smiley's friend Scott Slater . . . supported by crime**: Scott Slater and Felicity Slater interviews.

171 **residents in Sebec were similarly sent reeling**: Mallet and Lello interviews.

171 **Moriartys . . . celebrated**: Kim Martineau, "From life among the elite to charges of theft," *Hartford Courant*, October 25, 2005.

171 **stunned, unable to breathe**: Hudson interview.

171 **renovations to Room 117**: Glenn Collins, "Restoring vivid palette of library's map chamber," *The New York Times*, December 12, 2005.

171 **called Kelleher immediately . . . "consider yourself at fault"**: Ron Grim, "For the record," notes from phone conversation with Steve Kelleher, July 8, 2005; handwritten notes from phone conversation with Steve Kelleher, July 8, 2005; both from Norman B. Leventhal Map Center (LMC) archives at the Boston Public Library.

171 **fielding calls from other libraries**: Kelleher interview.

172 **insisted he hire a private attorney**: Slater and Statt interviews.

172 **"You're cooked" . . . "best to answer"**: Smiley interview. (Reeve did not respond to multiple requests for comment.)

172–74 **devil's bargain . . . for the federal government**: Kelleher interview; Christopher Schmeisser, interview with the author; United States' Memorandum in Aid of Sentencing (22), September 20, 2006, US v. Edward Forbes Smiley, US District Court, District of Connecticut, Crim No. 3:06CR189, 6–8.

174 **page through thousands of call slips . . . Grim later joked**: Grim interview.

174 **two months and one hundred hours**: Boston Public Library, "Impact of Smiley theft on rare books department," undated, LMC archives.

174 **ten items missing**: Boston Public Library, "Status of Smiley inventory," August 5, 2005, LMC archives.

174 **dozen missing maps**: Grim interview.

174 **identified four books**: Jim Akerman and Kelly McGrath, interviews with the author.

174 **bad copy of John Smith's map**: Ralph Hall, "Virginia," in Gerard Mercator, *Historia Mundi*, 1636, Newberry Library, 3880 1636.H3.

174 **Thornton map of South Carolina**: John Thornton, "New map of the Cheif [sic] Rivers, Bayes, Creeks, Harbours, and Settlements of South Carolina," in Frederik de Wit, *Atlas*, 1694, Newberry Library, VAULT oversize Ayer 135 . W8 A, no. [141] (PrCt).

174 **"lowest of the low"**: Tonya Maxwell, "The story of a map quest, a notable dealer's arrest—and now, a Chicago twist," *Chicago Tribune*, August 6, 2005.

174 **"Full disclosure will be embarrassing"**: Robert Karrow, "A plea for full disclosure," MapHist Listserv, August 13, 2005.

175 **Alexander map of Canada (1624)**: William Alexander, untitled, from *An Encouragement to Colonies*, London, 1624, British Library, G. 7139; Burden, *Mapping of North America*, (208), 257–258.

175 **Best map of world (1578)**: George Best, untitled, from *A True Discourse of the Late Voyages of Discouerie . . .*, London, 1578, British Library, C.13.a.9; Kim Martineau and Lisa Chedekel, "Map thefts not so rare after all: several more

top-tier libraries report visits by accused dealer," *Hartford Courant*, August 5, 2005.

175 **Apian map of world (1520):** Peter Apian, "Tipus Orbis Universalis iuxta Ptolomei Cosmographi Traditonem . . . ," from Caius Julius Solinus, *Ioannis Camertis . . .* , Vienna, 1520, British Library, C.32.m.5(2); Lester, *Fourth Part of the World*, 376–377; Schwartz, *Putting "America" on the Map*, 127, 285.

175 **provenance of this map:** British Library, victim impact statement; British Library's Sentencing Memorandum (19), US *v.* Smiley, 10–11.

175 **only person who had looked at all of these books:** Peter Barber, Judith Barnes, and Bob Goldman interviews.

175 **Boston Public also went public:** Jenna Russell, "Dealer faces probe in map thefts: 'perfect gentleman' is charged in Conn.," *The Boston Globe*, August 9, 2005; Christina Silva and Jenna Russell, "More maps turn up on list of missing," *The Boston Globe*, August 10, 2005.

175 **Smiley, too, kept quiet:** Maxwell, "The story of a map quest."

175 **finally respond to the charges:** Transcript, State of Connecticut *v.* Edward Forbes Smiley III, Superior Court, Judicial District of New Haven, Recorded by Tonia Speringo, August 9, 2005; Matt Apuzzo, "Collector pleads innocent to charges of stealing rare maps from library at Yale University," Associated Press, August 9, 2005; Kim Martineau, "Map searches continue as expert pleads not guilty," *Hartford Courant*, August 10, 2005; William Finnegan, "A theft in the library," *The New Yorker*, October 17, 2005.

176 **biannual International Conference:** Finnegan, "A theft in the library."

176 **rumors swirled about:** Anonymous author interviews. Smiley said the rumor about his son was untrue. Ashley Baynton-Williams and Barry MacLean declined comment on the facsimile rumor.

176 **"personal betrayal was worse":** Newman interview.

176–77 **loudest cries came from Tony Campbell . . . dealers could know what to watch out for:** Tony Campbell, interview with the author; Tony Campbell, "Issues arising out of the Smiley affair," post to MapHist Listserv, August 12, 2005.

177–78 **filed into the third-floor trustees' room . . . share their experiences:** "Meeting of curators of map collections at public libraries and universities," September 28, 2005, LMC archives.

178 **Grim had completed his own review:** "Subject inventory of missing items from publications used by Smiley at the Boston Public Library," October 27, 2005, LMC archives.

178 **Smiley had looked . . . during that period:** Ron Grim, memorandum to Bernard Margolis, Ruth Kownal, and Roni Pick, May 8, 2006, LMC archives.

178 **sent the list to the FBI:** Ron Grim, e-mail to Tony Campbell, June 22, 2006, LMC archives.

178 **since Kelleher had started . . . the dealers themselves:** Kelleher interview.

179 **All three dealers . . . acquiesced:** Kelleher, Schmeisser, and Newman interviews; Cohen and Burden interviews; Kim Martineau, "Rare documents going digital; Yale may join libraries using technology against theft of originals," January 15, 2006.

179 **Newman was asked . . . copy was missing?:** Newman interview; Alison Leigh

Cowan, "Thefts rattle the sedate world of rare maps," *The New York Times,* October 3, 2005.

179 **"not a bag lady":** Alison Leigh Cowan, "A rival is charged, and a map dealer wants to say, 'Told you so," *The New York Times,* October 20, 2005.

179 **faxed a list of maps:** Kit Schmeisser, fax to Boston Police, October 26, 2005.

179 **portolan chart of the Atlantic:** Grim and Kelleher interviews.

179 **immediately seeing a map:** "Doncker, Hendrick [Blaeu, Willem Janzzon], West-Indische Paskaert . . . 1659," Richard B. Arkway, Inc., Catalog 59, 2003.

180 **Grim went searching:** Hendrick Doncker, "West Indische Paskaert," 1655, Boston Public Library, Map 130.1655; Grim interview; catalog card on microfiche and call slip in LMC archives.

180 **"sketchy information from the FBI":** Ron Grim, e-mail to Tony Campbell, June 22, 2006.

180–81 **Sterling Memorial Library had no records . . . maps Smiley traded in:** Kaye, Miles, Parrish, Reese, and Schroeder interviews with the author; list of missing maps, undated, Sterling Memorial Library Map Collection archives; Kathrin Day Lassila, "Paper trail: close-ups—and some recent history of Sterling's rare maps," *Yale Alumni Magazine,* July–August 2007; Ross Goldberg, "Librarians say more maps are missing," *Yale Daily News,* Sunday, July 30, 2006; Martineau, "Rare documents going digital"; Kim Martineau, "Gift to help Yale preserve its maps," *Hartford Courant,* August 17, 2006. (Fred Musto did not return requests for comment.)

181 **included only eleven:** Plea Agreement as to Edward Forbes Smiley III (3), US v. Smiley, Exhibit A: Smiley Admissions.

182 **olive jacket:** Photos by Bob Childs/Associated Press, Laura Beach/*Antiques and the Arts Weekly,* June 22, 2006.

182–83 **ready to make a plea . . . "Guilty! Guilty!":** Information as to Edward Forbes Smiley, III (1), US v. Smiley; Plea Agreement as to Edward Forbes Smiley III (3), US v. Smiley; Transcript of Guilty Plea (6), US v. Smiley, transcribed by Sharon Montini, June 22, 2006; US Attorney, letter to Daniel Linsky, Boston Police, June 26, 2006; Alison Leigh Cowan, "For dealer, stolen maps point way to prison," *The New York Times,* June 23, 2006; Randall Beach, "Dealer guilty in $3M theft of 97 maps," *New Haven Register,* June 23, 2006; Kim Martineau, "Thefts off the chart: pleading guilty, dealer admits to stealing 97 rare maps worth more than $3 million," *Hartford Courant,* June 23, 2006; John Christoffersen, "Collector pleads guilty; admits stealing rare maps," Associated Press, June 22, 2006; "Map dealer pleads guilty," States News Service, June 22, 2006; Randy Boswell, "Earliest Canadian map thief's passion: antiquarian admits swiping 97 rare maps from world's libraries," CanWest News Service, June 27, 2006; James Kinsella, "Chilmark resident admits map theft," *Vineyard Gazette,* June 23, 2006.

183 **plead again in state court:** Transcript, State of Connecticut v. Edward Forbes Smiley III, transcribed by Dawn M. DeRose, June 22, 2006.

184 **"We're all a lot of mixed bags":** Martineau, "Thefts off the chart."

184 **"tip of the iceberg":** Kim Martineau, "For map thief, a world of deceit: Forbes Smiley's elite clientele are left feeling betrayed, humiliated; 'I took it personally,' says one," *Hartford Courant,* June 25, 2006.

184   **amended that date to 2002:** Defendant's Memorandum in Aid of Sentencing (20), US *v.* Smiley, 28.

CHAPTER 12

186   **owned by King George III:** "George III Collection: The King's Library," British Library, http://www.bl.uk/reshelp/findhelprestype/prbooks/ georgeiiicoll/george3kingslibrary.html.

186   **first met Forbes Smiley . . . Apian map:** Peter Barber, interview with the author; British Library, victim impact statement.

187   **"entertain serious doubts" . . . admit more thefts:** Kim Martineau, "New allegations against map thief; the British Library says that E. Forbes Smiley III stole four maps, not just one," *Hartford Courant,* June 30, 2006; "Libraries say more maps missing than those that were stolen," Associated Press, July 30, 2006; Kim Martineau, "Libraries suspect more maps taken: Yale University and other prominent institutions fear federal authorities may not have been thorough enough in their investigation of map dealer E. Forbes Smiley III, right," *Hartford Courant,* July 30, 2006.

187   **"minded to make common cause":** Peter Barber, e-mail to Ron Grim, et al., July 3, 2006.

187   **"cartographically semi-literate":** Tony Campbell, "Suggestions for Smiley's judge(s)," MapHist Listserv, July 2, 2006.

187–88   **Bob Goldman thinks . . . "other maps might be":** Bob Goldman, interview with the author; Kim Martineau, "History's policeman: with the fervor of a missionary, a former prosecutor helps track down those who would steal our heritage," *Hartford Courant,* August 14, 2006; G. Patrick Pawling, "The bounty hunter: Robert Goldman has traveled he globe tracking down stolen art," *Super Lawyers,* 2006; John Shiffman, "A TR 'nut' savors his big find: Theodore Roosevelt's revolver caps a career investigating art crimes," *The Philadelphia Inquirer,* June 16, 2006; Chris Mondics, "His career in art theft: lawyer Robert Goldman specializes in recovering stolen art, cultural treasures, historical pieces," *The Philadelphia Inquirer,* July 15, 2007.

189   **Sterling Memorial Library went public:** Kim Martineau, "Yale posts lists of missing maps; getting word out might thwart efforts to sell," *Hartford Courant,* July 20, 2006.

189   **Ellicott map of DC:** "Andrew Ellicott. Territory/of/Columbia," E. Forbes Smiley III website, www.efsmaps.com (site discontinued; accessed through Internet Archive, www.archive.org).

189–90   **listed it on the cover . . . no longer had its copy:** The Old Print Shop *Portfolio* 62, no. 1 (September 2002).

190   **missing maps in Arkway's catalogs:** Richard B. Arkway, Inc., catalogs 55, 58, and 62.

190   **"unfortunate that Yale has lost":** Martineau, "Yale posts lists of missing maps."

190   **Harvard released its own list:** "Missing map alert," Harvard College Library, http://www.rbms.info/committees/security/theft_reports/harvard-maps- 20060801.pdf; Janice O'Leary, "Stolen rare maps will find their way home," *The Boston Globe,* July 23, 2006; Martineau, "Libraries suspect more maps taken."

190 **"all of the affected institutions believe"**: Jenna Russell, "BPL, Harvard renew map quest," *The Boston Globe*, August 1, 2006.

190 **Grim had identified thirty-five maps . . . to Arkway**: Ronald E. Grim, letter to Christopher Schmeisser, August 29, 2006, LMC archives.

191 **back to the right places**: Nancy Cline and Alice Prochaska, e-mail exchange, July 1, 2006; Brittney L. Moraski, "New twist in Smiley case: libraries suspect that map dealer might have stolen more maps than admitted," *The Harvard Crimson*, August 4, 2006.

191–92 **curators from all the affected libraries . . . evidence they'd brought**: Goldman interview; Grim, Cobb, Hudson, Schroeder, and Kelleher interviews with the author; Brittney L. Moraski, "Status of stolen maps in limbo: libraries agree to keep 'positive and productive' meeting private," August 11, 2006; "Confidential," list of maps, undated, LMC archives.

192 **claim the map of Charleston . . . claim a map of New York**: "Confidential," list of maps, undated, with markings, LMC archives; Grim, letter to Schmeisser, August 29, 2006, LMC archives.

192 **working buffet lunch**: "Agenda for map meeting," August 9, 2006, LMC archives.

192 **urged them to go further . . . wouldn't be participating**: Goldman interview.

192 **rebuffed in his requests**: Robert Goldman, letter to Christopher Schmeisser, August 10, 2006; Goldman and Kelleher interviews; Schmeisser interview.

192 **victims the right to argue separately**: 18 US Code sec. 3771—"crime victims' rights", Paul G. Cassell and Steven Joffee, "The crime victim's expanding role in a system of public prosecution: a response to the critics of the Crime Victims' Rights Act," *Northwestern Law Review Colloquy* (2011); Jefri Wood, "The Crime Victims' Rights Act of 2004 and the federal courts," Federal Judicial Center, June 2, 2008.

193 **British Library filed . . . "16th century"**: British Library's Sentencing Memorandum (19), US v. Smiley; Kim Martineau, "British want stern justice: legal brief asks U.S. judge to punish rare-map thief harshly," *Hartford Courant*, September 14, 2006; Alison Leigh Cowen, "Map dealer deserves stiffer term, British say," *The New York Times*, September 14, 2006; John Christoffersen, "British Library says map-stealing collector robbed future generations, deserves punishment," Associated Press, September 14, 2006.

193–94 **Reeve, shot back . . . "next activity to try"**: Defendant's Sentencing Memorandum (20), US v. Smiley.

194 **government submitted its own memo**: Sentencing Memorandum by USA (22), US v. Smiley.

194 **warranted a "downward departure"**: Motion for Downward Departure by USA (21), US v. Smiley.

194–99 **Smiley arrived for sentencing . . . friends who had accompanied him**: Transcript of Sentencing Hearing (24), US v. Smiley; Slater and Statt interviews; Kelleher, Schmeisser, and Hudson interviews; John Christoffersen, "Map thief sentenced to 3½ years in prison," Associated Press, September 27, 2006; "Map thief sentenced to 42 months," States News Service, September 27, 2006; Kim Martineau, "Thief's next 3½ years mapped out: judge says prison term reflects dealer's cooperation in recovery of treasures," *Hartford*

Courant, September 28, 2006; Randall Beach, "Map thief going to prison; Mass. man draws 3½-year sentence after helping with recovery of items," *New Haven Register,* September 28, 2006; James Kinsella, "Chilmark man jailed for rare map theft," *Vineyard Gazette,* September 29, 2006; Laura Beach, "Mapping a new future: Smiley is sentenced," *Antiques and the Arts Weekly,* October 3, 2006.

199 **placed them in the backseat:** Kelleher interview.

CHAPTER 13

201 **"Obviously we are disappointed":** Laura Beach, "Mapping a new future: Smiley is sentenced," *Antiques and the Arts Weekly,* October 3, 2006.

201 **"doesn't send any message of deterrence":** Kim Martineau, "Thief's next 3½ years mapped out: judge says prison term reflects dealer's cooperation in recovery of treasures," *Hartford Courant,* September 28, 2006.

201 **"judge forgive a car thief":** "Unjust break for map thief," *Hartford Courant,* October 5, 2006.

202 **Smiley appeared . . . no additional jail time:** Transcript by Sarah Burke, October 13, 2006, State of Connecticut *v.* Edward Smiley; "Map thief gets 5 years; Smiley's state sentence is symbolic," *Hartford Courant,* October 14, 2006; Randall Beach, "Map thief handed 5-year sentence in city," *New Haven Register,* October 14, 2006.

202 **restitution order:** Restitution Order (29), US *v.* Smiley.

202 **Cohen and Taliaferro never merged with Arkway:** Cohen interview.

202 **forced to sell a valuable painting:** Newman interview.

202 **"lucky to still be talking":** Cohen interview.

202 **sold his Sebec farmhouse and shops:** Quitclaim Deed, August 25, 2005, Piscataquis County Registry of Deeds, Book 01681, Page 128; Warranty Deed, August 21, 2007, Piscataquis County Registry of Deeds, book 01868, page 281.

203 **forbidden from seizing a person's home:** William Francis Galvin, *Questions and Answers: The Homestead Act, Massachusetts General Laws, Ch. 188, §1–10,* Massachusetts Secretary of State, http://www.sec.state.ma.us/rod/rodhom/Homestead_q_ and_a.pdf.

203 **"he gets to keep his house?":** Burden interview.

203 **NYPL finally released its list:** "Missing antiquarian maps," New York Public Library, http://www.nypl.org/locations/tid/36/node/49189; "Rare Book Division missing maps," New York Public Library, http://www.nypl.org/locations/tid/36/node/29551.

203 **never be able to recover . . . "so uncooperative":** Hudson and Kelleher interviews.

203 **chart of Carolina:** Grim interview; Ron Grim, e-mail to Schmeisser, November 6, 2006, LMC archives.

204 **Dudley map of the Chesapeake:** Grim and Gordon interviews.

204 **both on the phone for a conference call:** Ron Grim, summary of phone conversations with Kit Schmeisser and Steve Kelleher, November 22, 2006, LMC archives, Boston Public Library.

204 **Moll map of the colonies:** Herman Moll, "New and Exact Map of the Dominions of the King of Great Britain on Ye Continent of North America," in *The World Described,* 1708, Boston Public Library, G1015.M65 1709 (Atlas 10.4. 1715).

204 **Seller chart of the West Indies:** John Seller, "Chart of the West Indies from Cape Cod to the River Oronoque," from *Atlas Maritimus,* 1672, Boston Public Library, G1059 .S45 1672 OR E672.SC4A.

204 **paid $12.87 for lunch:** Ron Grim, expense report, December 11, 2006, LMC archives.

204 **confirmed Grim's suspicions:** Ron Grim notes, "Observations at Arkway," undated, LMC archives.

204 **the John White map of Virginia:** John White, "Nunc Virginia Dicta, Americae Pars," in Theodor de Bry, *Collections, Segunda Editio,* vols. 6–7, 1591, Boston Public Library, G.281.51 vol. 6; Burden, *Mapping of North America* (76), 96–98; Ron Grim, letter to Jonathan Lupkin, January 16, 2007.

204 **agreed to return all three maps:** Ruth Kowal, e-mail to Maribeth Cusick and Edward Maheigan, April 19, 2007, LMC archives; Jonathan Lupkin, e-mail to Ron Grim, December 14, 2006, annotated with handwritten notes by Ron Grim, LMC archives.

205 **Boisseau map of New France:** Jean Boisseau, "Description de la Nouvelle France," 1643, Yale University Library, 755.1643; Richard B. Arkway, Inc., *Catalog 58: America and the World, Rare and Unusual Works 1522–1833* (14).

205 **Harry Newman closely examined . . . in Smiley's defense:** Newman interview; Kim Martineau, "Map with a legend; rare woodcut of Aztec city finds its way back to Yale," *Hartford Courant,* January 27, 2007.

205 **Norman chart of Carolina:** D.L. Dunbibin, "Chart of the coast of America from Cape Hatteras to Cape Roman," from Andrew Allen, *The American Pilot,* 1816, Boston Public Library, G1106.P5 A4 1816x.

206 **agreed it was Boston's map:** Ron Grim and Kit Schmeisser, e-mail exchange, May 4, 2007; Ron Grim and Jim Curtis, e-mail exchange, May 7, 2007; Ron Grim, handwritten notes regarding Jim Curtis, undated, LMC archives.

206 **new order for restitution:** United States' Unopposed Motion for an Amended Restitution Order (31) US *v.* Smiley. Amended Restitution Order (32), US *v.* Smiley (31–2), Amended Restitution Order.

208 **January 4, 2007 . . . 15867-014:** "Public information inmate data, Smiley, Edward Forbes III," US Bureau of Prisons, January 15, 2010; Randall Beach, "Map thief begins serving 3½-year sentence," *New Haven Register,* January 5, 2007.

208 **locked in a cell for twenty-three hours . . . "when I saw return addresses":** Smiley interview, corroborated by contemporaneous letters written by Scott Slater.

209 **gathered for their annual weekend:** "Boys' Weekend," Santa Cruz, California, October 5, 2007, order of ceremonies.

209 **"stripped of all the furnishings":** Scott Slater, "A Lament for Sebec."

209 **"I hear the boys a drinkin'":** Forbes Smiley, "Devens Prison Blues."

210 **work-release program:** Smiley interview; Scott Slater interview.

210 **furlough on December 23, 2009:** Ibid.

210 **officially earned parole:** "Public Information Inmate Data, Smiley, Edward Forbes III," US Bureau of Prisons, January 15, 2010.

210 **"five percent has been returned":** Arader interview.

211 **"cause of the loss was incorrect":** Ben Sanderson, e-mail to the author, November 29, 2013.

211 **"he turned in the dealers":** Arader interview.

211 **"no better protector of items than themselves":** Goldman interview.

211 **"have stolen maps in your collection?":** Cobb interview.

211 **Sotheby's announced it was auctioning . . . record $250,000:** Randy Boswell, "Rare map of Canada under scrutiny after Harvard thefts," Canwest News Service, October 12, 2008; Randy Boswell, "Champlain map cleared for auction," Canwest News Service, October 14, 2008.

212 **master list of all the missing maps:** John Woram, "Missing Maps," New York Map Society, http://www.newyorkmapsociety.org/MISSING/WORAM.HTM.

212 **"you have to put a photo out":** Woram interview.

212 **"not the map librarians who are the problem":** Campbell interview.

212 **James Brubaker:** Steve Twomey, "To catch a thief," and "Pay dirt in Montana," *Smithsonian*, April 2008; "Great Falls man pleads guilty to stealing rare library books," *Great Falls Tribune*, June 24, 2008.

212 **César Gómez Rivero:** Federal Bureau of Investigation, "Tesoros Nacionales: FBI returns stolen maps to Spain," press release, November 8, 2007, http://www.fbi .gov/news/stories/2007/november/stolenmaps_110807; Thomas Catan, "Library map thief gives himself up," *The Times* (London), October 22, 2007.

212 **Richard Delaney:** Ross McCarthy, "Worker stole historic maps; court: items worth pounds 89,000 taken from university," *Birmingham Evening Mail*, August 5, 2008.

212–13 **Farhad Hakimzadeh:** Sandra Laville, "History's missing pages: Iranian academic sliced out sections of priceless collection, *The Guardian*, November 20, 1998.

212 **Hungarian thief:** "Multiple map thief behind bars," thinkSpain, August 12, 2009.

213 **Czech Republic, a thief stole two maps:** "Czech court imposes five years on Pole for theft of rare maps," Ceske Noviny, August 19, 2009, cited by Tony Campbell, "News about map thefts," http://www.maphistory.info/theftnews .html.

213 **British library . . . as a fingerprint:** Barber and Sanderson interviews.

213 **ambitious digitization project . . . install cameras:** Grim and Janet Spitz, interviews with the author; Jenna Russell, "Stolen rare maps find their way back to library's collection," *The Boston Globe*, January 2, 2008.

213 **installed a new camera . . . after each use:** Parrish interview.

213 **$100,000 donation from Bill Reese:** "Yale Map Collection Receives Important Gift," Yale University Library, www. library.yale.edu/development/news/map-collection.html.

214 **numerous bags and coats:** Author visits to NYPL map room, 2012–2013; The New York Public Library did not respond to repeated requests for an interview.

214 **still get checks:** Newman interview.

214 **Smiley's mother passed away:** Parties' Joint Motion for Distribution of Estate Proceeds and for Clarification of the Amended Restitution Order (33), US v. Smiley.

214 **withdrew from the map community . . . one year short:** Hudson interview; Dawn Youngblood, "Alice Hudson: New York Public Library's treasure among maps," *Journal of Map and Geography Libraries* 6, no. 2 (2010): 151–173.

214 **"the end of the world":** Hudson interview.

215 **donating all his wealth:** Arader interview; Graham Arader blog, http://grahamarader.blogspot.com; Graham Arader, user profile, http://www.blogger.com/profile/08725182968958751913.

215 **gift of fifteen thousand antique maps:** Megan Sexton, "Natural history treasures coming to USC," University of South Carolina website, May 2, 2013.

215 **official opening of the Norman B. Leventhal Map Center:** Joseph P. Kahn, "BPL charts modern course: high-tech exhibit will expand access to vast trove of maps," *The Boston Globe*, January 3, 2011; "Boston Public Library to open new space for the Norman B. Leventhal Map Center," States News Service, October 6, 2011; "Leventhal Map Center opens," *Newton TAB*, January 4, 2012.

215–16 **got out of prison . . . "let them down":** Smiley interview.

216 **"something wrong with the guy":** Statt interview.

216–17 **opposite feeling . . . disabled son:** Slater interview.

217 **grants of $200 to $5,000:** Tony Omer, "Center for the visual arts accepting grant applications," *Martha's Vineyard Times*, March 5, 2013.

218 **"When painters paint":** Forbes Smiley, letter to Paul Statt, April 24, 2008.

Epilogue

221 **"After a well-known dealer" . . . US Coast Guard surveys:** "Map quest: seeking owners of stolen artwork," FBI, http://www.fbi.gov/news/stories/2013/july/fbi-seeking-owners-of-stolen-artwork/fbi-seeking-owners-of-stolen-artwork.

221–22 **case has since passed . . . box or tube:** Lisa McNamara, interview with the author.

Appendices

The information in the appendices is derived from a number of sources, starting with the list of missing maps compiled by New York Map Society member John Woram, who consolidated the various lists released by the FBI and the affected libraries. I have supplemented this list with my own research and reporting, verifying the information whenever possible with the curators at the institutions, most of whom were very open to assisting me. I also visited each of the six affected institutions and examined the books and maps themselves, in most cases personally viewing and photographing the items that have been recovered. While inevitably there may be errors in the listings, the final lists are as close to definitive as I have been able to make them.

Index

Note: Page numbers in *italics* type refer to illustrations.

ALSO BY MICHAEL BLANDING

"Put down your soda, read *The Coke Machine*, and join the global movement to rein in unaccountable corporations."
—BARBARA EHRENREICH, author of *Nickel and Dimed*

The *Coke* Machine

THE DIRTY TRUTH BEHIND THE WORLD'S FAVORITE SOFT DRINK

MICHAEL BLANDING

The Coke Machine is a shocking investigation of the accusations that one of the world's largest companies has systematically torpedoed health, labor, and environmental standards internationally.

AVERY